FINANCIAL
FIASCO

JOHAN NORBERG

FINANCIAL FIASCO

HOW AMERICA'S INFATUATION
WITH HOMEOWNERSHIP AND EASY MONEY
CREATED THE ECONOMIC CRISIS

CATO
INSTITUTE
WASHINGTON, D.C.

First Paperback Printing: 2012

Library of Congress Cataloging-in-Publication Data

Norberg, Johan, 1973–
   Financial fiasco : how America's infatuation with homeownership and easy
money created the economic crisis / Johan Norberg.
     p. cm.
   Includes bibliographical references and index.
   ISBN 978-1-935308-13-3 (alk. paper)
   1. Home ownership—Government policy—United States.   2. Financial crisis—
United States—History—21st century.   3. Keynesian economics.
I. Title.

HD7287.82.U6UN67 2009
330.973—dc22   2009026629

Cover design by Jon Meyers.

Printed in the United States of America.

CATO INSTITUTE
1000 Massachusetts Ave., N.W.
Washington, D.C. 20001
www.cato.org

For Alexander
—who will look back on these as the good old days.

We will not have any more crashes in our time. I find the markets very interesting, and the prices low. So where should a crisis come from?

—John Maynard Keynes, 1927

The most common beginning of disaster was a sense of security.

—Marcus Velleius Paterculus, *Compendium of Roman History*

Contents

Preface to the Paperback Edition

In the last three years, policymakers in the United States, Europe, and China have responded forcefully to the great recession. A crisis caused by cheap money, indebtedness, and bad investments has been met with even cheaper money and more debt and by subsidizing and protecting bad investments and overproduction in the housing sector, the infrastructure, and the car industry. In short, they are trying to do what the Federal Reserve did in 2001, when it saved the economy from a bursting bubble by inflating a new one, with disastrous results.

In this new edition, I have not changed the original text, but I have added a new chapter about government action in the wake of the crisis and about how the financial fiasco resulted in the euro crisis. It is much too early to tell whether these actions will have the intended effect. It could instead result in investors fleeing governments suffering under unsustainable debts. There might be a hard landing in China, the euro could collapse, and there might be a crisis of confidence in the dollar.

But there is also the chance that these short-term measures will succeed in inspiring our animal spirits more than market opportunities and hard data could have done on their own. In that case, we will have another episode of short-term investments, new bubbles, and a reinforced belief that investors will always be saved by taxpayers and the printing presses, no matter how much they engage in reckless lending and speculation.

At times when listening to politicians and businessmen these last few years, it has felt like we are living in a 2008 article from the satirical newspaper *The Onion*:

> "A panel of top business leaders testified before Congress about the worsening recession Monday, demanding the government provide Americans with a new irresponsible and largely illusory economic bubble in which to invest."

Unfortunately, the reality we face is much less amusing.

Stockholm, Sweden, March 2012

Preface to the First Edition

I can calculate the motions of the heavenly bodies, but not the madness of people.

—Isaac Newton, after losing a fortune in the South Sea
Bubble in 1720

In the fall of 1991, a high-pressure system from northern Canada collided with a powerful low-pressure system over the coast of New England. The large temperature contrast in such a small area gave rise to a cyclone. The cyclone, in turn, absorbed a nearby dying hurricane, which created an enormously powerful storm. The winds at times attained 75 miles per hour, and 35-foot waves shook unfortunate seafarers. The biggest individual wave measured was 100 feet high.

Meteorologist Bob Case at the National Weather Service in Boston explained that circumstances were perfect for the emergence of a storm. Three independent weather phenomena happened to occur at the exact times and places required for them to interact to create the most severe storm in living memory, causing great loss of human life and property. Circumstances were—unfortunately—perfect for devastation.

The world has just been struck by a perfect financial storm. A series of circumstances that individually would not have had to lead to disaster—low- and middle-income countries starting to save money; the head of a central bank's wishing to avoid a crisis; political demands to expand homeownership; new financial instruments; and new banking regulations, credit-rating requirements, and accounting rules intended to prevent cheating—came into existence at the same time and reinforced one another into what Alan Greenspan has called "a once-in-a-century event." Circumstances were perfect for a financial storm so tremendous that few people now alive have seen anything like it. The monster waves are swallowing gigantic banks and long-established industrial companies alike. The wind gusts are tearing apart entire economies.

Many politicians and businesspeople who use the "perfect storm" metaphor for this crisis do so to explain its catastrophic consequences. They believe they took all the necessary precautions and sailed their ships the way they should, but that they happened to find themselves in a storm beyond their control. As a result, they cannot take responsibility for the losses and problems that have arisen. However, my intention in writing this book is to show that each circumstance that led to the crisis—each low and high, and each colliding hurricane—was the result of conscious actions on the part of decisionmakers in companies, government agencies, and political institutions.

What makes today's crisis unique is that it has taken such a short time to wash over practically every corner of the world. Other countries have been negatively affected by the backwash of national crises throughout the 20th century, but never before has a financial crisis as such happened in so many places at the same time and in such a similar form. The panic went global in a moment. Two hundred years ago, the Rothschild brothers could earn a fortune by being spread across many European cities: Nathan lived in London, Amschel in Frankfurt, James in Paris, Carl in Amsterdam, and Salomon sometimes here and sometimes there. This enabled them to obtain information from one another immediately, so that before anyone else, they could buy securities and resources where they were cheapest and sell them where they were dearest.[1]

Today computers, satellites, and global media have given us a global market where each player can be a mini-Rothschild. This makes it harder for anyone to profit from being better informed, and it makes the division of labor and the use of resources more efficient, which gives us all greater opportunities. But it has also given rise to new risks, as bad news now travels so fast across the globe—especially since the media are becoming ever more likely to shout at the top of their voice. In fact, a comparison shows that they have been significantly more alarmist this time than they were after the 1929 stock market crash.[2] And when people are alarmed, they all simultaneously stop consuming and lending. Trouble on Wall Street soon leads to a 99.7 percent fall in the sale of trucks by Volvo in Sweden, to riots in eastern European democracies, to half of

China's toy exporters having to close up shop, and to Taiwanese animal shelters receiving lots of dogs that households can no longer afford to care for.[3] The globalization that only yesterday seemed so relentless has changed into its opposite. Right now we are experiencing a fall in global trade, investment, transportation, migration, and tourism. People all over the world are losing their jobs, their businesses, and their homes—and yet what we have seen so far is just the beginning of the recession.

We are experiencing the first global financial crisis in history, and that has rapidly given rise to a widespread reaction against globalization and free markets. Faith in big and active government has made an improbably fast comeback. To someone like myself, who believes that the free-market economies and globalized markets that have evolved over the past few decades have created fantastic opportunities for rich and poor countries alike, it has felt particularly important to understand this crisis.

This is the story of what happened and why it happened. It was written during the most dramatic months, when the sky seemed to be descending on our heads. It builds on the observations of participants and onlookers during these months and on the background to the events that unfolded. It is inevitable that our field of vision is restricted at this time, since we are still so close to the events. Journalists and researchers are hard at work right now analyzing and explaining the anatomy of the crisis in a wide range of fields. Our knowledge will grow, and it will be revised on many counts. Some of the low- and high-pressure systems that I describe may turn out to have been much more important for the storm than I believe now, others perhaps less. I expect us eventually to find out that some events actually occurred in an entirely different way from what we believe today. This book is an attempt to solve a jigsaw puzzle showing a changing picture. I would like you to consider it a first historical sketch.

Why should someone whose specialty is the history of ideas write a book about a financial crisis? Like many economists, I consider it a problem today that academic training in finance provides ever more advanced knowledge in an ever-narrower field.[4] Many of the brightest students now major in finance or business, but they leave college without having an overall idea of the function and interlinkages of the economic system or in-depth knowledge of economic history. The typical career in the financial market lasts a quarter of a century, meaning that the average person will experience only one major crisis. Lessons are thus lost, and each generation repeats the same mistakes.

Moreover, as a historian of ideas, I have learned that the interaction of ideas, politics, and economics is what governs the fate of the world. Economic crises in particular have led to political paradigm shifts and to the transformation of entire societies. Those who do not study economics are doomed to repeat the big economic mistakes of history. Crises strike us all hard. There is something deeply unsatisfactory—bordering on undemocratic—about the fact that people may have their lives shattered because of monetary policy and financial instruments that are sometimes felt to be the preserve of a small circle of economists and market players. Seldom have so many people been so heavily struck by something of which they understand so little. War is simply too important to be left to generals, and the financial markets are too important to be left to financial analysts and economists.

For this reason, I have tried to write this book for those who have no previous knowledge of financial markets. The first three chapters deal with the prelude to the crisis—the various factors that then meet in chapter 4 and reinforce one another into an historic financial chaos whose consequences I describe in chapters 5 and 6.

Chapter 1: Monetary policy. How the U.S. central bank (the Fed) and the surpluses of fast-growing emerging economies made money cheaper than ever in the past decade, and why that money ended up in people's homes.

Chapter 2: Housing policy. The story of how U.S. politicians—both Democrats and Republicans—worked systematically to increase the share of families who owned their homes, even when that undermined traditional requirements of creditworthiness.

Chapter 3: Financial innovations. How to transform big risks into smaller risks by repackaging them, labeling them, and selling them. How regulations and bonuses caused everybody to flock into the market for mortgage-backed securities, and why even cows could have made a fortune from such securities.

Chapter 4: The crisis. The story of how the fall of an investment bank gave the global economy cardiac arrest, a CEO was knocked to the floor by a subordinate, and a country went belly-up.

Chapter 5: Crisis management. About the largest government bail-outs in history, the constant comparisons with the Great Depression of the 1930s, and ways to make a crisis worse than it already is.

Chapter 6: Conclusion. But also the beginning of something new—and worse.

I will give you a single piece of advice on how to read this book. If you approach it as a whodunit, you will not be disappointed. You will encounter a great many Wall Street tycoons, politicians, heads of central banks, and credit-rating agencies that are perfect for the role as perps.

But if we are to search for scapegoats, we might as well take a look in the mirror, too. Who was it that did not care how our pension funds were invested? Who is it that wants mortgages to be as cheap as possible? Who is it that plans home purchases that will influence our lives for decades on the basis of this week's interest rate? Who is the first to call for regulations and bailouts whenever there is a crisis, without giving a moment's thought to the fact that those very regulations and bailouts may cause the next crisis? The answer is ordinary people, ordinary voters, ordinary savers. The answer is you and I.

As you read in this book about all those who acted in a completely thoughtless and sometimes reckless way, please also try to think a little about your own role in the perfect storm.

* * *

By the way, there are lots of figures and large numbers in this book. It is easy to lose contact with reality, as did many of the senior executives and politicians who juggled such numbers daily. So just let me give you this one thought for the road before you start reading:

One billion is a one followed by nine zeros, or 1,000 million.

One billion *seconds* ago, Leonid Brezhnev became leader of the Soviet Union, which was then at the height of its power.

One billion *minutes* ago, the Gospel of John was written.

One billion *hours* ago, language started evolving.

One billion *days* ago, the ancestors of humans began to walk upright.

One billion *years* ago, multicellular life began to develop on earth.

One billion *dollars* is what the stock markets of the world lost every 17 minutes in 2008 and what the federal government was spending on half an hour's worth of crisis fighting as Barack Obama assumed the presidency.

Stockholm, Sweden, February 2009

1. Preemptive Keynesianism

The law of supply and demand is not to be conned. As the supply of money (of claims) increases relative to the supply of tangible assets in the economy, prices must eventually rise.

—Alan Greenspan, "Gold and Economic Freedom"

Like so many other stories about our time, this one begins on the morning of September 11, 2001, with 19 terrorists and four passenger planes. Their attack, which cost almost 3,000 people their lives, shook our known universe. All U.S. aircraft were ordered to land immediately, and North American airspace was closed down. Routes of trade and communication were blocked as fear of additional attacks paralyzed the entire world, and speculation arose about long wars. The U.S. stock exchanges were closed; when they reopened, the New York Stock Exchange fell by more than 14 percent in one week. The United States was in a crisis, and the global economy was therefore under threat.

But there was one man on whom the world could pin its hopes. A New York economist of Hungarian-Jewish extraction with a bad back, who prefers to read and write lying down in his bathtub. A former jazz-band saxophone player who used to move in the laissez faire circles around writer Ayn Rand. A man whose dark clothes and reserved demeanor had caused his friends to nickname him "the undertaker." After a career in the financial sector and a few stints as a presidential adviser, however, Alan Greenspan had become a pillar of the U.S. establishment.

Even so, few had predicted the next step in the career of this man, who had advocated both in speech and in writing that the Federal Reserve, or "Fed," the U.S. central bank, should be closed down and that the market should instead determine the price of money, which should preferably be backed up by gold. In 1987, Greenspan was appointed chairman of the Fed at the age of 61. He soon acquired a reputation for expressing himself unintelligibly. This is probably a personality trait, but many believe he consciously adopted it to avoid scaring market players by using excessively strong words. In fact, this belief is symbolic of how commentators would always read into Greenspan's behavior an element of careful thinking and cleverness. Indeed, he was soon declared a genius in his new role.

Less than two months after starting his new job, Greenspan had his baptism of fire. There is still disagreement on exactly what triggered it all, but an international dispute about exchange rates and an unexpectedly weak figure for the U.S. balance of trade gave rise to concern, and computer models with preset sell prices for stocks caused the decline in prices to spread quickly. In a single day—October 19, 1987—the New York Stock Exchange fell by almost 23 percent. It was Greenspan's reaction to this "Black Monday" that laid the foundation of his fame. His response was to make an historically large cut in the benchmark interest rate and to offer freer credit. The market stabilized very quickly, and the ink of the magazines warning of a repeat of the Great Depression had hardly dried before the economy had shaken off the stock market crash and was back on track. A hero had been born.

With Greenspan at the helm, the Fed used the same modus operandi whenever crisis loomed: quickly cut the benchmark rate and pump liquidity into the economy. That is what it did at the time of the Gulf War, the Mexican peso crisis, the Asian crisis, the collapse of the Long-Term Capital Management hedge fund, the worries about the millennium bug, and the dot-com crash—and on each occasion, commentators were surprised by the mildness of the subsequent downturn. In someone with Greenspan's clear-cut opinions about the importance of free markets, this readiness to throw money at all problems was surprising. However, to a direct question in Congress about his old laissez-faire views of monetary policy, Greenspan replied, "That's a long time ago, and I no longer subscribe to those views."[1] And even though he hung onto most of his other market-friendly views, he no longer felt bound by ideological principles. As an economist told the *New York Times* when Greenspan was appointed Fed chairman:

> He isn't a Keynesian. He isn't a monetarist. He isn't a supply-sider. If he's anything, he's a pragmatist, and as such, he is somewhat unpredictable.[2]

But regardless of what theory Greenspan's actions built on, they caused him to be declared a genius in some circles, where he was viewed as a magician who had lifted growth and tamed the business cycle. Journalist Bob Woodward, of Watergate fame, chose the title *Maestro* for his book about Greenspan, who is there credited with orchestrating the 1990s boom in the United States. During the 2000 presidential election, the Republican primary candidate John McCain joked that he would reappoint the then 76-year-old Fed chairman—even if he were to die: "I'd prop him up and put a pair of dark glasses on him and keep him as long as we could."[3]

An Inflationary Boom of Some Sort

After September 11, 2001, the world once more looked to Alan Greenspan, the Fed chairman who, like Archimedes, got his best ideas in his bath. And he did not hold his fire. The Fed started to increase the amount of money in the economy. All of a sudden, the annual rate of increase of "M2"—one of the most common measures of the money supply—soared to 10 percent. In mid-2003, it remained as high as 8 percent. In other words, the metaphorical printing press in the Fed's basement was running red-hot. This was part of an effort to force down the Fed funds rate—the benchmark interest rate at which banks can borrow money in the short term, which is one of the Fed's tools to control the economy. In fact, Greenspan had already been lowering this rate rapidly throughout 2001 to prepare for a looming economic downturn, and after 9/11 he pushed it down aggressively. At the beginning of 2001, banks had to pay 6.25 percent interest on the money they borrowed; at the end of the year, they could get away with 1.75 percent—and they would not have to pay more until almost three years later. But this was not enough for the Fed, and the market players were clamoring for more to cope with the downturn.

Basically, this desire to help the economy squares well with the task that the Fed has been given by Congress. Unlike most other central banks in the world, the Fed has a duty not only to maintain price stability but also to ensure that the unemployment rate is as low as possible and that long-term interest rates are low. This has made many European politicians view the Fed as a model. What's more, there was concern at the Fed that prices would start falling. One Fed governor who was an expert on the Great Depression,

Ben Bernanke, convinced Greenspan and their colleagues that the country was at risk of entering a deflationary spiral as it had in the 1930s and as Japan had done in the 1990s.

But there was in fact no collapsing economy in need of being propped up. Only two months after 9/11, the stock exchange was back at a higher level; in 2002, the United States saw economic growth of 1.6 percent. Even so, the Fed worried that higher interest rates could halt the rise and thus continued making cuts. Alan Greenspan himself has admitted that at least the last rate cut, down to 1 percent in June 2003, was not necessary:

> We agreed on the reduction despite our consensus that the economy probably did not need yet another rate cut. The stock market had finally begun to revive, and our forecasts called for much stronger GDP [gross domestic product] growth in the year's second half. Yet we went ahead on the basis of a balancing of risk. We wanted to shut down the possibility of corrosive deflation; we were willing to chance that by cutting rates we might foster a bubble, an inflationary boom of some sort, which we would subsequently have to address.[4]

One percent was the lowest the rate had been in half a century, and in August the Fed promised it would remain at that level "for a considerable period." In December, promises were again made about very low interest rates for a long time to come.[5] The most ardent defender of the record-low rates was Bernanke. The Fed ended up keeping its benchmark rate as low as 1 percent for a full year; once it finally began edging it upward, it did so in tiny, cautious steps even though the wheels of the economy were by then turning very fast. Only in June 2004 did the Fed funds rate reach 1.25 percent, and it took almost two more years to attain 5 percent. The overall effect of this for borrowers was that, over a period of two and a half years, inflation reduced the value of their loans by more than the total cost of interest. In other words, borrowing was not just free—you were actually paid to borrow.[6] And while short-term rates thus stayed low, long-term rates were affected by other factors as well and never came down any further than to just under 3.5 percent. That made it a particularly profitable proposition to take out short-term loans and then lend the money long term, but doing so always involves large risks because the people you have borrowed from short-term may suddenly decide that they want their money back (or that they will not renew your short-term loan) while you have passed on that money to others and promised them they will not have to repay you for a long time.

As Greenspan admitted, the Fed took a conscious risk, and the result did indeed turn out to be an inflationary bubble of some sort. It is true that people were not keen on general consumption, as unemployment was rising at the time and they had just gotten their fingers burned on the stock market—but if you pump new money into the economy, it will always end up somewhere or other. This time it went into real estate.

The U.S. political establishment had actually paved the way for a real-estate boom long before this. Homeownership is viewed as part of the American dream, as a route from poverty and social exclusion to independence and responsibility. For this reason, ever since the United States introduced an income tax its government has been helping out its citizens by allowing them to deduct mortgage-interest payments from that tax—similarly to some other countries, including Sweden. This support for homeownership was reinforced by President Ronald Reagan and Congress in 1986, when the tax deduction for home mortgage interest was retained, while tax incentives favoring rental development and ownership were removed. In addition, the deduction for other consumer loans, such as car and credit card loans, was abolished, which had the effect of steering more and more lending toward the housing market. In 1994, 68 percent of home loans were in fact used to pay down debts for other consumption, for example, car purchases.[7] Some people therefore see the mortgage deduction as an annual $80 billion subsidy for the house as an investment object.

"Clearly, we've gotten some bang for all these bucks," as the economics writer Daniel Gross explained in *Slate* in 2005:

> The United States has an enviably high rate of homeowner-ship and a highly developed infrastructure—secondary markets in mortgage-backed securities, online mortgage companies, etc.—that supports the construction and purchase of homes.
>
> But the once-modest deduction has evolved into a very large and highly inefficient rent subsidy. The deduction plainly causes distortions. People are willing to pay more

for houses and buy bigger houses than they otherwise would because they can deduct the interest from their taxes.[8]

Homeownership was favored even more after 1997, when President Clinton abolished the capital gains tax on real estate (up to $500,000 for a couple) but kept it for other types of investment, such as stocks, bonds, and people's own businesses. "Why insist in effect that they put it in housing to get that benefit? Why not let them invest in other things that might be more productive, like stocks and bonds?" asked the then head of the Internal Revenue Service, but to no avail. The money was going to the housing sector and that was that. A Fed study showed that the number of home deals during the decade starting in 1997 was 17 percent higher than it would have been without this selective tax cut.[9]

As far back as August 2001, James Grant, publisher of the financial newsletter *Grant's Interest Rate Observer*, noted with concern that U.S. home prices had increased by 8.8 percent over the past year even though the dot-com bubble had burst and the economy was virtually in recession. "What could explain a bull market in a non-earning asset in a non-inflationary era?" he wondered—replying himself that the reason was simply that credit was too easily available at too-low an interest rate, and that we did not realize there was hidden inflation in the background.[10]

It is hardly surprising, then, that further rate cuts stoked the fire. The economic columnist Robert Samuelson suddenly discovered that his wife understood the housing market vastly better than he did. Houses in their neighborhood were being sold for one-fourth more than he thought they were worth, but his wife was not in the least surprised. Americans had started exploiting the low interest rates to take out new and bigger loans. My home was no longer my castle, but my ATM. Since homes were suddenly worth more, their owners could go back to the bank and borrow even more money against the same collateral. In the past, most people used to take out loans that they would actually pay off, but now more and more borrowers were obtaining loan agreements under which they would only have to pay interest or at least would not have to pay back any of the principal until after a decade or so.

In 2002 alone, U.S. households borrowed $269 billion more on their homes, usually for consumption or home improvement. In

Samuelson's words: "Fed up with the stock market, Americans went on a real-estate orgy. We traded up, tore down and added on. Builders started almost 1.7 million new homes, up 5 percent from 2001. Existing home sales were a record 5.5 million."[11]

In a speech to a number of credit institutions in February 2004, Alan Greenspan effectively reprimanded borrowers for taking out costly fixed-rate mortgages. The Fed's research showed that many homeowners could have gained tens of thousands of dollars in the past decade if they had let the interest rates on their mortgages move freely instead of locking them at a certain level. Greenspan called for new, freer types of loans: "American consumers might benefit if lenders provided greater mortgage product alternatives to the traditional fixed-rate mortgage."[12] More and more Americans took this lesson to heart and obtained adjustable-rate mortgages instead. In January 2004, the Washington Mutual bank stated that the proportion of its customers who chose adjustable rates had increased from 5 to 40 percent in a single year.[13]

Between 2000 and 2005, the value of U.S. single-family homes increased by $8 trillion.[14] More than 40 percent of all new jobs were related to the housing sector, and new mortgages were financing record consumption. The American people could finally draw a sigh of relief. The crisis was over; money was flowing. Happy days were here again. The Fed had saved the economy once more, this time from the dot-com bubble—but it had done so by inflating a new bubble.

A financial worker living outside Atlanta, Georgia, was pleasantly surprised to realize that he could buy his dream home even though he was unable to sell his old home, as it was being renovated. He simply took out an interest-only mortgage at the end of 2001 and became the owner of two homes. One year earlier, he would have had to pay around 7 percent interest, but now the loan cost him only 2.8 percent. And that was before tax deductions. He felt as though he "was getting a house for free."[15]

It is important here to note that the bubble manifested itself very differently in the various parts of the United States, depending on how hard it was to build new homes there. The economist Paul Krugman, who is usually no enemy of economic regulation, wrote in August 2005 that from the perspective of housing policy, the United States consists of two different countries: one in the middle and the other along either side. In the inland region, or "Flatland," building is fairly simple and cheap, and no housing bubbles ever arise. Along the west and east coasts, however, stretches "the Zoned Zone," where land-use regulations place a series of obstacles in the way of new developers. If people grow enthusiastic about real estate there, for example because of low interest rates, that causes the prices of existing homes to explode.[16]

Statistics prove Krugman right. The real-estate bubble proper actually occurred in only about a dozen states. The environmental economist Randal O'Toole identifies their common denominator in that they were almost the exact same states that apply various types of regulations restricting how much cities may expand, how much the population may grow in a particular area, or where new developments may be located. A rise in prices does not necessarily mean that an area has become more attractive. Often it is instead the result of actions the authorities took a few years earlier to restrict supply. Such restrictions increase the density of housing and therefore push up the prices of single-family homes with gardens in particular. Home prices rose by more than 130 percent in heavily regulated states such as California and Florida between 2000 and 2006. By contrast, they increased by only 30 percent in Texas and Georgia, which, even though they are two of the fastest-growing states, allow people to put up new buildings as they please. The regulated Silicon Valley was hit by an economic crisis and unemployment but still saw soaring home prices. The unregulated cities of Atlanta, Dallas, and Houston each grew by at least 130,000 people during six years of the housing bubble without prices taking off.[17]

But the big-bubble states were the ones calling the tune. An increasing share of U.S. home purchases was pure speculation. People bought, perhaps renovated a bit, and then sold quickly at prices that had risen in the meantime. Many started to earn a living from "flipping" real estate in this way. On June 23, 2005, the TLC television network first aired a reality series called *Property Ladder*, where viewers get to follow a person or group who has the idea of buying a home, fixing it up, and then trying to sell it for more. Three weeks later, the Discovery Home Channel launched *Flip That House*, which is about someone who has just bought a house, often in southern California, and does what it takes to sell it quickly at a good profit. And 10 days after that, on July 24, 2005, the A&E Network premiered a new TV series with a not entirely dissimilar name, *Flip This House*, whose subject is a company based in Charleston, South Carolina, that is in the business of buying, fixing, and selling.

A specifically American phenomenon contributed to making so many potential buyers willing to take a chance. In many parts of the United States, there exists something called a "nonrecourse mortgage," meaning that a home loan is linked to the home, not to the person who has taken it out. The home is collateral for the loan, and the home is the only thing that the lender can get back if the borrower decides to stop paying. People can thus buy houses that they cannot really afford on the assumption that they will be able to negotiate a better deal on interest rates later (lenders are often willing to lower the rate rather than risk having to take over the house) or that prices will rise so that they can sell at a profit. In most countries, homebuyers who stopped paying their loans would be saddled with a mountain of debt; but in about half of the U.S. states, buyers can return the keys to the bank and walk away debt-free. As it also became increasingly common that households did not even have to put down a deposit, they stood to lose nothing at all by taking a wild gamble. In some states with nonrecourse mortgages, including California, lenders do have a theoretical possibility of going to court and requesting more money from a defaulting borrower if the selling price does not cover the loan, but this is a long and costly process that is typically used against borrowers who have large assets.

An article in the *Wall Street Journal* in early 2005 informed readers that a growing minority of Americans was even buying a *third* home, often to flip it or to rent it out during part of the year. Even though rising home prices gave the impression that homes were safe investments, the article did warn that having a third home can be a bit of a nuisance:

> Homeowners have to deal with upkeep on yet another property, and keep a third set of everything from clothes to kitchen utensils. Some homeowners also may feel obligated to vacation in their third home, even when they might prefer to travel elsewhere.[18]

The housing market defied gravity. U.S. home prices had recently increased by another 15 percent in a year, and they had almost

9

doubled since the turn of the millennium. To return to the trends they had followed in the 30 years before that, they would have to fall by around one-fifth. But the builders' associations and the banks' magazines explained soothingly that home prices never fall nationally. This did not impress James Grant, who noted that, since the Great Depression, the United States had experienced 29 market bubbles—strong rises in the prices of securities or other assets. Twenty-seven of them had burst. The two exceptions were stock and real-estate prices in June 2005. Not understanding why bubbles no. 28 and no. 29 should be exceptions, Grant gave his readers some good advice:

> Does your brother-in-law, the real estate broker, owe you money? Now is the time to collect.[19]

The Fed Is Our Friend

When Alan Greenspan left the Fed in January 2006, *The Economist* warned that the popularity he had garnered from recurrent rescue efforts such as the aggressive interest-rate cut after 2001 was the most dangerous of his legacies:

> Investors' exaggerated faith in his ability to protect them has undoubtedly encouraged them to take ever bigger risks and pushed share and house prices higher. In turn, American consumer spending has become dangerously dependent on unsustainable increases in asset prices and debt.
>
> In December Mr Greenspan was made a Freeman of the City of London. One of the traditional perks of this honour is that he can be drunk and disorderly without fear of arrest. The snag is that his policies have also encouraged drunk and disorderly asset markets and intoxicated consumers. When the party ends, Mr Greenspan will not be there to clean up the mess. But end it surely will.[20]

The thankless role of central banks is often described as having to take away the punch bowl just as the party is getting going. As soon as investors and markets grow too happy, central banks must hold back—only what they must keep down is not blood-alcohol content but inflation levels. Theirs is an important task because governments are invariably tempted to finance their spending by simply printing more money (except that the actual printing press is too slow for present-day administrations, which usually speed up the process by issuing bonds and ordering their central bank to buy them with new money). The printing press may look less intimidating than the taxman, but in practice it is worse. Creating more money not only entails an indirect tax in that it reduces the value of citizens' savings but also, and more importantly, undermines the price system by giving businesses incorrect information about demand. The additional money created does not end up everywhere at the same time but percolates into the economy in certain places, where it leads to price increases, which businesses interpret as an increase in demand, causing them to hire more people and step up production. Only after a while do businesses realize that the prices of everything else have also risen and that their costs are increasing even though they are not selling any more than their competitors. In fact, the price increase did not indicate an increase in demand, only a deterioration in the value of money. As a consequence of these incorrect market messages, resources have thus been brought to places where they should not have ended up, meaning that the businesses now have to cut down on production and lay off people.

It is important to get the printing press under control, but that is not quite what central banks do. Instead, they aim to control price increases. Their formal objective is often to prevent consumer prices from increasing more than 2 percent in a year, or something along those lines. The Austrian economist Ludwig von Mises and his Nobel Prize–winning pupil F. A. Hayek identified a problem inherent in such a policy. In a dynamic economy with constant innovation in technology and business models, the prices of goods and services often decrease. Let's assume that the real underlying cost of all goods and services falls by 2 percent owing to increased efficiency but that this development is counteracted by an increase in the money supply so that the price tags in stores actually indicate a price increase of 1 percent. In this situation, the central bank is likely to grab hold of the wrong end of the stick by concluding that there is no inflation worth mentioning, and that will prompt it to cut interest rates.

But if interest rates are too low, it no longer pays to save, meaning that there will be an increase in consumption—for example, of homes, which are not included in our inflation indexes. Companies will want to borrow more to make bigger investments, in parts of the economy that would never have been given a boost without the increase in the money supply. This means that the stabilization of consumer prices may give rise to various asset bubbles. James Grant notes that the price of a basket of goods exposed to international competition had fallen by 31 percent in the 20 years prior to 1886, before the United States had a central bank. Since the 1990s, the country has experienced another period of technology break-throughs and strong competition that should have pushed prices down. Indeed, cheaper imports from Asia and enhanced efficiency in U.S. corporations, for instance, the new logistics of Wal-Mart, did cause prices to fall. This made the central banks believe that there was no actual inflation and that there was thus no need for them to hold back. But there was inflation. It showed up not in the consumer price index but in suburbia. Grant, who warned of the real-estate bubble as far back as 2001, points out that "falling prices are a natural byproduct of human ingenuity. Print money to resist the decline, and the next thing you know, there's a bubble."[21]

The Fed chairman Alan Greenspan did not stand idly by watching that bubble grow. Rather, he huffed and he puffed at the top of his lungs. The Fed's power over interest rates makes it similar to any government agency wishing to regulate prices in an industry; the difference is that by regulating the price of money, the Fed to some extent controls all prices. Many have spoken admiringly of how Greenspan would sit in his bathtub perusing statistics of manufacturing, inventories, and trade to understand what was going on in the economy so that he could determine the appropriate price of money. After 10 years at the Fed, Greenspan had doubled the number of data series monitored by his institution to over 14,000, including a complex system to monitor inventories that his colleagues joked only their boss understood. This enabled him to spot economic shifts long before anyone else and quickly change the direction of monetary policy.[22]

This adulation is an expression of the dream of the planned economy—the idea that some enlightened man in a bathtub will understand the market better than all the millions of market players and that he will be able to use his insights to steer them in the right direction. There can be no doubt that Greenspan was unusually talented at reading the economy, but giving him such huge powers also made huge mistakes possible. Grant notes:

> If you accept that interest rates are the traffic signals of the financial economy, Greenspan said, "Turn them all green."

> By imposing this 1 percent interest rate, the Fed invited
> everyone and his brother and sister-in-law to go out and get
> a new mortgage and take on more debt.[23]

In a speech on December 19, 2002, Greenspan rejected the critics' claims that the Fed should fight asset bubbles. He said that central banks could not possibly tell a bubble from a nonbubble while it was expanding. What they were capable of, however, was "dealing aggressively with the aftermath of a bubble," for instance by pumping liquidity into markets.[24]

In a sense, this is the opposite of the usual job description for central banks. It means that the Fed does not take away the punch bowl when the party takes off. Instead, it treats the guests to its own bowl, filled to the brim with cheap credit, and it does not cut the supply until consumer prices start to show signs of being under the influence. But if this puts a damper on the atmosphere, the Fed immediately announces an afterparty and brings out even larger bowls to avoid losing momentum. In the market, this policy has been dubbed the "Greenspan put." Buying a "put" option means that you agree to sell something in the future at a predetermined price—if there is a crisis, Greenspan will ensure that your investments still fetch a reasonable price, as if you had bought such an option. His successor Ben Bernanke has acted similarly, so people in the market are now talking of the "Bernanke put" instead. In a 2002 speech, Bernanke presented arguments almost identical to those of Greenspan. Bubbles cannot be avoided, he said, but "the Fed should provide ample liquidity until the immediate crisis has passed. The Fed's response to the 1987 stock market break is a good example of what I have in mind."[25]

In each case, at the time of each crisis, it does of course seem necessary to stabilize financial markets and rebuild confidence. The alternative could be a recession, widespread manufacturing bankruptcies, and high unemployment. Politicians, voters, and the media all demand rapid action to minimize all problems. At the same time, however, each time there is a rescue operation, the risk of a new crisis increases. If somebody puts up a safety net, more and more people will try ever more advanced acrobatics; if the Fed always steps in to cure hangovers, people will be boozing uncontrollably. Greenspan and Bernanke both said it straight out in their 2002 speeches: The Fed will never do anything to reduce the value of stocks or homes, but if prices start plummeting, it will step in and tidy everything up. In late 2000, Ed Yardeni, the chief investment officer of Deutsche Bank Securities, said he was not worried about there being a deep crisis after the dot-com crash: "I am less concerned because I believe that the Fed is our friend."[26] Yardeni was right. His friend was there when he needed him, and that made investors even more confident that they could go on taking huge risks.

Not only outsiders considered the policy pursued by the Fed to be very risky. The minutes from the December 14, 2004, Fed meeting state that "some participants" warned that the Fed's low-interest-rate policy had encouraged "excessive risk-taking in financial markets" and that "speculative demands were becoming apparent in the market for single family homes and condominiums."[27] As the world's most important financial institution in the world's largest economy, the Fed also exerted a great deal of influence on the global economy by cutting interest rates.

The financial strategist George Cooper, who wants to rehabilitate a Keynesian analysis of the financial market, sees similarities between interventionist economist John Maynard Keynes's desire to stimulate demand in times of crisis and the behavior of the serial rate-cutters at the Fed—interestingly, however, he thinks the latter are more Catholic than the Pope in this respect. Keynes believed that an economy should be stimulated to escape from a deep depression. The Fed and the politicians of today have systematically stimulated the economy to keep it from ending up in a recession in the first place. This is what Cooper terms "preemptive Keynesianism." The difference is subtle but important. Recessions send important messages to market players, telling them that their investments have failed and that they have borrowed too much. That forces them to give up bad projects and get out of bad investment positions, moving the money to more productive parts of the economy. If the central bank and politicians step in every time to save the economy from a recession, it will lull borrowers and lenders into a false sense of security that will make them take ever-greater risks. They will be pushing a growing mountain of debt in front of them, and eventually the stimuli will not be large enough to prevent a collapse.[28]

On the 20th anniversary of the 1987 Black Monday, the "Buttonwood" column of *The Economist* noted that the market's continued faith in the "Bernanke put" may lead it straight to the precipice:

> One day, investors will realise central bankers are not magi-
> cians. That might be another Black Monday.[29]

Taking from the Poor and Lending to the Rich

"What is going on?" a surprised Alan Greenspan asked a colleague in June 2004. This time, the Maestro had come across a "conundrum" that not even he could figure out. After a whole year with 1 percent interest, he had finally started to feel concern about the housing boom, and consequently he had just raised the rate to 1.25 percent. But the long-term rate, which usually followed the short-term one, went not up but down, and Greenspan was flabbergasted. This pattern would repeat itself. As the Fed increased the interest rate step by step, it took longer than it had in the past to get the long-term rate—what the market is willing to pay for 10- and 30-year Treasury securities—to follow.

What happened was the Fed now had competition. It was no longer alone in pumping money into the U.S. economy: The low- and medium-income countries of the world had joined it. Globalization had allowed those countries to grow faster than ever before, and they now accounted for an increasing share of the global economy. That also led to explosive growth in global savings, and developing countries would invest more and more of their capital abroad.

As recently as 1999, the current account of the balance of payments of the developing world was negative—that is, developing countries were importing capital from the rest of the world to keep their economies going. But in the first years of the 21st century, that changed quickly, and China and the oil exporters in particular began to save their surpluses. In 2004, they amassed $400 billion of financial capital, and two years later they topped $600 billion. Most of those savings they exported to the United States by buying Treasuries, causing the price of money there—the interest rate—to stay low. This was one explanation for the much-talked-about global imbalances that involved Americans' borrowing and importing more and more while saving less and less.

Fed chairman Ben Bernanke has referred to this as a "savings glut." It is a paradoxical but well-known phenomenon that poor people often save a larger proportion of their income than rich people, because the poor need a buffer for bad times and unforeseen expenses. As the income of the poor has risen, so have their savings,

15

but investment opportunities are often limited in countries with many poor people, in part because the financial markets there are so underdeveloped that it would be impossible to gain a decent return. Since the United States is such a large and liquid market, most people feel it is one of the safest places to invest. You can always get your money back—which is not always the case in savers' home countries.

Even so, it does seem odd that the poor countries of the world should have been paying for consumption in its richest ones to such a large extent. In his book *Fixing Global Finance*, Martin Wolf, a leading economics writer at the *Financial Times*, argues that this is not the result of spontaneous saving and the free play of the market forces. Instead, these savings have largely been ordered by the governments of developing countries. The background to this can be found in these countries' recent experience of financial crises. Since their financial markets had lagged behind for so long, capital was rarely channeled into productive investments, creating a dependence on short-term foreign capital. The problem is that this is the sort of capital that will rush back out of the country at the first whiff of a crisis. The straw that finally broke the camel's back was the deep Asian crisis in 1997, when the Western world and the International Monetary Fund forced the countries hit by the crisis to meet humiliating requirements if they were to get any help. Many Asian countries decided then and there never again to be dependent on the generosity of the outside world. That is why they began to build their own buffers.

In Wolf's opinion, this saving had a very specific purpose: "At the heart of the story of the imbalances is official action to intervene in the foreign-currency market, to keep the currency down."[30] If, say, the Chinese government pushes down the exchange rate of its national currency, the yuan, China's exporters can sell more cheaply to other countries while its consumers have to pay higher prices.

If the market forces had had their full sway, huge export revenues would have been able to push up the value of the currency. That is because the rest of the world has to obtain yuan with which to buy Chinese goods. To avoid that, the Chinese immediately sent everything they earned back to the United States by making enormous purchases of U.S. Treasuries. Wolf calls this the biggest recycling operation in history. It is based on a series of systematic government actions. The Chinese government (to take one example) buys dollars from its exporters and has to ensure at the same time that it continues to have a surplus in the current account of the balance of payments. It therefore reduces private consumption nationally by maintaining high taxes, high interest rates, and strict credit controls. Through these actions, China has attained a level of saving that corresponds to almost 60 percent of gross domestic product. This has probably never been surpassed by any economy in history. One trillion dollars have been invested in U.S. securities.

In a world with more savings than ever before, the United States began to act as the borrower of last resort. There is nothing inevitable about this from a historical perspective. In fact, the world's leading economies have tended to be net exporters of capital, as the United Kingdom was in the 19th century. But now more than 70 percent of the surpluses found their way to U.S. stocks, bonds, bank accounts, direct investments—and above all Treasuries. However, this did not lead to more investments. Instead, it made U.S. households save less and consume more. This is not to say that American wastefulness is what created these imbalances. Martin Wolf points out that, if that had been the case, Americans would have demanded more capital, crowding out other willing borrowers by accepting higher interest rates. The wastefulness was an effect, not a cause. Governments of low- and medium-income countries were stepping up their saving and pushing down interest rates so far that Americans were able to spend. Until those countries allow the market to set exchange rates and develop financial markets that make it safe for them to invest in their own economies, these imbalances will remain.

The governors of the Fed, and many respected economists, have claimed that this policy means that the real-estate bubble should not be blamed on them. Greenspan could not possibly have resisted these floods of capital, they say. Regardless of what the Fed had done to short-term interest rates, the long-term rates would have been forced down. But this is wisdom in hindsight. When the Fed cut its benchmark rate, it took a conscious risk because it believed that otherwise, there would be a very deep crisis. Greenspan strongly widened the spread over long-term rates when he reduced the short-term one, which shows that the Fed was in fact calling the shots. If it was a real concern to him that the long-term rates took so long to turn upward from 2004 on, it is impossible to understand why he did not raise the Fed funds rate any faster. Even though the rate was increased, it was still so low that the Fed's major influence for a long time was to push more money into the economy, which also held the long term rate down. The belief that only external factors control the long-term rate is incorrect. Research in recent years shows that the Fed's adjustments to short-term rates strongly influence rates on 10- and 30-year loans as well.[31] In other words, the choices made both by the Fed and by developing countries played a large part in causing 10-year rates to fall from almost 7 percent in 2000 to less than 3.5 percent in 2003.

The low interest rates not only fed the housing bubble. Combined with the rapid rate of growth, they fueled a general hunt for risk. If you get no interest worth writing home about on bank deposits or safe bonds, you start looking for riskier investments that may give you a higher return. Investors now started falling over one another to find more exciting bets to make and more adventurous markets to enter, and if the return was too small, they did not mind borrowing a lot to make sure their tiny return would at least be multiplied many times over (this is called "leverage"). What's more, the U.S. government subsidizes corporate debt in that businesses may deduct interest payments from corporate income tax. The U.S. Treasury Department warned in December 2007:

> The current U.S. tax code favors debt over equity forms of finance because corporations can deduct interest expense, but not the return on equity-financed investment. . . . Excessive reliance on debt financing imposes costs on investors because of the associated increased risk of financial distress and bankruptcy.[32]

It had simply become cheaper to use other people's money than your own, and businesses worked hard to reduce their margins. The risk, of course, was that renewing the loans would be difficult if there was a crisis, but that seemed a far-fetched concern in a world awash with capital. In addition, the high growth rates made it seem as though there was a wide range of potential investment objects. James Grant once wrote a book entitled *The Trouble with Prosperity*, and U.S. economist Hyman Minsky claimed that "stability leads to instability." Their point is that nothing is more dangerous than good times because they encourage investors to borrow more and take bigger risks. If things look good, they are going to get worse.

"Investors said, 'I don't want to be in equities anymore, and I'm not getting any return in my bond positions,'" explains a financier who is the author of many financial innovations: "Two things happened. They took more and more leverage, and they reached for riskier asset classes. Give me yield, give me leverage, give me return."[33]

It's the Deficit, Stupid

U.S. households were not alone in opening wide their pocketbooks and bankbooks: The U.S. government did the same. By 2002, the Bush administration had turned a $127 billion surplus into a $158 billion deficit. This was not only the effect of the general economic downturn but also the result of conscious policy choices. The Democrats' classic "tax and spend" had been followed by Republican "borrow and spend." Immediately after his inauguration in January 2001, President Bush began to push for a $1.3 trillion tax cut over 10 years, but without a corresponding reduction in spending. Instead, he contributed to a very swift rise in government expenditures, particularly after 9/11, both through the wars in Iraq and Afghanistan and through new domestic spending. The 2003 Medicare prescription drug benefit was the biggest new U.S. government program since the 1960s.

The Bush administration represented a new form of conservatism—"big-government conservatism"—which stipulates that the large government sector is not going to be dismantled but rather is going to be used to achieve conservative goals. Treasury Secretary Paul O'Neill warned that the policies pursued were irresponsible and would soon require huge tax increases or spending cuts. Vice President Dick Cheney told him off, explaining that budget deficits do not matter. A month later, O'Neill was fired. The conservative *Weekly Standard* magazine, though, informed its readers that budget deficits do matter: they are a good thing because they help save the economy from a recession.[34] Keynesianism had made inroads among neoconservatives.

In many cases, Congress rather than the White House was the origin of proposals for cotton subsidies or bridges to nowhere. The spendthrift impulses of members of Congress had been kept in check since 1990 by a law under which all new expenditures and tax cuts had to be funded by other budget proposals—or else painful cuts that nobody wanted to be guilty of would automatically be made to the armed forces and entitlement programs. Alan Greenspan warned the House Budget Committee that the absence of such a mechanism would very soon make the inherent deficit-creating tendency of politics gain the upper hand. Half the members did not show up for his presentation, and the other half obviously did not want to listen. On September 30, 2002, the Budget Enforcement Act was put to sleep by a large majority. Members of Congress were again free to promise voters anything.

At that point, the country would have needed a president who could face down demands and veto irresponsible spending. Ronald Reagan used his veto 78 times during his presidency, often against spending bills. George H. W. Bush vetoed 44 bills during four years in the White House.[35] His son, however, became the first president in 176 years to go a whole term without using his veto. After five years in power, George W. Bush still had not vetoed anything. A dismayed Alan Greenspan pleaded with the president's aides to veto at least some spending items, if for no other reason than to send a message that Congress would not be able to get away with just about anything—only to be told that the president abstained out of consideration for House Speaker Dennis Hastert, thinking that he could control him better by not challenging him. That was further proof that one-party control of both the White House and Congress leads to open season on the taxpayers.

In 1989, the real-estate tycoon Seymour Durst put a digital counter on the sidewall of a building near Times Square in New York City. It was a "national-debt clock," and Durst's aim was to highlight the fact that the U.S. national debt had attained an unbelievable $2.7 trillion and kept growing. In 2004, it was replaced with a new clock that could count backward as well. That was overly optimistic. Up was the only way the clock ever had to go, and on September 30, 2008, it reached its upper limit as the debt passed $10 trillion for the first time. That meant the display had run out of digits. A new national-debt clock will soon be put up, with room for two more digits, just to make sure.

During the Bush presidency, billions of dollars of support was showered on the transportation sector, schools, agriculture, and the pharmaceutical industry. Overall, President Bush increased spending faster than any of his predecessors since Lyndon B. Johnson. A

Treasury official during the first Bush presidency, Bruce Bartlett, has issued a blistering opinion on the 43rd president:

> I think it is telling that Bush's Democratic predecessor, Bill Clinton, was far better on the budget than he has been. Clinton vetoed bills because they spent too much. Bush never does. Clinton not only reduced the deficit, but he actually cut spending. Bush has increased both. Clinton abolished an entitlement program. Bush created an extremely expensive new one.[36]

In the first years of the 21st century, Americans had a pleasant problem. They were surrounded by institutions that showered money on them. The Fed set interest rates at the lowest level in half a century; the administration increased spending to historically high levels while lowering taxes; and developing countries saved more than ever, sending their savings to the United States.

The economic crises that struck several Asian and Latin American developing countries in the 1990s were crucial to the economist Nouriel Roubini's choice of research field. He set about studying the preconditions and patterns of such crises. Their background often included large asset bubbles, financed by risky foreign loans, which could in some situations cause sudden panics in shaky financial systems. In 2004, Professor Roubini sat down to think about what country would likely be the next one to run into trouble. Where were the largest bubbles and the deepest deficits to be found? His answer was that the country that looked the most like a rickety developing country at that time was in fact the world's biggest economy: the United States of America.[37]

Ludwig von Mises had warned of this as early as 1944:

> True, governments can reduce the rate of interest in the short run. They can issue additional paper money. They can open the way to credit expansion by the banks. They can thus create an artificial boom and the appearance of prosperity. But such a boom is bound to collapse sooner or later and to bring about a depression.[38]

2. Castles in the Air

Come to see victory
In a land called fantasy

—From a song by Earth, Wind and Fire, who entertained
at Fannie Mae's big Christmas party in 2006

Henry Cisneros would often drive out to Lago Vista, a new housing development in the southern, and poor, part of San Antonio, Texas. This was an area characterized by pawnshops and used-car dealerships. Cisneros was anxious to ensure that the people living in the 428 homes were happy, because he was the one who had put them there. Literally, because his company, American CityVista, had initiated the development in 2000, but also spiritually, because as Bill Clinton's housing secretary from 1993 to 1997, he had carried out major changes to the system, causing explosive growth in this type of homeownership among low-income earners. The grandchild of Mexican immigrants, Cisneros had a particularly soft spot for ethnic minorities who were unable to buy their own homes—most residents of Lago Vista were Latinos. Cisneros's energy and charisma had made him the ideal housing secretary for President Clinton, whose campaign promises had included government support to help more people own their homes.

As one of the companies behind Lago Vista put it in a commercial, "One of the greatest misconceptions today is people who sit back and think, 'I can't afford to buy.'" Indeed, government subsidies made it possible for people to take out big mortgages without having to spend a cent of their own money. "This was our first home," explains one Lago Vista resident. "I was a student making $17,000 a year; my wife was between jobs. In retrospect, how in hell did we qualify?"

The policy to expand homeownership, which was pursued with equal enthusiasm by presidents Clinton and Bush, enjoyed unprecedented success. The proportion of people who owned their homes had been fairly stable for about 30 years but suddenly rose from under 64 percent to over 67 percent between 1993 and 2000, and in 2004 it exceeded 69 percent for the first time.[1] The left saw this as a way to reduce discrimination and marginalization; the right saw it as a way to build an ownership society and to give low-income earners a stake in the American dream. Both sides used the federal government to drive this development. In the recent words of left-wing economist James Galbraith, son of the legendary economist John Kenneth Galbraith:

> the housing sector exists on this scale thanks to a vast network of supporting financial institutions, subject to federal deposit insurance, the secondary mortgage markets provided by quasi-public corporations (Fannie Mae, Ginnie Mae, Freddie Mac), and the tax deductibility of mortgage interest. Since 1986, when the tax deductibility of other forms of interest was eliminated, homeownership rates rose—thanks to the state, not the market.[2]

On the other side of the political spectrum, enthusiasm was at least as strong. Former Fed chairman Alan Greenspan recently stated:

> I was aware that the loosening of mortgage credit terms for subprime borrowers increased financial risk, and that subsidized homeownership initiatives distort market outcomes. But I believed then, as now, that the benefits of broadened homeownership are worth the risk.[3]

But it did not take long for cracks to appear in the walls, and this whole political project now looks as if it had been jerry-built. Henry Cisneros rarely visits the Lago Vista development these days. Not only did the jogging tracks and swimming beach that had been promised never materialize, but more and more households are finding it hard to pay the huge loans that they were granted on such flimsy grounds. An increasing number of homes have been abandoned by their owners, and the banks are foreclosing on them— that is, they take over the houses and try to sell them cheap to cut their losses. The area is starting to decay, and residents complain of rising crime.

Foreclosures are now spreading like wildfire across the United States. In October 2008, more than 279,500 American homes were in foreclosure, and there are few buyers.[4] The whole noble project of expanding homeownership to new groups has collapsed, and the statistics are falling back toward the old levels—the difference being that many people have had their personal finances blown to pieces on the way. When the *New York Times* runs a profile on Henry Cisneros today, he is wise in hindsight: "People came to homeowner-ship who should not have been homeowners," he says.[5]

A Message to the Lending Community

The first government projects to increase homeownership were launched during the Great Depression in the 1930s. Because savings and loan associations were not allowed to expand across state bound-aries at that time, they could not develop a national market for mortgages to spread risk.[6] To compensate for that, President Franklin D. Roosevelt founded a federal mortgage corporation, the Federal National Mortgage Association, in 1938. In 1968, private stockhold-ers were allowed to take stakes so that Fannie Mae would not have to be recorded as an expenditure in the federal budget, which was already weighed down by the Vietnam War and burgeoning entitle-ment programs. Even so, there was no doubt whatsoever about the link to the federal government. The president of the United States appointed five of the members of Fannie Mae's board of directors, and there was an implicit federal guarantee for the mortgages. At the same time, the part of operations that directly generated mort-gage loans from the federal government was moved out of Fannie Mae and placed in a separate institution called the Government National Mortgage Association, or Ginnie Mae. On the pattern of Fannie Mae, Congress then established the Federal Home Loan Mort-gage Corporation in 1970. Freddie Mac was initially chartered to serve savings and loan associations, but later its authorities were expanded to directly compete with Fannie. Together they constitute the conventional secondary mortgage market.

That meant that Fannie and Freddie did not themselves lend money to homebuyers, but when a bank had done so, Fannie and Freddie would buy the loan from the bank, so that the bank got its money back and could lend even more to other prospective homebuyers. Sometimes Fannie and Freddie would keep mortgage loans that they had bought from banks, but they often packaged those loans with other loans and sold the packages to other investors, which freed up resources to buy even more mortgages. At the same time, Fannie and Freddie guaranteed that they would pay both interest and principal to the investors even if the borrowers could not afford to do so. For this generous insurance, they charged a fee, which they made huge profits on.

In the debate about how Fannie and Freddie inflated the housing bubble, the right has claimed that they were government corporations, whereas the left has argued that they were private businesses. But as we have seen, they were in fact an entirely different animal—a hybrid of public and private. The technical name for the hybrid that they represent is government-sponsored enterprise (GSE). A GSE is potentially the most dangerous type of enterprise since it may allow private owners to take any risks they can imagine, pocket any profits for themselves, but count on taxpayers to take care of any losses. Fannie and Freddie have been privately owned, but with a political mission and with an implicit federal guarantee in case they should fail. That guarantee has made their business concept a lucrative one. Thanks to the federal guarantee, they have been able to lend at lower interest rates than others (almost as low as the rate that the federal government pays on its own debt), and they have used the money that they have borrowed to buy mortgages for which they have been paid at market rates. The Congressional Budget Office has calculated that Fannie Mae earned $3.9 billion on this guarantee in 1995, of which $2.5 billion was used to reduce mortgage costs and the rest was pure corporate profit. What's more, Fannie and Freddie have been exempt from the usual capital requirements, as well as from both state and federal income tax. These exemptions are worth several hundred million dollars to them each year.[7]

Fannie and Freddie used to focus on reducing the housing costs of the broad middle class, but during the Clinton administration, they shifted their attention toward low-income earners. Candidate Clinton had stressed the need to expand homeownership to new groups, and all parts of the mortgage machinery had received the message. In March 1994, Fannie promised a "Trillion Dollar Commitment" to do for low-income earners and minorities what it had previously done for the middle class. A trillion dollars was spent to give 10 million low-income people their own homes.

Another sign that something new was in the offing was the 1995 tightening of the Community Reinvestment Act, a law first enacted in 1977 to reduce discrimination against minorities in the housing market. Some American inner-city districts were in decay at that time, and many believed it was because people with low incomes had difficulties taking out mortgages. The CRA prescribed that any bank or other institution covered by federal deposit insurance had to provide mortgage loans throughout its region of operation, including in poor areas. The task of checking that they actually did so fell to the government agencies in charge of supervising each lender in other respects.

This decentralized model of supervision had its limitations, but the 1995 amendment led to more standardized monitoring of compliance. The process underpinning decisions to grant a loan or not became less interesting; what counted instead was the number of loans made to households earning less than 80 percent of the median income. A bank scoring a low CRA grade could be prevented from expanding by opening new branch offices or from merging with another bank. In 1995, U.S. banks became free to merge with banks in any other state, meaning that it was very important for all those wishing to join in the expansion to keep an eye on their ranking and employ special CRA officers.[8]

One way to show your willingness to meet the needs of low-income earners was to buy loans granted to them. The amendment actually made this easier by allowing mortgages to be "securitized"—that is, gathered together, repackaged, and sold to investors as securities based on the risk each investor was willing to take. In October 1997, First Union and Bear Stearns proudly announced that they had performed a "unique transaction." They were the first in the industry to securitize CRA mortgages. The mortgages were guaranteed by Freddie Mac, and even though the securities they sold included risky loans, they were given the highest possible credit rating. The CRA officer of First Union trumpeted:

> First Union is committed to promoting homeownership in traditionally underserved markets through a comprehensive line of competitive and flexible affordable mortgage products. This transaction enables us to continue to aggressively serve those markets.[9]

The securities worth $384.6 billion were oversubscribed several times over. Another pioneer in the field could triumphantly proclaim that it doubled its profit by selling repackaged CRA mortgages to a certain New York bank in need of improving its CRA grade.[10]

One reason politicians decided to publicize information about mortgages and CRA grades was to encourage public debate about them. Their tactic worked: various citizens' groups started to pressure banks into expanding their lending. One of these groups was the Association of Community Organizations for Reform Now, and one of its most successful activists was Madeleine Talbott at ACORN Chicago. She launched meetings for banks that agreed to lower their creditworthiness requirements and reduce the down payments they demanded, and she organized protest rallies against those that did not. Her goal was to push banks—"kicking and screaming"—into more generous lending practices.[11] The CRA gave these groups real power because official complaints from them could be used against banks when their CRA grades were to be evaluated. For example, Chase Manhattan and J. P. Morgan donated hundreds of thousands of dollars to ACORN in conjunction with their application for permission to merge.[12] This gave nourishment to activists who demanded more federal action in support of cheap housing for low-income earners. The CRA in itself probably did not lead to any major increase in lending, and investments banks—which would go on to make the most mind-boggling deals—were not covered by it. But it did have a major indirect effect in that it fostered the development of new groups that increased the momentum of a political process. These groups, through their interaction with the Department of Housing and Urban Development, Congress, Fannie, Freddie, real-estate agents, and financiers, caused various types of housing programs to expand.

Madeleine Talbott of ACORN was a key player when several financial institutions agreed in 1993 to launch an innovative national $55 million package to give home loans to households on low incomes and with low creditworthiness. Fannie Mae bought the mortgages. Talbott had high expectations for the project: "If this pilot program works it will send a message to the lending community that it's OK to make these kind of loans."[13]

The message was loud and clear. Even in February 2008, economist Stan Liebowitz could find CRA-mortgage offers on the Internet with "100 percent financing . . . no credit scores . . . undocumented income . . . even if you don't report it on your tax returns."[14]

Stretching the Rules a Bit

Under Henry Cisneros, HUD continued its work on many fronts. It started guaranteeing mortgages to families that could prove only three years of stable income, where five years would previously have been needed. Cisneros also made it easier for lenders who wanted a federal guarantee. They no longer had to interview borrowers personally, and they no longer had to have houses appraised by an external party.

But nothing was more important than the requirements to expand lending that he imposed on Fannie Mae and Freddie Mac. In December 1995, Cisneros for the first time set a quantitative target for Fannie's and Freddie's mortgage portfolios. That target drew on a new federal regulatory structure introduced in 1992. At least 42 percent of all mortgages traded by Fannie and Freddie had to go to households with "low and moderate income," and targets were also set for the number of loans to be granted to marginalized areas and families with "very low income." HUD was pleased to see that Fannie and Freddie not only attained their targets but also actually exceeded them. Those who bought the mortgages from Fannie and Freddie risked nothing because the two government-sponsored enterprises guaranteed them, and Fannie and Freddie themselves also took little risk because the federal government guaranteed their operations.

But it was not always possible to reconcile those targets with traditional creditworthiness checks and requirements for down payments. To be able to extend loans to low-income earners who would not normally have been granted them, "lenders have had to stretch the rules a bit," as one of them put it.[15] The author of that statement was the CEO of Countrywide, a mortgage giant, who during a solemn meeting with Henry Cisneros had signed a pledge to use "proactive creative efforts" to expand homeownership to minorities and people with low incomes. In 1996, Countrywide opened a division dedicated to subprime mortgages.

"Subprime" is the label stuck on a borrower who is deemed more likely to end up being unable to repay a loan, perhaps because of past defaults or bankruptcies. Many U.S. institutions define "subprime" as a person who scores below 620 on the FICO scale from 300 to 850, which is the most commonly used creditworthiness scale. Since such people entail greater risk, they typically must pay several percentage points higher interest on their loans than "prime" borrowers. That subprime borrowers could now obtain loans constituted progress in and of itself, because if the blotches on their credit records were sins of the distant past, they would be given a chance to rebuild their lives. There were also examples of abuse in the credit industry, with small lenders conning people into taking out loans on exorbitant terms; the victims would often be offered reduced rates at first to trick them into disregarding the heavy blow that they would get soon after. Having large institutions enter the subprime market was initially viewed as a way to get it under control and weed out abuse.

Countrywide, which had grown into a true giant with, at its peak, over 60,000 employees and 900 branch offices, was the largest seller of mortgages to Fannie Mae. Theirs was a very close relationship; wags in the housing industry joked that Countrywide was a subsidiary of Fannie. The background to this was that Fannie had offered Countrywide special discounts and benefits in the early 1990s to be allowed to buy as many of its mortgages as possible.[16] Fannie explained in a public report that this conferred certain privileges on Countrywide:

> Countrywide tends to follow the most flexible underwriting criteria permitted under GSE [government-sponsored enterprise] and FHA [Federal Housing Administration] guidelines. Because Fannie Mae and Freddie Mac tend to give their best lenders access to the most flexible underwriting criteria, Countrywide benefits from its status as one of the largest originators of mortgage loans and one of the largest participants in the GSE programs.[17]

Senior management of Fannie Mae did not come away empty-handed either. In June 2008, the *Wall Street Journal* revealed that two former Fannie CEOs had been granted loans by Countrywide on particularly favorable terms. Those CEOs were referred to by another acronym in Countrywide's internal communication: "FOA," or "Friends of Angelo." "Angelo" referred to Angelo Mozilo, the CEO of Countrywide. Another friend of Angelo was the powerful senator Christopher Dodd (D-CT), who was both one of Congress's strongest supporters of Fannie and Freddie and the top recipient of campaign contributions from them.[18]

There was a background to the relaxation of underwriting standards carried out by Fannie and Freddie. As far back as April 1993, the Federal Reserve Bank of Boston published an influential and systematic attack on the lending criteria that have been considered the norm in the credit industry since the beginning of banking: creditworthiness, stable income, interest payments not exceeding a certain percentage of the borrower's wages, and so forth. This was important because the Boston Fed, like the other 11 regional Fed banks, is involved in the supervision and regulation of commercial banks and because the new ideas spread across the country. Its 27-page manual from 1993 aimed to explain what banks should do to avoid discrimination in mortgage lending. The key sentence of that manual instructs that, to attract minority customers, lenders must refrain from "unreasonable measures of creditworthiness" and instead use procedures that are "appropriate to the economic culture of urban, lower-income, and nontraditional consumers."[19]

The Boston Fed suggested, among other things, that lenders must not be overly skeptical of poor borrowers asking for loans that make up a larger proportion of their income than what is usual. It also pointed out that temporary sources of income such as unemployment benefits should count in such borrowers' favor and that citizens' groups or local governments could step in to make the down payment. The authors of the manual went so far as to say that lenders should not even exclude households having previously defaulted on their loans, because low-income earners may be hit by unexpected expenses. One way of assessing whether someone should be granted a loan could instead be to investigate whether he or she had participated in "credit counseling or buyer education programs." To give banks stronger motivation to make this new gospel their own, the report began with a warning that a bank sued for discrimination could be fined up to $500,000.[20]

There was no lack of criticism. The economists Theodore Day and Stan Liebowitz warned of raising expectations too high in a 1998 journal article:

> We are likely to find, with the adoption of flexible underwriting standards, that we are merely encouraging banks to make unsound loans. If this is the case, current policy will not have helped its intended beneficiaries if in future years they are dispossessed from their homes due to an inability to make their mortgage payments.[21]

But they were not the kind of economists who had the ear of policy-makers and who were to be found in the corridors of power. The foreword to the Boston Fed's clarion call for looser lending was signed by its president, Richard F. Syron. In 2003, he became CEO of Freddie Mac.

Henry Cisneros quit his job as housing secretary after a scandal in 1997 and embarked on a career course that had been opened up by the rule changes he himself had brought about. He became a member of the board of directors of Fannie's favorite corporation, Countrywide, and at the same time jointly started up a construction and development business with the building company KB Home, whose board he also joined, together with, among others, a former CEO of Fannie Mae. In his new role, Cisneros started constructing buildings in poor areas, guaranteed by—Fannie Mae. It's a small world.

Cisneros was replaced as housing secretary by the youngest-ever occupant of that post, Andrew Cuomo, son of former New York governor Mario Cuomo. One of his first duties was to set new targets for Fannie's and Freddie's lending. He prepared those by launching an attack against the duo, accusing them of discrimination on the grounds that not enough of their mortgages went to minorities. Cuomo's closest aide, William Apgar, demanded "flexibility"—code for less strict requirements for creditworthiness and down payments: "We believe that there are a lot of loans to black Americans that are good loans that could be safely purchased by Fannie Mae and Freddie Mac if these companies were more flexible."[22]

In July 1999, Andrew Cuomo proposed stricter requirements for Fannie and Freddie. The share of mortgages to be granted to those earning less than the median income in their area was raised from 42 to 50 percent, and the share that should go to people on very low incomes increased from 14 to 20 percent. The chairman of Fannie Mae, Franklin D. Raines, was very receptive to the new message: "We have not been a major presence in the subprime market, but you can bet that under these goals we will be."[23]

Fannie Mae kept that promise, launching a large subprime project in September 1999. Twenty-four banks in 15 markets would help Fannie roll out mortgages to people who would not normally qualify as borrowers. They would have to pay only one extra percentage point of interest on their loans, and if they made all payments on time during the first two years, even that distinction would be removed. Fannie hoped that, by buying such mortgages, it would encourage other banks and mortgage institutions to lend more and more along similar lines. The project would be launched nationally in the spring. In the same year, Fannie set itself the goal of doubling its profits in five years, and its employees were rewarded with stock options when that goal was achieved.

In 1999, Steven Holmes noted in the *New York Times* that, by pushing through such projects, the administration could cause a repeat of the housing crisis of the 1980s:

> In moving, even tentatively, into this new area of lending, Fannie Mae is taking on significantly more risk, which may not pose any difficulties during flush economic times. But the government-subsidized corporation may run into trouble in an economic downturn, prompting a government rescue similar to that of the savings and loan industry in the 1980s.[24]

But there was nothing tentative about the actions of Fannie Mae. The following year, it announced that its Trillion Dollar Commitment from 1994 had been completed. Instead it launched an "American Dream Commitment," under which $2 trillion would be spent on expanding homeownership to 18 million low-income earners and minorities. In 2000, Fannie Mae bought only $1.2 billion worth of subprime mortgages, but it also pledged that only 10 years later, it would buy risky loans to low-income earners for almost 1,700 times more money. The extreme rate of subsequent growth showed that this was a reasonable forecast. In 2001, Fannie bought subprime mortgages for $9.2 billion, and in the next year, it spent $15 billion on them. That was also the year when Fannie launched a program for mortgages with no down payment whatsoever. In 2004, it and Freddie Mac had already spent $175 billion together.[25]

Fannie Mae and Freddie Mac's large-scale subprime expansion made it profitable for other institutions to grant subprime mortgages in order to sell them to Fannie and Freddie. But that was not the extent of their influence. By systematically, over a series of years, opening up the market for owning homes to people who had previously rented, they had also pushed up house prices. As more and more people were trying to squeeze into a limited stock of housing, the bubble increasingly inflated until home construction caught up with the new demand. Now that Fannie and Freddie were also rushing headlong into the young and underdeveloped subprime market, they sent a clear message to all those who had been glancing warily at high-risk borrowers and complex loan structures: "Pull out all the stops!" And if the two government-sponsored giants of the mortgage market say it's OK, that's the way it is.

At the same time, Fannie and Freddie reassured the world that their new commitments involved no new risks. In 2002, Fannie paid the Nobel laureate Joseph Stiglitz, the future federal budget director Peter Orszag, and economist Jonathan Orszag to conduct a study that found that there was "extremely low probability" that Fannie and Freddie would become insolvent. The study talked about scenarios with a likelihood of one in more than 500,000 and claimed that the risk to the government was "effectively zero."[26]

However, Fannie and Freddie's new, cocky attitude was out of all proportion to their ability. When mortgages were to be rolled out at such breakneck speed to a group that had not been allowed to borrow before, neither its systems nor its credit analysts could keep up. "We didn't really know what we were buying," admits Marc Gott, a former director at Fannie. "This system was designed for plain vanilla loans, and we were trying to push chocolate sundaes through the gears."[27]

HUD stated in its own documents that the new requirements it was imposing on Fannie and Freddie might need to be accompanied by more explicit monitoring of the loans made. Concerned that lending might grow irresponsible, many citizens' groups also called for such monitoring. But when the targets were established in October 2000, HUD Secretary Cuomo had dismissed all thoughts of reporting requirements or lending rules. For example, Fannie and Freddie could buy mortgages where borrowers faced a penalty for early repayment, meaning that they would be forced to pay high rates of interest even if interest rates fell in society. In 2005, 1 in 10 Fannie mortgages had such penalty clauses. And many of the mortgages that Fannie and Freddie bought were designed to attract borrowers by offering very low interest rates to begin with but raising them significantly after some time. As it turned out, the all-out political effort did not get the subprime market under control—rather, that sector ended up making politics subprime.

Andrew Cuomo also opened up the Federal Housing Administration for ever-riskier mortgages. The FHA, which was founded during the New Deal, insures millions of mortgages by giving compensation to lenders whose customers cannot pay their loans. The price of such insurance is the same for subprime borrowers as for those with a good credit record. Cuomo almost doubled the upper limit for an FHA mortgage, raising it to $235,000. He also reduced the required down payment to 3 percent while initiating programs to ensure that borrowers would not have to pay even that 3 percent out of their own pockets.

Such encouragement of subprime mortgages led the *Village Voice* to designate Andrew Cuomo as "the man who gave birth to the mortgage crisis." Although many politicians were pursuing similar policies because they were close to Fannie and Freddie or to activist groups demanding cheaper housing, the *Voice* claims that Cuomo's policies were dictated by his close ties to the banking and mortgage industry. Banks and mortgage institutions were the ones that profited from the extension of federal mortgage insurance; they were the ones that wanted Fannie and Freddie to focus on low-income earners so that they could have the well-heeled customers to themselves, and at the same time they were also the ones that wanted Fannie and Freddie to buy every single loan they made.

Cuomo was a popular guest at the Mortgage Bankers Association, a heavyweight lobby group. Two of his close aides moved from HUD to the MBA, and several top MBA officials donated money to him. *Real Estate Finance Today*, the MBA's weekly magazine, regularly paid tribute to Cuomo. Groups such as ACORN shared the objective of wringing out more subprime mortgages, but the differences were clear from the details. The consumer groups also called for stricter rules to ensure that borrowers would not be saddled with costly subprime mortgages even though they could have qualified for cheaper ones. Cuomo, by contrast, was the first U.S. housing secretary to establish that institutions could not be sued for tricking people into accepting more expensive mortgages than they were entitled to—a clarification welcomed by the industry in the pages of *Real Estate Finance Today*.[28]

"It was a mistake" is how William Apgar, then Cuomo's closest aide, today describes HUD's guiding of the government-sponsored enterprises toward the subprime market. "In hindsight, I would have done it differently."[29] But some people in politics have more lives than a cat. Andrew Cuomo has moved on: Since 2006, he is attorney general of New York State, and he is spoken of as a possible governor or senator.

The Ownership Society

When Fannie Mae and Freddie Mac collapsed in 2008, the Bush administration quickly circulated the story of how it had seen the problems coming years ago and had tried to gain control over operations but how the Democrats in Congress blocked the attempt. White House officials even penned a talking-points memo entitled "G.S.E.'s—We Told You So." It described a 2003 report from Armando Falcon Jr. at the Office of Federal Housing Enterprise Oversight, whose job it was to keep an eye on Fannie and Freddie, where he warned that the two government-sponsored enterprises engaged in such irresponsible lending practices and risk management that they could become insolvent. According to Falcon, this could have a domino effect, causing liquidity shortages in the market.

There was just one small detail that Bush's aides left out of their talking-points memo: The same day that Falcon published his report, he received a call from the White House personnel department informing him that he was fired.[30]

President Bush's aim was to create an "ownership society" where citizens would be in control of their own lives and wealth through ownership, which would promote both independence and responsibility. But that did not just mean free markets based on private-property rights—it was the expression of a willingness to use the levers of government to treat ownership more favorably than other contractual relationships in the marketplace. One of Bush's key objectives was to increase the proportion of homeownership, and two of his best friends in that endeavor were called Fannie and Freddie.

One sunny day in June 2002, President Bush visited the home of police officer Darrin West in Park Place South, a poor neighborhood of Atlanta, Georgia. Officer West had just been able to buy a house there thanks to a government loan that covered his down payment. The president had dropped in on him to explain the problem of blacks and Latinos not owning their homes to the same extent as whites, and to tell him what he proposed to do about it. The number of members of various minority groups who owned their homes would be 5.5 million higher by 2010, and that would be achieved by means of Fannie, Freddie, federal loans, and government subsidies. In Bush's own words:

> It means we use the mighty muscle of the federal government in combination with state and local governments to encourage owning your own home.[31]

Indeed, the Republicans endorsed virtually all the decisions made by Henry Cisneros and Andrew Cuomo—and upped the ante. Bush designed new federal subsidies for first-time buyers, whom he wanted to be covered by federal insurance even if they did not deposit a single cent as down payment. In 2004, it was time to set new targets for the government-sponsored enterprises. Cisneros had demanded that 42 percent of Fannie's and Freddie's mortgages go to low-income earners, and Cuomo had raised that to 50 percent. The Bush administration raised it once more, stipulating 56 percent in 2008. An even more remarkable change was that the proportion of loans to be made to people with very low incomes was to increase from 20 percent all the way up to 28.

"No one wanted to stop that bubble," according to Lawrence Lindsey, Bush's senior economic aide. "It would have conflicted with the president's own policies."[32] And to some extent, housing policy had acquired a momentum of its own. As more people could get mortgages more easily, more of them entered the housing market and prices went up. That in turn made it more difficult for those who had not yet ventured into that market to afford a home, meaning that new political interventions were required to make it even easier to get a mortgage, which pushed prices even higher. And yet the huge mortgages looked harmless, exactly because prices kept rising and you could easily take out a new loan on your old home.

The administration's attitude toward Fannie and Freddie did not begin to change until after a startling scandal. In June 2003, only a few months after its regulators had declared Freddie Mac's accounts "accurate and reliable," it was revealed that the enterprise had stashed away profits of $6.9 billion in the previous three years for use in harder times. Scrutiny of the government-sponsored enterprises' accounts then showed that Fannie Mae had cooked its books, too, but by overstating profits to ensure that its bosses would get their full bonuses. A series of other irregularities was also exposed, and the senior executives were sent packing.

It came as a shock that the GSEs, seen by many as a type of charitable society—President Bush liked to say that they did business from their hearts—appeared to have learned their bookkeeping skills from Enron. Only a few days before the scandal at Freddie Mac broke, its supervisor, the Office of Federal Housing Enterprise Oversight, had stated the following in a report to Congress:

> Freddie Mac's proprietary risk management programs and systems are effective. Management effectively conveys an appropriate message of integrity and ethical values. Management's philosophy and operating style have a pervasive effect on the company. The organizational structure and the assignment of responsibility provide for accountability and controls.[33]

Now the OFHEO had to talk about large-scale fraud at the government-sponsored enterprises instead, and it fined them more than half a billion dollars. The accounting scams strengthened Fannie's and Freddie's skeptics in the Bush administration. Alan Greenspan sharply criticized them for exposing the economy to risk, and President Bush reinstated Armando Falcon Jr., the critic of Fannie and Freddie who had in fact been fired, in his job as their supervisor. The administration decided to tighten supervision of the two enterprises and wanted a bank-like receivership process in the event of a crisis that would stipulate that the federal government did not guarantee all their liabilities. This would have dealt a disastrous blow to the enterprises' business model, which was built solely on the "big, fat gap" (in Greenspan's words[34]) between the cheap interest rates at which they could borrow thanks to the federal guarantee and the market rates they earned on their lending.

But the administration would not get the last word. At an investors' meeting in 1999, Fannie Mae's CEO Franklin Raines had declared, "We manage our political risk with the same intensity that we manage our credit and interest rate risks."[35] If anything, that was an understatement. As Fannie was progressively losing control of the mortgages it bought, it devoted more and more time and money to monitoring all political threats to its financial position. Over the years, it had also used its profits to build a lobbying organization with local offices and a network of politicians that few institutions could match. In the past decade, Fannie has spent $170 million on lobbying and donations to political candidates.[36] Fannie and Freddie often hired politicians' relatives to work at their local offices, and friendly politicians could themselves find well-paid employment with the government-sponsored enterprises during periods when they were out of elected office. In exchange for political support, Fannie and Freddie regularly let members of Congress announce large housing developments for low-income earners—in practice, political decisions that never had to pass through political decision-making processes. By contrast, members of Congress who wanted to whittle down the privileges of Fannie or Freddie would be drowned in angry calls and letters, and voters would receive automatic phone messages: "Your congressman is trying to make mortgages more expensive. Ask him why he opposes the American dream of homeownership."[37]

The strategy had been outstandingly successful, and the critics of the two enterprises had been beaten back time and again. In 1999, President Clinton's Treasury secretary Lawrence Summers was concerned about Fannie and Freddie, but his reform proposal was shot down. They could even flout the rules of the New York Stock Exchange, under which a corporation that does not present annual reports on its financial position must be removed from trading. When Fannie failed to do so, the NYSE introduced an exemption—applicable if "delisting would be significantly contrary to the national interest." The Securities and Exchange Commission approved the exemption, and Fannie Mae could remain listed.[38]

One of those who got a taste of Fannie's and Freddie's wrath was Rep. Richard Baker (R-LA), who had obtained information in 2003 from their supervisory authority about how much they paid their top executives. Fannie and Freddie threatened to sue him if he went public with the information, which made him keep it under his hat for a year. Baker, who has now left Congress, told the *Washington Post* that he had never experienced anything like it: "The political arrogance exhibited in their heyday, there has never been before or since a private entity that exerted that kind of political power."[39]

When the Bush administration had turned its back on them, Fannie and Freddie set their entire lobbying machine in motion to mount a violent attack on the reform proposals. They mobilized the housing and real-estate finance industry and activist groups they had often donated money to, and they went for a large-scale advertising campaign on TV and radio. "But that could mean we won't be able to afford the new house," a dejected woman in one of the TV spots concluded about the consequences of the proposals. Fannie and Freddie won. The Democrats put up strong resistance, managing to remove the receivership provisions from the House bill, leading the bill to become so watered down that the administration no longer wanted to support it. In the Senate, Robert Bennett (R-UT) managed to weaken the provisions regarding securities disclosures and capital requirements.

Senator Bennett's second-largest donor was Fannie Mae. His son worked for Fannie in Utah.

Anybody Could Have Seen It

To Fannie Mae and Freddie Mac, their defeat of the Bush administration was as costly as the Greek commander Pyrrhus's original Pyrrhic victory over the Romans at Asculum. They used to enjoy broad support from both political parties, but now that the administration had turned against them, they had to rely more and more on the congressional Democrats, who wanted even faster expansion of the two enterprises' most popular operation: loans to low-income earners and minorities. Fannie and Freddie's only chance of survival was to cultivate the Democrats' support by letting go of all restraint with regard to credit checks and lending. They had also lost time because of the accounting scandals, which had allowed other lenders to take market share from them. And at this point, most low-income earners who could handle a mortgage on normal market terms already got one long ago. The government-sponsored enterprises therefore had to venture into even riskier territory in their attempt to regain lost ground.

Daniel Mudd, the CEO of Fannie Mae, left no doubt about the future strategy. He told his workers to "get aggressive on risk-taking, or get out of the company." A former employee explained to the *New York Times* that everybody knew they had started buying mortgages in an unsustainable way, "but our mandate was to stay relevant and to serve low-income borrowers. So that's what we did."[40] In mid-2004, Freddie Mac's chief risk officer David Andrukonis told the CEO Richard Syron that credit checks had become increasingly lax and risked exposing both the enterprise and the country to great financial risks. But Syron refused to heed the warnings, explaining dejectedly to Andrukonis that Freddie Mac could no longer afford to say no to anybody.[41]

Even though the Bush administration had criticized Fannie and Freddie for their reckless risk taking, it inexplicably helped drive them further down that road by decreeing in October 2004, at the height of the lending craze, a drastic *increase* in their targets for the number of mortgages to low-income earners. As previously mentioned, the share of such mortgages was to increase each year, from 50 percent in 2000 to 56 percent in 2008. The share of loans to people on very low incomes was to rise from 20 to 28 percent.

There was a defeatist atmosphere at Fannie Mae and Freddie Mac even at that point. Their senior executives had given up trying to serve all their masters: the stockholders' demands for long-term profitability could not be reconciled with the politicians' directives to step on the gas. One employee described how discussions at the office would increasingly be about how long it would take before they were exposed:

> It didn't take a lot of sophistication to notice what was happening to the quality of the loans. Anybody could have seen it. But nobody on the outside was even questioning us about it.[42]

In fact, there were political reasons for not wanting to see what was going on. The intentions were good, and the objectives were almost beyond criticism. As late as July 2008, Paul Krugman, a left-wing economist who would soon win the Nobel Prize, attacked the critics of Fannie and Freddie, pointing out that the duo had nothing to do with risky lending and had not made a single subprime loan.[43] Krugman may have been mixing things up: It is true that Fannie and Freddie did not lend to subprime borrowers, because they did not lend at all; but they did buy loans, and a growing share of those loans were subprime. But Fannie and Freddie also tried to cover up their risky lending by applying narrower definitions of "subprime" than most other players in the market. In July 2007, the chief risk officer of Countrywide proudly told analysts during a conference call that his institution was selling mortgages to Fannie Mae that were "far below" even generous limits for subprime but that were still considered "prime" by Fannie.[44]

The message sent out by Fannie and Freddie around 2004 that they would be buying just about anything that moved was a large part of the reason banks and other institutions started pumping out new mortgages that were subprime and Alt-A. "The market knew we needed those loans," a Freddie Mac spokesperson explained.[45] "Alt-A" was a type of loan considered riskier than "prime" but less risky than "subprime." Since loans were often given this label because there was no documentation of the borrower's income, another name for them is "liar loans." In practice, they turned out to be about as risky as subprime loans, and it has been suggested that subprime and Alt-A should be merged into the less opaquely named category of "junk loans." In 2003, junk loans accounted for only 8 percent of all U.S. mortgages, but that increased to 18 percent in 2004 and to as much as 22 percent in the third quarter of 2006. About 40 percent of the mortgages that Fannie and Freddie bought in 2005–2007 were subprime or Alt-A.[46]

The grandiose objectives had forced Fannie and Freddie to change their strategy. Instead of just buying mortgages and repackaging them into securities, they now bought more and more such securities from others. In fact, Fannie and Freddie soon became the largest buyers of the safest "tranche"—that is, the specific group with the highest credit rating—of each such security. Many commentators think that was decisive for the uncontrolled spread of subprime-mortgage securities across the world. The reason is that the yield on the safest tranche was barely higher than the interest paid by banks on deposits, meaning that investors were not exactly lining up to buy. But to Fannie and Freddie, which were able to borrow cheaply because of their government backing, it could still look like an attractive deal. And once they had supplied capital for that tranche, it was easier to find other investors who were willing to buy the riskier ones, which yielded much bigger returns—sometimes up to 20 times more. That prompted companies such as New Century and Ameriquest to design securities solely to make Fannie and Freddie buy them: it was no coincidence that the amount of the mortgages those securities were based on was just below $417,000, which was the ceiling for loans that could be part of Fannie's and Freddie's portfolios.[47]

Fannie's and Freddie's joint exposure to the housing market was huge. At the end of 2007, the sum of the liabilities and mortgage-backed securities that they had guaranteed and issued equaled the

U.S. national debt. For every $100 they had guaranteed or lent through securities, they had only $1.20 of equity.[48] In August 2008, Fannie and Freddie owned junk loans and securities based on junk loans worth over $1 trillion—more than one-fifth of their entire mortgage portfolio.[49] In the words of Nassim Nicholas Taleb, author of the book *The Black Swan*, about how people underestimate low-probability risks, they were "sitting on a barrel of dynamite." Their army of analysts, however, claimed that the risks were small. They had sophisticated models to manage risks. That is, all risks but one— a fall in home prices.[50]

As Freddie Mac's former CEO Richard Syron looked back on what went wrong, he blamed the bad mortgages on politicians' pushing through an expansion of homeownership even to households that could not afford to own a home. That was the price the government-sponsored enterprises had to pay for their privileges. But 15 years earlier, it had been on Syron's watch that the Boston Fed had started its systematic efforts to loosen banks' requirements for creditworthiness, and at Freddie Mac, he had led a huge expansion of the sub-prime market. When the *New York Times* recently asked him if there was nothing he could have done differently, he replied: "If I had better foresight, maybe I could have improved things a little bit. But frankly, if I had perfect foresight, I would never have taken this job in the first place."[51]

3. How to Build Financial Weapons of Mass Destruction

The mercantile community will have been unusually fortunate if during the period of rising prices it has not made great mistakes. Such a period naturally excites the sanguine and the ardent; they fancy that the prosperity they see will last always, that it is only the beginning of a greater prosperity. They altogether over-estimate the demand for the article they deal in, or the work they do. Almost everything will be believed for a little while.

—Walter Bagehot, *Lombard Street: A Description of the Money Market*

In July 2007, a mad ride was coming to an end at IKB Deutsche Industriebank. IKB, a small government-owned bank in Düsseldorf, Germany, specialized in lending to medium-sized businesses but had in recent years diversified into the international market. Above all, it had placed large bets on the U.S. housing market. Toward the end, it had a portfolio worth almost 13 billion euros ($17.8 billion) of securities based on repackaged mortgages—and securities based on securities based on repackaged mortgages. Some people claim that this tiny bank was paying investment banks and credit-rating agencies $200 million a year to design and appraise packages with the highest credit rating.

IKB put these securities in a special off-balance-sheet vehicle that it financed by taking out short-term loans. It was a brilliant business model for as long as home prices kept rising and revenues kept flowing in from U.S. households paying their loans on time. But IKB bought ever-riskier mortgages to boost its income, and then something went wrong with the housing market. In the summer of 2007, nobody dared lend anymore, so IKB itself had to finance its special vehicle, which seemed to be outside the bank—and since IKB could not afford to do that, its principal owner, KfW, which is owned by the German federal and state governments, had to take over IKB's bad business.[1]

A tiny Düsseldorf bank whose real business was to make loans to medium-sized German manufacturing companies had been wrecked by its enthusiasm for exotic packaged securities that most of its customers had never heard of. But what exactly was it that IKB had paid so much to have packaged, and that eventually caused the whole ship to go under?

Alchemy

The first building block of these mind-boggling housing deals is called a mortgage-backed security. It is a kind of bond that is put together, for example, by a bank that first goes out and buys several thousand mortgage loans from those who have made them to house-holds. Since so many households are included, the risk associated with some of them being unable to pay back the money is reduced. What's more, the bank buys mortgages from different parts of the country to ensure that a local housing-market collapse or a natural disaster will not have a big negative effect.

These mortgages are then fashioned into securities of varying riskiness. The basic design can be compared to an irrigation canal providing fresh water from, say, the north. If there is enough water, all landowners will get what they need for their crops, including those farthest to the south. But those who own the southernmost fields run a bigger risk, because they will be the first to be left dry when there is insufficient water in the canal. Mortgage-backed securities work in the same way. Interest payments from households are passed on to those who hold the safest securities or tranches— those rated "Aaa"—even if a lot of households default, while those who have bought the riskiest securities—with ratings starting with "B" or even "C"—take the first hit if anything goes wrong. If some households stop repaying their loans, regardless of the credit rating they were given when they took them out, the investors holding the riskiest tranches are the ones who are left without income. For investors to want to buy these higher-risk securities, they must get a much larger share of payments when the going is good. Those who own Aaa tranches, by contrast, lose nothing until all other holders have lost their income, but instead they get a much lower return.

We now have a mortgage-backed security: we have "securitized" mortgage loans and created a bond. Basically, this is a clever way to distribute risk. The large number of mortgages from various parts of the country reduces exposure, and investors can choose what bonds to buy based on the level of risk they are willing to take. This resembles the insurance business, where it is important to ensure that those covered by similar policies have different risk profiles so that they do not all fall victim to the same type of accident at the same time. Securitization of this kind began to develop in the bubbling laboratory of U.S. housing policy from the 1970s onward. Ginnie Mae premiered it in February 1970 by buying large numbers of mortgages and selling them to investors who then received the regular incoming payments. Lenders no longer had to wait 10, 20, or 30 years to get their money back. They could get all their income immediately by selling their loans, meaning that they had fresh money to lend to someone else. This was a successful experiment and attracted capital to regions where the market had been rather reluctant to invest before.

The mortgage giants Fannie Mae and Freddie Mac soon followed suit, and in June 1983, Freddie broke new ground by commissioning Salomon Brothers and First Boston to package mortgages and slice them up according to the level of risk investors wanted. One of the inventors of securitization, Lewis Ranieri of Salomon Brothers, had succeeded in convincing first Freddie and then Fannie to guarantee such securities. This was the starting signal for the entire mortgage industry, because the position of the government-sponsored enterprises made other investors treat these securities as if they were guaranteed by the U.S. Treasury. Other Wall Street firms soon set up their own securitization departments to share in the profits.[2]

In the 1980s, this idea spread to new areas, such as car loans and credit-card debt. But it was not until the 1990s and above all the 2000s that securitization went from snowball to avalanche. What made the concept really lucrative was that it turned out that you could put subprime mortgages in your packages and still convert them into securities whose safest tranche would get a top grade from credit-rating agencies, such as Moody's and Standard & Poor's. This was remarkable because, contrary to some people's belief, a person who buys an Aaa security does not receive only the Aaa mortgages. In practice, he owns all the mortgages that went into the package—from the safest to the least safe. That his security is safer means only that he will be the last to lose money if the entire package of mortgages goes bad. In other words, here we had this machine that you could feed unsafe loans made to households with low creditworthiness, and it would churn out securities that were deemed as safe as an investment could be—almost as safe as Treasuries. And the credit-rating agencies claimed that even the risky tranches were investment grade. It goes without saying that this attracted players to the market like flies to a lamp.

Increasingly sophisticated varieties of securitization also began to evolve. When large bunches of mortgages have been resold as securities, other investors can buy a few hundred such securities of different origins, for example medium-risk ones, and repackage them once more into a new kind of security, a "collateralized-debt obligation," or CDO. That will also be split into tranches depending on the level of risk that buyers are willing to take. The original idea of CDOs was to spread risk by including a wide variety of assets, but in 2003, Wall Street firms started to create CDOs backed exclusively by mortgages. Similar to an ordinary mortgage-backed security, the buyer who picks the riskiest tranches gets paid the most but also has to suffer the first loss if the CDO investments fail.

The remarkable thing was that the riskiest tranches of those CDOs could also get top grades from the rating agencies. Since they are one step further removed from the actual housing market, you might think that CDOs were less exposed to price fluctuations or to bad loans. In fact, the risk could be significantly higher because the creators of CDOs would often buy the riskiest mortgage-backed securities and repackage them. But even if a CDO designer used only building blocks rated BBB or BBB-, 75 percent of the CDOs they were packaged into were awarded an AAA rating because they, in turn, were insured with a major insurance company. "Here is a miracle of faith," concluded the investment writer James Grant.[3]

Anyone who cared to could even buy bits of CDOs, repackage them into a "CDO-squared," and resell them based on the risk involved, and someone else could buy bits of that and slice it up anew, into a "CDO-cubed." The advantage for issuers, of course, was that they could charge fees at each stage of the process. The most money of all was to be made by developing synthetic CDOs that consisted of no real loans at all but imitated, through a complicated design involving various credit derivatives, a security consisting of parts of securities that consisted of parts of mortgage loans.

Even though the terminology was becoming increasingly bizarre, most commentators felt that this packaging and repackaging of assets and risks represented an important innovation. It made it possible to spread risks and thus to reduce them. The risks were taken away from those who could not bear them and given to those who considered that they could, to the extent that they wanted to take them on. The fact that securities that were largely based on mortgages considered to be of inferior quality obtained excellent grades from the credit-rating agencies convinced most people that the financial market had finally discovered the secret of alchemy— how to turn lead into gold. Inevitably, this brought on a gold rush.

How Banks Joined the Moving Business

In the mid-1990s, the securitization of mortgages got a boost from an unexpected corner—from attempts by governments and central banks to make banking less risky. The world's richest countries were unhappy that differences across countries in the level of regulation enabled banks to move their operations to the place with the most favorable rules. In 1988, after six years of negotiations in Basel, Switzerland, banking authorities and central banks from those countries produced a collection of standards and rules, nicknamed "Basel I," which laid down how much capital a bank must have to cover its risks.

The need for governments to impose capital and reserve requirements on banks at all was a result of other, more fundamental public interventions that had transformed the entire financial sector, namely, governments' tendency to rescue banks that are in danger. Once upon a time, savers had to pay attention to how likely a given bank was to take risks, and banks had to build sizable buffers or people would not dare entrust them with their savings. The classic problem of banking is that savers typically have the right to withdraw their deposits at any time, while the same money has been lent long term to businesses and for homes. As the banker George Bailey, played by James Stewart, says to the worried crowds trying to force their way into his bank to get their money back in the movie *It's a Wonderful Life*:

> You're thinking of this place all wrong. As if I had the money
> back in a safe. The money's not here. Your money's in Joe's
> house; that's right next to yours. And in the Kennedy house,
> and Mrs. Macklin's house, and a hundred others.

If everybody wants his or her money back at the same time, the bank cannot pay it all out. It is not that the bank does not have the money, it just cannot get it back fast enough from all those it has lent it to. The bank has the capital, but it lacks liquidity. This means that banks are at risk of runs: Mere concern that others are going to withdraw their money may make people want to hurry and get theirs out first. Rumors and fears may be self-fulfilling.

That is why central banks were set up as "lenders of last resort" to banks without liquidity. The aim, naturally, was to prevent or mitigate banking crises. When the United States got a central bank (the Fed) in 1914, its bank supervisor, the Office of the Comptroller of the Currency, happily declared that "financial and commercial crises or panics ... seem to be mathematically impossible."[4] That, unfortunately, was wrong, because another effect was that banks and investors no longer stayed clear of big risks once they knew that they would be bailed out if there was a crisis. In fact, they were all of a sudden given an incentive to act irresponsibly, as they could privatize any gains but socialize any losses. This is usually referred to as "moral hazard." In his classic history of financial crises, Charles Kindleberger explains it thus: "The dilemma is that if investors knew in advance that government support would be forthcoming under generous dispensation when asset prices fall sharply, markets might break down somewhat more frequently because investors will be less cautious in their purchases of assets and of securities."[5]

What's more, in 1933 the United States introduced deposit insurance, meaning that savers would get their money back even if their bank went out of business. One of those who opposed that decision was President Franklin D. Roosevelt. He threatened to use his veto because he believed that deposit insurance would punish prudent banks and subsidize irresponsible ones, as customers would start choosing the bank that offered them the highest interest rate, however great the risks that bank might be taking. But Roosevelt had to accept deposit insurance as part of a compromise. Before the United States had a central bank and deposit insurance, banks usually had equity amounting to 20–30 percent of their total lending.

During the rest of the 20th century, banks' capital ratio never again exceeded 10 percent.[6] Developments have been similar in western Europe.

When the U.S. administration decided during the present crisis to increase the level of deposit insurance and start guaranteeing interbank loans, it was presented as a way to create security and stability. Later, however, Treasury Secretary Henry "Hank" Paulson admitted that this unfortunately encourages banks to take excess risks, but said that he was forced to do it because the Europeans had started it, and American banks would otherwise have found it hard to compete.[7]

As Martin Wolf of the *Financial Times* puts it, "Financial markets are indeed risky . . . but the interventions of government often make them less safe, not more so." Wolf believes that if there were no government safety nets, banks would set aside more capital, take longer-term deposits, and lend more in the money markets where they can cash out quickly. That may not be a solution that he himself advocates, but he still thinks it would be better than today's system: "Given the frequency of banking crises, this might be a big improvement."[8]

To limit the risk taking that government protection has encouraged, governments may demand to know more about what banks are up to, and if banks get into trouble, they may bail out depositors but let stockholders and senior executives lose their money and jobs. Another way to deal with moral hazard is to require banks not to lend too much relative to their capital. Under Basel I, capital requirements were calculated on the basis of a five-way breakdown of banks' assets. The assets that were deemed not to be in the least dangerous, such as cash or lending to Organization for Economic Cooperation and Development governments, did not count as risks at all, whereas the most precarious assets, such as lending to most corporations, counted at a rate of 100 percent. For the three intermediate categories, percentages varied depending on how risky the claims were considered to be. That yielded a risk-adjusted sum of assets for each bank, which was the minimum sum of capital it had to have. Banks with international operations had to hold 8 percent of capital against their risk-adjusted assets. It goes without saying that one aim of this requirement was to reduce the exposure of banks to the risk that a counterparty may be unable to pay what it owes.

The Basel I standards began to be applied in most developed countries in the 1990s and rapidly spread across the world. Now risk was under control and the economy was safe. Or so it was thought. But, as Raghuram Rajan, a former chief economist of the International Monetary Fund, has noted, "Since the business of banking is to take on and manage risk, any broad-based attempt to thwart risk-taking is likely to see it reappear in less transparent forms."[9]

Basel I did not place risk taking under control. It just established a price list. Banks soon learned to take exactly those risks that were cheapest with regard to capital. As many old risks were made more expensive by Basel I, the banks chose instead to take new ones, in less open and more convoluted ways.

Above all, it became incredibly lucrative to remove items from the balance sheet, that is, to have business that did not show up in a bank's own summary of its assets and liabilities. If you simplify heroically, you can say that a bank wanting to sweep risky investments under the rug may create a special company, a "conduit" or "structured investment vehicle." That company (not the bank) then makes investments, and it finances its operations by taking out cheap short-term loans directly in the financial market. The bank usually makes a commitment to finance the special company if capital cannot be raised in the market, but the special company is a separate legal entity and is not owned by the bank. And that is what makes the whole difference. If the bank itself had invested $100, it would have had to have $8 of capital, but if the investment takes place through the special company, the bank needs only 80 cents of capital (and in some countries, nothing at all). If you invest $100, this may not be such a big deal; but if you invest $100 billion, you actually save $7.2 billion on this simple operation.[10]

That gave the world of finance an irresistible impetus to bundle mortgage loans into packages and put them outside the balance sheet. Since the securities created were awarded top grades by the credit-rating agencies, they were believed to be safe investments, meaning that the proceeds could be reinvested in new loans. The new standard solution in banking was to remove, posthaste, anything that showed up on the balance sheet. After Basel I, banks were no longer in the storing business but in the moving business, as *The Economist* concluded.[11] A parallel "shadow banking sector" developed where operations lacked transparency and had little capital to back them up. This was banking without banks, and since it was credit-financed, it helped increase the leverage of the global economy significantly: More and more capital entered the market and was lent to borrowers who lent it again. It is interesting to note that, even though nobody had intended the regulations to stimulate such a shadow banking sector, most regulators welcomed this development as a wise way to spread and thus reduce risks.

That the new regulations did encourage the use of such devices is clear if you look at a country that chose a different path. Spain was a party to the negotiations in Basel, but its central bank let the same capital requirements apply to assets regardless of whether they were on or off the balance sheet. "We did not do anything special," says José María Roldán of the Bank of Spain. He and his colleagues simply thought that off-balance-sheet banking operations looked just like ordinary banking. Since there were no rules favoring special companies, Spanish banks simply did not create them and instead conducted their operations in the open.[12]

But the system still had weaknesses, or so the financial authorities thought. When banks bundled mortgages into securities that they sliced up according to the level of risk, they were able to sell the tranches with lower risk and lower yields to others but keep the riskiest ones, because the latter did not require any more capital than the former. That meant that banks could take greater risks without having to set aside more capital. To plug this hole, the U.S. authorities drastically raised capital requirements for the risky tranches. Suddenly banks had to hold capital against the entire investment for the riskiest tranches but against only 20 percent of the value of the safest ones.[13] This new regulation was intended to reduce the risks created by the old regulation. But the new one had an unintended effect, too. Banks of course began to sell the risky securities that now cost them so dearly, meaning that they would no longer be the ones to take the first and biggest hit if borrowers were to default. That reduced the incentive for banks to ensure that the mortgages they put in their packages were good ones.

Many of the problems with Basel I were apparent at an early stage, which is why the governments involved began to negotiate a new agreement in the late 1990s. The outcome was Basel II, which was ready in 2004. The aim was to avoid crude rules of thumb and instead impose more sophisticated requirements on individual banks based on the risks that each bank actually takes. Risk estimates are arrived at by analyzing historical data using mathematical models, meaning that the credit-rating agencies and the banks' own risk-management systems become more important in the computation of capital-adequacy ratios.

Most countries only recently started to implement Basel II, but U.S. regulation of investment banks—those that do not take deposits but whose main business is to provide advice and to issue and sell securities—started to develop in that direction as early as 2004. Capital requirements for the trading divisions of the big five investment banks were eased. In return, the Securities and Exchange Commission was granted unrestricted insight into the business both of these divisions and of their parent companies. In the future, the banks would submit reports each month and explain in detail how their internal risk models worked. For the first time, the SEC could prevent banks from taking risks that it deemed excessive. The SEC's John Heine described this as a clear tightening of the rules:

> The Commission's 2004 rules strengthened oversight of the securities markets, because prior to their adoption there was no formal regulatory oversight, no liquidity requirements, and no capital requirements for investment bank holding companies.[14]

The models—and the overall Basel II project—have one major limitation: they cannot predict an uncertain future, especially not when they are analyzing entirely new financial instruments that have only been tested in good economic times. The investment banks' securitized mortgages, which had been awarded top credit ratings, came across as absolutely safe, and so the banks could assume more and more debt without appearing undercapitalized.

In public debate, this 2004 rule change has been cited as one of the clearest examples of how "deregulation" and a "laissez-faire philosophy" caused the financial crisis.[15] But in fact it was the direct opposite. It is hard to imagine a more ambitious attempt to regulate every detail of the operations of individual banks. The problem was just that the SEC, as one of its former key officials puts it, "constructed a mechanism that simply didn't work."[16] Trying from the outside to understand myriad financial operations and control them to ensure that they all went right was a totally unfeasible proposition. In practice, the SEC ended up relying on the banks' own computer models to assess risk. But government agencies biting off more than they can chew is not the same as laissez faire.

As Long as the Music Was Playing

Each year that went by, Wall Street firms sold more securitized mortgages that had been guaranteed by Fannie Mae and Freddie Mac. The fees paid by investors, banks, pension funds, and insurance companies were a profit machine, which gave the firms an interest in gaining control over the entire process so that they would get all the fees. One by one, they set up their own departments to buy and repackage mortgages and sell them. They could not compete for the very safest mortgages—Fannie and Freddie had cornered that market, as their government guarantees meant they could borrow and buy cheaper—so they had to focus on other types of loans: those that were too big for the government-sponsored enterprises or those that were made to subprime borrowers.[17]

One of the most fleet-footed investment banks was Lehman Brothers, which had hired securitization experts as far back as the mid-1990s and started to build contacts with subprime lenders. It soon also acquired its own subprime-lending unit, BNC Mortgage, to ensure that it would not have to buy subprime mortgages from others. This led to higher fee income and greater control over the loans made. In practice, Lehman had built an assembly line and was making money at every station along the way. The bank lent money to homebuyers, it repackaged those mortgages into securities, it repackaged the securities into CDOs, and it sold the whole works on the market. After the Fed cut interest rates in 2001, the money really started to flow in. The seller of a CDO could charge a fee of more than 1 percent. That translates into more than $10 million per $1 billion deal.

When Stanley O'Neal took over as head of Merrill Lynch, another investment bank, in 2002, he wished he were in Lehman Brothers' shoes. The lucrative securitization of mortgages had passed by Merrill's stock traders completely. O'Neal, the first African American at the helm of a Wall Street firm, had worked his way up from the factory floor at General Motors to its financial division and from there to the financial center of the world. Now he was using all his energy and talent to catch up with the other investment banks. His message was crystal clear: Merrill Lynch, whose corporate symbol is a bull, was going to enter the subprime market and become the biggest player in the world. The bank recruited traders and started paying more for subprime mortgages than any other Wall Street firm.

Like Lehman, Merrill wanted to own the entire assembly line. In the two years following January 2005, it made 17 major investments in the global mortgage sector, from real estate to mortgage lenders. Its aim was to generate large amounts of its own mortgages to systematically securitize them. Concurrently, Merrill revved up its development of CDOs: In 2002, it created hardly any; four years later, it created more than anyone else in the world. And when there were not enough underlying assets to go around, it started manufacturing synthetic CDOs—the kind that are not made of mortgages, only of computer-generated imitations of mortgages. Because of their complexity, Merrill could charge even higher fees for them.

This strategy yielded a fantastic cash flow. In 2006, Merrill reported record profits and could pay record bonuses. That year, employees as a group took home more than $5 billion in bonuses: 100 people got more than $1 million, and those involved in securitization hit the biggest jackpot of all. The 42-year-old workaholic who headed up the bond division received $350,000 in salary that year but 100 times as much—$35 million—in bonuses. Those profits were gained at the price of completely insane risks, which would already start generating equally large losses the following year. At the end of 2005, the insurance company AIG no longer wanted to insure Merrill's securities. But the people at Merrill did not win bonuses that year by thinking about next year, they did so by generating as much business as possible here and now. So they continued.

"That's a call that senior management or risk management should question, but of course their pay was tied to it too," says a dispirited former employee. Risk management at Merrill Lynch seemed to be mainly about removing obstacles to risk taking. Its top risk manager streamlined away the employees whose task had been to conduct regular interviews with people on the floor about the deals they were making. One of the bosses told off traders who gave risk management an honest description of what they were up to. In 2006, that boss got a $20 million bonus.[18]

Another fearless player—at the bridge table—was James Cayne. He plays professionally and has won the North American Bridge

Championships several times. Since 1993, he had also found the time to be president, CEO, and eventually chairman of Bear Stearns, the investment bank that made much of not being like all the rest. While the other banks were nice suits with nice degrees, Bear Stearns was a working-class outsider that didn't give a hoot about appearance or tradition but instead worked harder and longer. When the huge hedge fund LTCM shook global markets in 1998, Bear Stearns was the only investment bank that refused to help rescue it.

Bear Stearns was smaller than the other investment banks and had not expanded internationally, so it had to play an aggressive game with the hand it had been dealt. It bet on the U.S. housing market, creating early on a financial structure called Klio Funding, which made large-scale purchases of securitized assets that it financed by short-term loans in the money market. This was a safe investment for savers because the giant bank Citigroup guaranteed these "Klios" in case the underlying assets should run into problems. Bear Stearns's huge revenues from fees inspired many other banks to create similar off-balance-sheet structures.[19] Bear Stearns also launched its own hedge funds, which operated according to the same principles. At the peak, James Cayne's personal fortune was $1.3 billion, most of it in Bear Stearns stock. But he did not give up his bridge, and on Thursdays in the summer, he would take a helicopter from New York City to have time for his afternoon golf in New Jersey.

In some cases, top bankers did not quite seem to have understood what they were trading. In late 2002, Citigroup's CEO Charles Prince said he wanted his bank to go all out for the CDO market. Citigroup was the outcome of a 1998 merger between a bank, Citicorp, and a financial corporation, Travelers Group. As a result, it was both an investment bank and a commercial bank accepting deposits, and that meant that it was more heavily regulated than ordinary investment banks. Since Prince (according to a former colleague) couldn't tell the difference between a CDO and a shopping list, he had to find people he could rely on. One of those he picked was Robert Rubin, Treasury secretary under President Clinton and then an adviser at Citigroup. Rubin advised him to move more and more resources off the bank's balance sheet and to go for large-scale securitization. In 2007, Citigroup created almost $50 billion worth of CDOs, making it the world leader. The new business was appreciated on the trading floor: "As long as you could grow revenues, you could keep your bonus growing," as one trader put it. Tight bonds of friendship between trading bosses and risk management caused problems to be swept under the rug, and warnings never reached top management. Provided that attention was paid to the rating agencies' assessments, the risks associated with this trade were tiny, those responsible promised.[20]

As late as July 2007, Charles Prince thought that the market was sound and that the money would keep flowing. When the *Financial Times* asked him a skeptical question about the financial outlook, he replied: "When the music stops, in terms of liquidity, things will be complicated. But as long as the music is playing, you've got to get up and dance. We're still dancing."[21]

The investor Warren Buffett has said that there are three Is in each bubble: the innovators, the imitators, and the idiots.[22] But while a bubble is inflating, a person may sometimes come across as an idiot for not wanting to join in. When a bubble is at its biggest, pyramid schemes involving various assets often start spontaneously. Since the prices of tulip bulbs or mortgage-based securities have risen so far and profits have been so easy to make, more and more people are attracted to the market. This boosts demand, meaning that the newcomers have to pay even more for the asset, and that increases profits even more for the early joiners. Banks that acquired mortgage-based securities to resell them may suddenly be tempted to keep them until their value goes up even more. Things never look as irresistibly attractive as just before the fall. It seems downright moronic not to play along and get a share of the easy money. And this in turn attracts even more people to the market, pushing up profits even further, which attracts even more people, and so on and on. Until the music stops.

Pimp My CDO

When a credit-rating agency such as Moody's is going to work out the rating of a financial product, which will determine whether that product will be a bestseller or a fiasco, the analyst first switches on his computer. He launches the company's rating software and types in a number of informational items about the structure, price, and duration of the security. Then he presses Enter. At this point, he may just as well go out and have a beer with his coworkers, go home to sleep, and then come back to work the next morning. In the meantime, his computer will be performing a million different simulations of various scenarios for what may happen to the ratings, the trades, and the underlying assets. The average of all these simulations shows the mettle of the security and how it should be rated.

If you are lucky you get Aaa, which is the lowest possible risk, or Aa or A. Baa is average risk and just about acceptable, but if you go as low as Ba or B you are in trouble, and Caa and Ca are nothing but junk.

In August 2006, after making all the usual simulations, Moody's European division was happy to be able to award an Aaa to a CPDO developed by the Dutch bank ABN AMRO. "CPDO" stands for "constant-proportion debt obligation." It is a bet on the overall credit risks of hundreds of companies, with a special twist: If the CPDO loses money, it will spend even more trying to win it back. This rating was an unexpected boon to ABN AMRO given that its CPDO yielded more than 10 times the return of comparable financial instruments with the same rating. Other banks rushed headlong into the market with their own variations on the CPDO theme, and Moody's had to work around the clock rating new products. The agency had never made so much money on a single type of financial instrument. Investors were flocking to the new security, which sounded more like a robot out of a *Star Wars* movie than anything else.

But as anyone who has ever been close to a computer knows, there are often "bugs" in the software, little mistakes in the computer code that cause big problems and give users stomach ulcers. The software Moody's used also contained such bugs. They were usually manageable, but this time there were more of them than there would typically be. In early 2007, the bug hunters discovered a minor coding lapse that had led to major consequences. In fact, the simulations were way off target, and CPDOs were significantly riskier than Moody's had thought. They were not even close to deserving an Aaa.

That came as a shock. Multibillion deals had hinged on the mathematical equivalent of a spelling mistake. And yet it was a tiny problem compared with what the future had in store. In short order, the members of the rating committee discreetly gathered to deal with the crisis. The *Financial Times* has reported that they fixed the bug, but that before rerunning the simulations, they also chose to slip in three major changes to the methodology. One of them they later skipped because "it did not help the rating," as an internal document expressed it. The changes they did keep included a lowering of their assessment of volatility in the credit market. One million simulations later, they obtained the result they wanted. Against all the odds, the CPDO managed to keep its Aaa grade even after the bug had been fixed.[23]

The credit-rating agencies are absolutely crucial to our modern financial economy since virtually all investors swear by their ratings. They were the decisive factor behind the explosive development of securitized mortgage loans. If securities backed by B-rated mortgages had never risen past a B rating themselves, there would not have been a market for them. The agencies' generous use of their A stamp is what made investors across the world believe in alchemy and scramble for the securities. But how reliable and independent are these agencies, anyway? The CPDO incident reveals an uncomfortable truth: Sometimes the agency will first decide on a rating and then program its computers to obtain that rating. And Moody's is actually reputed to be one of the more conservative agencies.

Brian Clarkson, one of the driving forces behind the enthusiasm for securitization at Moody's, has said, "You start with a rating and build a deal around a rating."[24] For example, the people at ABN AMRO spent months designing and analyzing when they were trying to put together a CPDO that would bring home the top grade. Part of that work was to run innumerable simulations themselves to identify a structure capable of attaining a high rating. Another was to have discussions with the rating agencies. They will deny it adamantly, but many people in the industry claim that the agencies' involvement amounts to full-fledged negotiations about what would be required for an instrument to get the highest rating. In a sense, the agencies and their customers build the products together. And if one agency is unwilling to be of service, the other one across the street will happily offer a second opinion. Moody's and its main competitor, Standard & Poor's, both gave the CPDO their highest grade. The third major competitor, Fitch, by contrast, said it could not understand how the CPDO could be so highly rated since its own models indicated it was only one notch above junk. Needless to say, not a single bank came to Fitch to have its CPDOs rated. Honesty had a cost.

How was it possible for the credit-rating agencies, which used to be viewed as the most conscientious, most intractable, and grumpiest of all bean counters, to become eager participants in rating inflation? Two major changes that occurred in the 1970s started to transform their business model. One change concerned their financing and the other their legal status. They previously got their money from potential investors who subscribed to their ratings of various institutions and instruments. Buyers naturally like to know what they are buying. But because of the growing number of bonds and derivatives, and their increasing complexity, the agencies simply did not have time to value them all without a much larger organization. That made them charge potential sellers instead.

Even this presented a certain amount of danger. The buyer of a house pays to have it valued for the simple reason that it is hard to trust an appraiser paid by the person who wants to sell and who obviously wants the house to be worth as much as possible. It is a manageable problem provided that you do not have to rely on such partisan appraisals, but a rule change made at about the same time meant they could no longer be disregarded. The SEC, which wanted to bring the risks taken by banks and stockbrokers under control, started to demand more in terms of regulations and capital adequacy from those who held risky securities. To arrive at an official definition of "risk," the SEC in 1975 formally recognized three credit-rating agencies—Moody's, Standard & Poor's, and Fitch (which have since been joined by a few more). That was just the beginning. Similar regulations soon followed for insurers, pension funds, mutual funds, and all other financial institutions. Many were completely banned from buying anything that the rating agencies considered to be "speculative" rather than "investment grade."

In this way, the federal government granted the credit-rating agencies, which had previously been rather marginal players, an oligopoly entailing guaranteed profits. If a company had its creditworthiness rating lowered by them, it would suddenly lose its ability to finance its operations, and that could sound its death knell. Anyone wanting to sell securities had to go to the agencies to obtain what was in practice a license to sell. And if you succeeded in lifting your securities from Ba to Baa3 (on the scale used by Moody's) or from BB+ to BBB- (on that used by S&P or Fitch), the world was your oyster. In 1996, the *New York Times* columnist Thomas Friedman informed his readers that there were two superpowers in the world—the United States and Moody's—and that it was sometimes unclear which of them was more powerful. The only question was how unscrupulous use the agencies would make of their new super-strength. Long-established principles and traditions may permeate their walls, but there was bound to come a point when the temptation of making a sale would overwhelm the principle of determining a correct rating.

In fact, Moody's and several other agencies have criticized the federal authorities for giving them such a regulatory task, which they claim will distort the motivation of their employees. For example, the director of corporate development at Moody's, Thomas McGuire, put their case in a speech before the SEC: "Rating agencies are staffed by ordinary people with families to support and bills to meet and mortgages to pay. Government regulators are inadvertently subjecting those people to improper pressure, and share accountability for any scandals which may result."[25]

At Moody's, the turning point appears to have been when the company went public in 2000. The focus on immediate profit increased, and the employees were spurred on by stock options. Its CEO, John Rutherford, is said to have declared that he wanted each analyst (Moody's has 1,200) to pull in at least a million dollars a year. That was a strong incentive to perform as many ratings as possible, as quickly as possible. The key was to make customers come to them rather than go to the competition, and they would be more likely to do so if they could count on being made to feel welcome and on getting good ratings. Moody's, which used to be a bit sulky in its outward behavior, suddenly began to spend a lot of time with its customers on numerous golfing trips and karaoke nights.

The number one growth industry at that time was the securitiza-tion of mortgages. Moody's held out for a long time, sticking to its principle that no CDO consisting solely of mortgages could get a top rating since there was too little diversification of risk—a national fall in home prices would have a devastating effect on its value. But other rating agencies were making out like bandits by awarding top grades to such securities, even though some of the people working there were already suspicious. One S&P employee warned in an internal e-mail that the CDO market they were creating was a "mon-ster," concluding, "Let's hope we are all wealthy and retired by the time this house of cards falters."[26]

The CEO of Moody's explained the development much later at an internal meeting: "It was a slippery slope. What happened in 2004 and 2005 with respect to subordinated tranches [the riskiest bits of CDOs] is that our competition, Fitch and S&P, went nuts. Everything was investment grade."[27] The conservative rating agency must have felt an overwhelming temptation to go a little crazy itself: Moody's abandoned its diversification requirement in 2004 and started bringing out its Aaa stamp when customers came calling with mortgage-backed securities. From a business point of view, this was exactly the right thing to do. A single rating assignment could earn the company more than $200,000, and it did not have to take more than a day and could sometimes be done in a few hours. Moody's became one of the world's most profitable businesses, and various kinds of securitization accounted for more than 40 percent of the company's sales in 2005.[28]

The potential profits were huge because good ratings were what created the necessary conditions for the securitization industry in the mortgage market—the possibility to shake a bunch of risky mortgages until they were rated as a risk-free investment. "The whole creation of mortgage securities was involved with a rating," as securitization pioneer Lewis Ranieri points out.[29] This engendered not only rating inflation but also pure and simple cheating. Gretchen Morgenson describes in the *New York Times* how Moody's gave a package of securities from Countrywide a rating that made them nonviable. Countrywide (which we remember as Fannie Mae's biggest customer) complained that the assessment had been too rigid. The analysts at Moody's then went back to their computers and returned the next day with a top grade—without any new information having been added.[30]

A young analyst described to me how a rating committee gathered around an oblong table. Each member had to say what rating he or she thought a security should be given. When it was finally the boss's turn, he was unhappy with the low ratings the others had proposed. He asked if they were positive, took out his calculator, entered a few numbers. He explained that the diversification of risk looked good, that history showed that house prices can only go up, and that similar products had been given higher ratings. Then he suggested a second turn around the table, taking all this into consideration. Now everybody suddenly agreed that a higher grade was more appropriate. It was "totally absurd," the analyst said, but what are you supposed to do when you are 23 years old, fresh out of college in a small town in Nebraska, and your boss with all his authority explains to you how the industry works?

At a hearing about the credit-rating agencies, the House of Representatives gained insights indicating that this was hardly an isolated event. The documents obtained by the House included an Internet chat between two S&P analysts who were going to assess a new security:

> 1: By the way, that deal is ridiculous.
> 2: I know, right, model definitely does not capture half the risk.
> 1: We should not be rating it.
> 2: We rate every deal. It could be structured by cows, and we would rate it.
> 1: But there's a lot of risk associated with it—I personally don't feel comfy signing off as a committee member.[31]

And then they went on to rate and sign off.

At this stage, the public authorities intervened—though not to rein in rating inflation but to force the pace! In 2005 and 2006, the SEC threatened to ban an activity called "notching," which it considered contrary to antitrust law. Notching is when the creator of a CDO that had been rated by one agency went to another agency for a second rating and that agency offered two options: either it would make a full (and more expensive) assessment based on the mortgage components of the CDO, or it would automatically (and more cheaply) give the CDO a rating one notch (hence the name) lower than that awarded to it by the first agency. The rating from the second agency could be crucial because many investors had to have ratings from two agencies before they were allowed to make a purchase. I don't understand why a ban on notching would help small competitors. Wouldn't it just require the company to get a full, expensive second rating? How would that help small agencies? That would have made more and more customers go to the small agencies, which were the main culprits behind rating inflation, since the customers could then have hoped to obtain automatic endorsements from the most conservative agencies. As already intimated, the small agencies managed to get the SEC on board, but it eventually abandoned the proposal after a flood of criticism. However, econo-mist Charles Calomiris thinks the mere threat of legislation was enough to tear down the last remaining barriers in the industry: "Trying to swim against the tide of grade inflation would put conser-vative rating agencies at risk of running afoul of their regulator."[32]

But what was the actual procedure when a mortgage-backed secu-rity was to be rated? The financial journalist Roger Lowenstein was allowed to watch this happen at Moody's. To preserve some confi-dentiality, they called it "Subprime XYZ." This was a package of 2,393 mortgage loans made in the spring of 2006, at a value of $430 million. Moody's received broad, general information about the borrowers from the New York bank that had created the pack-age—for instance, that three-fourths of them had adjustable-rate mortgages and that 43 percent had not confirmed their reported income. However, Moody's did not get access to individual loan files and made no attempt to confirm any of the data.

"We aren't loan officers," explained Claire Robinson, the manager responsible for rating mortgage-backed securities at Moody's. "Our expertise is as statisticians on an aggregate basis." Their aim was to forecast, based on historical data about mortgages, how large a share of the households would be unable to pay back their loans. Once Moody's had rated such securities, someone else would package them into a CDO and bring it to Moody's to have it rated. The group in charge of doing that would investigate the overall structure and its components, but it would never examine the sustainability of the real mortgage loans that made up the packages. "We're structure experts," said Yuri Yoshizawa, head of the derivatives group at Moody's. "We're not underlying-asset experts." The analysts were experts at checking the math, but nobody was in charge of scrutiniz-ing the underlying risks. Except of course those who lent the money in the first place, but they had sold those risks a long time ago.[33]

The historical data that Moody's used indicated that the mortgage-loan package in Subprime XYZ would lose only 4.9 percent. Since even the riskiest tranches could cope with a 7.25 percent loss, it seemed a fairly safe investment. The problem, however, was that the most recent statistics available to Moody's were from 2002 and concerned the losses incurred during that economic downturn. But that downturn was a unique one. The Fed had pushed down interest rates as far as they would go and house prices continued to rise although times were bad. Even those who ran into difficulties making repayments could take out a second mortgage to cover their costs. And the rating agencies also ignored the fact that the mort gages singled out for securitization were not just any mortgages. The mortgages put in packages were the most toxic ones, the ones that lenders preferred to get rid of quickly. One study shows that a set of mortgages that had been securitized ran about a 20 percent higher risk of failure than a set of mortgages with the same risk profile that had not been securitized.[34]

To this should be added an even more fateful circumstance: As the housing bubble inflated, mortgage amounts became higher and the demands made of borrowers became laxer. James Grant had a look at a representative sample and found that, in 2000, 0 percent of subprime mortgages were interest only, just 1 percent were second mortgages to exploit price rises, and just 25 percent lacked proper documentation of income or the like. In 2006, the corresponding shares were 22, 31, and 44 percent, respectively.[35]

One person who was in the bond business and worked for one of the world's biggest banks tells me that they were under constant pressure from management to cram as many risky mortgages as possible into their packages. They were constantly comparing themselves with other banks, and whenever someone else upped their level of risk slightly they felt they could do the same. In other words, more and more junk was being put in the packages to be sold. And yet the rating agencies guaranteed that they were of the same high quality as before. Some people were attentive to the fraud that was going on, such as Pimco, the manager of the world's largest bond fund, which abandoned the mortgage market as far back as the end of 2004, when it saw packages being filled with riskier and riskier loans to less and less creditworthy households. In fact, distrust should have been a very lucrative niche. If it was obvious that the prices of derivatives were built on wishful thinking by all parties involved, speculators should have been able to exploit it. The strategy used to do that is called "selling short." A speculator who thinks that a bond is overvalued borrows that bond and sells it at the current price. If the price has fallen when it is time to return the bond, he can buy a new bond cheaper and return that to the lender (pocketing the price difference). If that had been done on a large scale with mortgage-backed instruments, it could have kept prices down even at an early stage, thus choking off the supply of air to the bubble.

But the problem was that there was no exchange for mortgage-backed securities. The trade in them was so new that there was no open and liquid market where different investors had strong incentives to assess real risk at all times, thus pushing prices down. A large share of trades took place behind closed doors between two people who were often more interested in achieving a large volume of sales than in making good deals, since sales volume was what earned them their bonuses. There was no real market price.

In early 2006, the banks finally opened a marketplace for mortgage-backed securities: the ABX.HE. For the first time, various appraisals and interests were aggregated into a market price. This very soon revealed that the securities were worth much less than everybody had assumed. "ABX.HE is the acting weatherman of the sub-prime mortgage market, predicting a rough storm ahead," said Kiet Tran at the financial company Markit.[36] In the second half of 2006, prices fell slowly but steadily, and after the turn of the year, they began to tumble. Toward the end of 2007, the big indexes of mortgage-backed securities had fallen by 80 percent, and everybody had to reconsider his or her view of the housing market. The ABX.HE was too late to prevent the bubble, but it was just in time to pop it.

At the same time, the analysts at Moody's who were constantly monitoring ratings to see if they needed to be changed discovered that something was very wrong with Subprime XYZ. Many borrowers had fallen behind with their payments right from the start, and 6 percent of the loans were in default after only six months—a record level. Concern spread, and the people at Moody's contacted the lenders to find out what was going on. What they were told made them realize that the U.S. housing market was on the edge of the abyss. Many of the houses had not been lived in, and no lawns had been laid. Most of the loans had been made in states where a family could return the keys to the bank and walk away debt-free. In some cases, things had not even gone that far. Many mailboxes contained the house keys. The borrowers had never even moved in. They had just bought the houses so they could resell them at a higher price in a market that could only go up. When house prices started to fall, they just quit paying their loans, staying in their old homes or buying a cheaper one somewhere else.

Six months later, 13 percent of the mortgages included in Subprime XYZ were in default, and the percentage kept rising each month. Tranche after tranche of securities based on these mortgages lost all its value. This was alchemy in reverse. The losses first hit the riskiest securities but soon found their way up to the Aaa-rated tranches, like a flooding river that has invaded the basement, starts to submerge the lower stories, and is now slowly rising toward the highest floors.

4. Hurricane Season

When sorrows come, they come not single spies,
But in battalions.

—William Shakespeare, *Hamlet*

On Tuesday, September 16, 2008, it was distressingly easy to get a table at the usually overbooked gourmet restaurant Esperanto in central Stockholm. At first it looked as though the exclusive eatery, which boasted one star in the *Michelin Guide*, would be chock-full that night, the maitre d' recounts, but suddenly people began to cancel their reservations. First a few phone calls, then some more, and suddenly all the others calling at once. When evening came, the large restaurant felt deserted. A couple of business travelers and a family with children celebrating somebody's birthday received a level of attention from the staff that they could not have dreamed of.

"The first law of bubbles is that they inflate for a lot longer than anybody expects," *The Economist* noted in the summer of 2004. "The second law is that they eventually burst."[1]

This particular bubble burst on the morning of Monday, September 15, when the 158-year-old investment bank Lehman Brothers was declared bankrupt. That started a series of events that provoked a global financial panic. Lehman was one of the world's largest issuers of commercial paper (a type of short-term interest-bearing security typically issued by big corporations and banks), which it used to finance its assets. Its commercial paper now became worthless, causing problems for all those who had bought it expecting to get their money back soon. At about the same time as the family with children at Esperanto were served their tarred pigeon with pastella classique and almond, a money-market fund of great renown yet obscure to the general public, the Reserve Primary Fund, posted a message on its website:

> The value of the debt securities issued by Lehman Brothers
> Holdings, Inc. (face value $785 million) and held by the

> Primary Fund has been valued at zero effective as of 4:00PM
> New York time today. As a result, the NAV [net asset value]
> of the Primary Fund, effective as of 4:00PM, is $0.97 per
> share.[2]

This message may not sound very dramatic, because money-market funds are not—or are at least not supposed to be—dramatic. Investing in such a fund is a way of lending short term to a diversified group of stable institutions, such as governments, banks, and large corporations. Most people see investing in them as a more profitable version of keeping their money under their mattress. In almost 40 years of history, hardly any money-market fund had ever lost money. Now that the Primary Fund's loss on Lehman paper had caused its funds to drop in value from $1.00 to $0.97, it had happened again—but on a huge scale. The upshot was a mass flight from money-market funds, on which many institutions were dependent for their financing, not least the special companies that the banks had crammed full of mortgage-backed securities and put outside their balance sheets.

The message posted on the Reserve Primary Fund's website was tantamount to crying "Fire!" in a crowded theater. Panicking investors trampled one another as they tried desperately to get to the exits. Thousands of miles away, the usual guests at Esperanto in Stockholm suddenly had other things to do. And many of them had started wondering whether they would ever again be able to afford that kind of meal.

A Run on the Shadow Banking Sector

The first, huge domino to fall was the U.S. housing market. Commentators had been sounding warnings for many years, and *The Economist* came close to boring its readers stiff by repeating in issue after issue that the bubble was soon going to burst. The only question was when; and the longer it took, the more unsustainable investments households and market players would have time to make. Mark Zandi, an economist at the forecasting division of Moody's (which is separate from the rating division), published a report in May 2006 warning that a growing number of mortgages had gone to households with low creditworthiness, that the indebtedness of Americans was at a record high, and that there were no margins left: "The environment feels increasingly ripe for some type of financial event."[3]

The Fed had just raised its funds rate 0.25 percent and would raise it another 0.25 percent the next month. The climb had been slow but the total increase, from 1 percent three years earlier to 5.25 percent now, was dramatic. Households with adjustable-rate mortgages experienced a quick increase in their housing costs, and those who had received a discount on early interest payments and were only now beginning to pay back in earnest did not believe their eyes. That was when the biggest housing bubble in history was at its absolute peak. The past year had seen only very marginal price increases, and now property values were starting to fall. The number of households that were unable to repay their loans grew fast.

If a household runs into trouble in a state that allows borrowers to return the keys to the bank and walk away, the mortgage is usually renegotiated. It is better for the bank to have someone living in the house, who may be able to pay back the loan in the longer term, than to be forced to take over the house and try to sell it just when prices are lowest. But the securitization of mortgages had led to an unexpected consequence: The original lender no longer owned the loan, because it had been repackaged and sold and then chopped up and sold as part of a collateralized-debt obligation. Households in default no longer had an individual lender to negotiate with, which made more and more of them just abandon their homes and either buy something cheaper or start renting.

On July 24, 2007, the mortgage giant Countrywide held one of its regular conference calls with investors and analysts from Bear Stearns, Merrill Lynch, Morgan Stanley, and the rest of the Wall Street elite. The task of its CEO, Angelo Mozilo, was to explain why Countrywide's profit had fallen by one-third in the second quarter and why around one-fifth of its subprime borrowers were behind on their payments. He talked about falling home prices, pointing out that the big investment banks had also failed to see this coming. When the hard questions would not stop, the famously no-nonsense Mozilo chose to make sure that there could be no doubt whatsoever that Countryside was not alone: "We are experiencing a huge price depression, one we have not seen before—not since the Great Depression."[4]

Most cultures have a taboo against naming dangerous or evil things because it is believed that doing so can bring them forth. Perhaps Mozilo should have borne that in mind. The next day, Countrywide's stock plummeted 11 percent and the Dow Jones index also fell rapidly under heavy trading. A possibly superstitious investment banker attacked Mozilo for using the D word: "He started it."[5] Countrywide soon found it hard to renew its loans as investors lost faith in the soundness of its assets. The company barely stayed afloat for the rest of the year, until Bank of America bought it in January 2008. The media started reporting how Countrywide had tricked people into taking on bad subprime mortgages to make big bucks. Betsy Bayers, who was stepping down as Countrywide's compliance executive, unequivocally denied one of these claims, namely, that her company had made any money: "All those years it was losing money. . . . They were spending too much money building it out, opening one subprime center after another."[6]

One week after that conference call, two of Bear Stearns's hedge funds collapsed. Those funds, valued at $40 billion, had made large bets on mortgages, especially subprime mortgages, and had now sustained severe losses. Nobody wanted to inject new money. At that fateful hour for the aggressive investment bank, its chairman and CEO, James Cayne, was playing bridge in a tournament in Nashville, Tennessee, and could not be contacted either by cell phone or by e-mail. Bear Stearns's third-quarter profit would fall by 61 percent.[7] During a conference call on August 3, its chief financial officer said that the bond market was in worse shape than it had been for 22 years. The stock plummeted, and surprised CNBC viewers were treated to the spectacle of Jim Cramer, the host of the somewhat bizarre investment show *Mad Money*, walking back and forth, jumping up and down, moaning and shouting that the Fed had "no idea!" how disastrous the situation was and that it had to lend to the investment banks, finally concluding, "We have Armageddon."[8]

In April 2007, even the people at the rating division of Moody's had finally understood that they had to update their hopelessly outdated calculations for the housing market. When the analysts ran simulations based on the new assumptions, they realized that the alchemy had never worked. The bad mortgages were just as bad no matter how they were repackaged; lead had never turned into gold. On August 16, Moody's downgraded 691 mortgage-backed securities in a single day, citing "dramatically poor overall performance."[9] Analysts at Moody's and the other rating agencies then worked around the clock for the rest of the year to lower the ratings of investments previously viewed as safe. Between the third quarter of 2007 and the second quarter of 2008, securities worth $1.9 trillion had their ratings cut.[10]

This was the agencies' way of sealing off a bridge that had already collapsed. The number of families who had not paid their mortgages was over 5 percent and rising by the week. About 10 mortgage-financing companies went to the wall each week. It was too late for the agencies to salvage their reputations. "If you can't figure out the loss ahead of the fact, what's the use of using your ratings?" an angry executive at Fortis Investments asked in an e-mail. "You have legitimized these things, leading people into dangerous risk." An anonymous executive at Moody's stated to an internal evaluation team, "These errors make us look either incompetent at credit analysis or like we sold our soul to the devil for revenue, or a little bit of both."[11]

The loss of money was problematic, the loss of confidence catastrophic. For every mortgage-backed security that was downgraded, the market's faith in credit ratings was further undermined. In an economy that had increasingly come to consist of complex and not very transparent structured products, it was a disaster. Since investors themselves did not know what the packages contained, the "Aaa" label was what gave them their value. And now it turned out that most of them had been mislabeled. As if on command, investors stopped buying mortgage-backed securities. All the financial institutions and special companies whose business model was to take out short-term credit to keep their trade in securities going discovered that they could no longer renew their loans.

It was a bank run. As it concerned the shadow banking sector, it did not involve actual crowds of depositors rushing to the bank to get their savings out before everybody else did, but the mechanism and the effect of causing the bank to go belly-up in the process were the same. All the special companies, conduits, and structured investment vehicles filled to the brim with mortgage-backed securities that the banks had placed off their balance sheets depended on regularly being able to renew short-term loans of maybe $1 billion, $10 billion, or $30 billion for maturities ranging from as much as nine months to as little as 24 hours. The investors had treated these special companies as if they were as safe as ordinary banks, but now they no longer knew what mysterious risks they were being asked to finance and therefore shut the taps. They demanded their money back and refused to lend any more. One-third of the special companies' financing disappeared in the second half of 2007.[12]

This was a dramatic development, given that at this point more money was flowing through the shadow banks than through the ordinary ones. The entire economy had become dependent on the shadow banking sector. The banks that had deemed it a stroke of genius to place large assets off their balance sheets now realized that nobody else wanted to finance those assets. They had to come to the rescue using their own money, often because they had a legal obligation to do so and in other cases to preserve market confidence in them. The banks had built boomerang structures. No matter how far away they had thrown these structures, they were now back on their balance sheets. Banks were forced to make huge commitments, and the law required them to hoard capital to cover those commitments, but the market was in no lending mood. In just a few moments, a stable bank could seem to be teetering on the brink of insolvency. Citigroup saw its balance sheet grow by $49 billion in a single day in December 2007. There was no other way out for the banks but to pull the emergency brake so that they could build up more capital, and several of them also started borrowing directly from the Fed. The drawn-out bank run can be said to have begun on August 9, 2007. That was when the French bank BNP Paribas took the unusual step of preventing investors from withdrawing money from three money-market funds invested in U.S. mortgage-backed securities. Only one week earlier, its head had made assurances that the bank's exposure to the subprime crisis was absolutely negligible, but now BNP explained that the collapse in prices made it impossible to assess the value of the funds. Concern arose that many, many other institutions were in similarly dire straits, and stock markets took a sharp downward turn. The European and American central banks responded by pumping liquidity into the financial market.

Four years earlier, the successful investor Warren Buffett had described in his annual letter to stockholders how ever-greater risks were accumulating in a small group of market players who also traded among themselves to a large extent. This meant that a single major event affecting one of them could bring them all down, causing a large systemic crisis. The financial instruments that made these risky links possible should therefore be seen as "time bombs" or "financial weapons of mass destruction," potentially lethal to the entire financial system. Buffett was not thinking of securitized mortgages, which did not account for a particularly big market at that time, but of various types of derivatives involving money changing owners at some point in the future based on the value of some other asset. Even so, his description of risk concentration and of everybody standing or falling with everybody else felt disturbingly apt at the end of 2007. The problem was just that the weapons of mass destruction were hidden away in different places in the financial system. They were what Donald Rumsfeld would call "known unknowns"— things we know that we do not know. The only question was whether there would be time to locate and defuse them before the "megacatastrophe" that Buffett felt had to be included in the overall picture of risk.[13]

A Rational Panic

Financial reporting over the next 12 months felt as though it were stuck on "Repeat": the housing market deteriorated even more, banks announced new losses, central banks lowered interest rates and came up with new, innovative ways to shower liquidity on the markets. Each time the commentators would ask whether the worst was over. But it never was, because the problem was not only about liquidity, as it is when people lose confidence in banks out of pure fear and take home their money. That could have been fixed with temporary loans from central banks. The banks had in fact done some really lousy business, which would come across as progressively worse as time passed. It was not a shortage of liquidity but a lack of solvency. As Paul Krugman maintained, the panic was not irrational—it was rational.[14]

The write-down of bonds caused Merrill Lynch, whose employees had been taking ever-bigger risks to get ever-bigger bonuses, to lose $100 million a day in August and September 2007. That did not prevent its CEO Stanley O'Neal from playing 20 rounds of golf in those months, including 3 rounds on three different courses during a single day. In October, he was finally forced to stand down, but he did not come away empty-handed from Merrill Lynch, which gave him a platinum handshake of more than $161 million.[15] And as the corporation was hemorrhaging more and more severely, O'Neal's successor John Thain decided to accelerate bonus payments of $4 billion to employees and to spend $1.2 million renovating his personal office and adjoining spaces. Among other things, he bought a wastepaper basket for $1,400.

Citigroup's Charles Prince (the man who stood accused of being unable to tell a CDO from a shopping list) found out for the first time at a board meeting in September 2007 that his bank was sitting on $43 billion in various types of mortgage-backed securities. He asked the person responsible whether this was a problem and was told that no major losses could be expected. Only two months later, however, the bank estimated its subprime losses at $10 billion. Prince chose to step down—taking $38 million in bonuses, stocks, and options with him.

In September 2007, the United Kingdom was hit by a classic bank run taking place on real streets and squares. In scenes that the country had not witnessed for over 140 years, long lines of worried depositors wanting to withdraw their money were forming outside the branch offices of Northern Rock. This Newcastle bank had derived two-thirds of its financing from money-market loans, capable of being canceled at any time, and used the money for decade-long securitized mortgages whose value exceeded that of the actual homes.[16] As Martin Wolf has concluded, government guarantees for the banking system meant that savers saw only the high rates of interest paid by Northern Rock, not the risks it was taking. But this daredevil business concept did not survive a nervous market that would no longer touch mortgage-backed securities with a 10-foot pole. The Bank of England, the UK central bank, expressed its willingness to support Northern Rock on September 14, but that did not make savers any calmer—on the contrary, this was when the bank run started in earnest. It took three more days until the lines dissolved, after the government had declared that taxpayers would indirectly guarantee deposits. That was the first step toward nationalization.

Only days before the run, a trader at Lehman Brothers had underlined in an e-mail that now was the perfect time to buy: "Load up on Northern Rock for your children, your mum, your goldfish."[17]

And that was not a lone optimist. Despite a whole series of alarms going off and a number of meetings with the bank, the UK Financial Services Authority had not noticed any major problems. On the contrary, the FSA approved Northern Rock's dividends and models briefly before the end. It was "asleep at the wheel," as an inquiry report put it.[18]

The government-sponsored mortgage giants in the United States also remained optimists to the very end. In January 2007, Fannie Mae's chief economist gave a soothing message at a press conference: "I think the worst in housing is over. The biggest declines are behind us."[19] In the subsequent month, Fannie Mae's CEO Daniel Mudd launched a plan to buy additional subprime mortgages for $11 billion. He conceded that there had been problems with earlier mortgages but was now convinced that the quality of the class of 2007 would be better. However, it did not take long before that year's mortgages proved to be the worst ever. In March, Mudd admitted that the subprime business was experiencing a "partial meltdown," but he claimed that stress tests of Fannie's assets showed that it would not suffer any losses.[20]

By contrast, *The Economist* warned that even small write-downs of securitized mortgages could make Fannie and Freddie insolvent since their government guarantee had enabled them to work without margins. They had only $83 billion in capital to cover liabilities and commitments of $5 trillion. This amounts to a leverage ratio of more than 60 to 1, about twice that of the investment banks that were generally seen as horribly undercapitalized. Growing and yet undeclared mortgage losses could break Fannie and Freddie, and the mere suspicion of that could make it impossible for them to borrow in the market to cover their current expenditures. That, in turn, could have a domino effect on the financial system since banks were allowed to hold unlimited liabilities to the government-sponsored enterprises. What's more, many foreign central banks were also holders of Fannie's and Freddie's bonds. The magazine gave vent to its worries: "This raises the spectre of a broad financial crisis if either of the mortgage giants were to collapse."[21]

The duo lost more than $5 billion in 2007 but still paid dividends of over $4 billion to stockholders. "The thinking was that if something really bad happened to the housing market, then the government would need Freddie and Fannie more than ever, and would have to rescue them," says David Andrukonis of Freddie Mac in retrospect.[22]

The Treasury and the Fed explained to Fannie and Freddie in secret talks that they had to raise more capital. Ben Bernanke even threatened to attack the enterprises in public if they did not bring about capital infusions. Fannie reduced its mortgage portfolio and started to take in new capital from stockholders, but Freddie went on expanding and only took minor actions. In March 2008, at a conference for analysts and investors in New York City, Freddie's CEO Richard Syron defiantly declared, "This company will bow to no one." But as the value of its stock and the U.S. economy both deteriorated, Freddie found it increasingly hard to raise new capital. In October 2007, its stocks traded at over $60. At the turn of the year, they were worth only half that, and in July 2008, they had lost almost 90 percent of their value.

The government-sponsored giants were now accelerating on their way to total collapse. And yet Treasury Secretary Hank Paulson insisted as late as July 10, 2008, that "their regulator has made clear that they are adequately capitalized." William Poole, who had just left his post as president of the Federal Reserve Bank of St. Louis, had long warned of the government-sponsored enterprises. Convinced that, under normal accounting rules, both of them were as good as bankrupt, he could not believe his ears. Three days later, the administration was indeed forced to bail out the pair. Paulson declared that Fannie and Freddie could borrow directly from the Fed and that the taxpayers could step in and buy their stock. The bailout legislation also gave the administration explicit control over the enterprises, as well as the ability to increase the national debt by $800 billion so that it could cover Fannie's and Freddie's debts. Interviewed on CNBC, Paulson clarified his July 10 statement: "I never said the company was well-capitalized. What I said is the regulator said they are adequately capitalized."[23]

A top executive at Freddie Mac concluded, "It basically worked exactly as everyone expected—when things got bad, the government came to the rescue."[24] Even Joseph Stiglitz had had enough. Six years earlier, the Nobel Prize–winning economist had declared in a report paid for by the government-sponsored enterprises that their level of risk was "effectively zero." Now he attacked them and the administration in a vitriolic article in the *Financial Times*:

> We should not be worried about shareholders losing their investments. In earlier years, they were amply rewarded.

The management remuneration packages that they approved were designed to encourage excessive risk-taking. They got what they asked for. Nor should we be worried about creditors losing their money. Their lack of supervision fuelled the housing bubble and we are now all paying the price. . . .

A basic law of economics holds that there is no such thing as a free lunch. Those in the financial market have had a sumptuous feast and the administration is now asking the taxpayer to pick up a part of the tab. We should simply say No.[25]

The administration's commitments would soon become much larger, as it emerged that its earlier measures were not enough to calm investors and others. On September 7, Fannie Mae and Freddie Mac were for all intents and purposes nationalized. Their CEOs and boards of directors were sent packing, and the government injected $200 billion into the enterprises and promised future loans in exchange for a controlling stake. The government had now grown tired of privatizing gains and socializing losses. In the future, the gains—if any—would also be socialized.

Bill Clinton, who during his presidency had taken Fannie's and Freddie's commitments to entirely new levels, now admitted what his critics had been saying all along: "Frankly, it was never an ideal structure. They were government operations—but not."[26]

Richard Fuld Takes One on the Chin

As more and more write-downs and losses were announced, it increasingly appeared that the subprime wave was big enough to drown the investment banks of Wall Street. They were the ones who more than anyone else had surfed that wave, and yet this came as a surprise to many politicians, such as the President's Working Group on Financial Markets, because they had foreseen that the crisis would come from unregulated hedge funds rather than the more regulated investment banks. Paul Atkins, a former commissioner of the Securities and Exchange Commission, thinks that one of the reasons why the SEC missed the real causes of the crisis is that it was so busy trying to find ways to regulate hedge funds.[27]

On March 16, 2008, the Fed took the dramatic step of beginning to lend directly to investment banks. This had previously been the exclusive domain of commercial banks, those that accept deposits from the general public. The stock of Bear Stearns—the slightly different and slightly more aggressive investment bank that had run into trouble with its hedge funds at an early stage—had been trading at $133 before the crisis. On Monday, March 10, it was down to $62, and persistent rumors that Bear Stearns had liquidity problems caused it to fall further to $30 by the end of the week. Meanwhile, James Cayne, who had by then quit his job as CEO but remained chairman, was taking part in a bridge tournament in Detroit, Michigan, and the financial blog of the *Wall Street Journal* was keeping its readers up to date about his performance.[28]

The stockholders who went to sleep on Friday regretting that the Bear Stearns stock was deemed to be worth no more than a lousy 30 bucks still had the worst shock ahead of them. As they woke up on Monday, March 17, they discovered that J. P. Morgan Chase had offered to buy a majority stake in Bear Stearns for $2 per share and that the Federal Reserve Bank of New York was guaranteeing $30 billion of its assets. Over a single weekend, 84 percent of the company's remaining value had been annihilated.[29] On the revolving doors at Bear Stearns headquarters on Madison Avenue, somebody with a black sense of humor taped a $2 bill. That was all the 75-year-old corporation was deemed to be worth. On May 30, the deal was concluded at $10 per share, but it was the memory of the $2 bill at the entrance to the 43-story office building that brought to mind the slave riding on Wall Street's triumphal chariot whispering, "You too are mortal."

Throughout the weekend, people from the Treasury Department, the Fed, Bear Stearns, and its major rivals had been sitting in that office building, going through the books and the contracts in an attempt to find a way to prevent the problems of one investment bank from leading to systemic collapse. Eventually, they had to settle for a hasty marriage of convenience where the government provided the dowry. This was the full-dress rehearsal. A few months later, during the weekend of September 12–14, bureaucrats, lawyers, and market players were again sweating over charts and Excel spreadsheets to save a subprime-damaged investment bank, one whose stock had fallen 48 percent the day after Bear Stearns was bought up. That was the 158-year-old Lehman Brothers with 23,000 employees. And the first night did not go as well as the dress rehearsal. That was the weekend before the Monday that emptied the gourmet restaurant in Stockholm.

It was later claimed that the people in the White House decided to let Lehman fail because they were dyed-in-the-wool advocates of laissez faire. The Bush administration's expansion of public spending and its bailouts of Bear Stearns, Fannie Mae, and Freddie Mac shows that there is little truth to that. What is true, though, is that the administration had been under heavy fire for those bailouts and very much wanted to find a way to save other institutions without putting the taxpayers' money at stake. In fact, however, they tried to do more or less what they did with Bear Stearns, but they ran into unexpected problems.

Lehman's CEO for the past 16 years, Richard Fuld, had spent a long time trying hard to find a buyer for his company. Treasury Secretary Paulson had also encouraged him to do so on several occasions. Fuld took on this task with the great intensity and aggressiveness that had earned him the epithet "the Gorilla." Unlike other Wall Street titans who were keen golfers or bridge players, Fuld could just about manage to squeeze in the odd game of squash. Those who served under him testified that he was an authoritarian boss with an ice-cold gaze who could scare the living daylights out of his subjects. He had no time for rivals or naysayers. There are countless stories of people in high positions being told off or thrown out for contradicting him. You would only come to his office on the 31st floor if you brought good news.

Because of this homogeneous culture, nobody contradicted Fuld in late 2007 when, believing that subprime-mortgage securities had bottomed out, he started expanding Lehman's mortgage portfolio. This culture also created generous views on levels of remuneration. In the previous eight years, Fuld had taken home almost $350 million, and his second-in-command would go to work by helicopter. In June 2008, people at a Lehman subsidiary suggested that top management should abstain from taking bonuses to send a message that they took responsibility for the poor financial performance. One member of Lehman's board, President Bush's second cousin George Herbert Walker IV, immediately killed that suggestion by e-mail: "Sorry team. I am not sure what's in the water at Neuberger Berman. I'm embarrassed and I apologize." Fuld calmed his execs by saying that the idea came from people who could not think beyond their own wallets. On the very last Friday, while the company was asking for the taxpayers' help to survive, it was planning to give three senior executives severance pay of more than $23 million.[30]

Perhaps the White House just wanted to find a scapegoat and set an example by eventually allowing Lehman to go under if this proved necessary, as some people claim. Opinion is divided on that point. But even so, it would definitely have been easy to find worse candidates for that part than Richard Fuld.

As he was making increasingly desperate attempts to save his company, the main obstacle at first was not government passivity but rather government interventions and regulations. Fuld's attempts to find a buyer failed not only because people felt that Lehman was overvalued but also because of what two Bloomberg journalists called the "Bear Stearns Precedent." Since the government had stepped in to bail out Bear Stearns, the potential buyers of Lehman now wanted to put off making a deal until the government would make a desperate offer of similar or preferably better terms. Another proposed solution was to turn Lehman into a "bank holding company" so that it would be allowed to accept deposits from the general public. Fuld went to Timothy Geithner at the New York Fed (now Barack Obama's Treasury secretary) and asked whether a green light would be forthcoming, but Geithner did not much like the idea. Lehman also suggested that the bad assets be transferred to a separate company and new capital injected into the old one. But the SEC replied that under the rules in force, that would take three months— and by then there would be no Lehman Brothers.[31]

That last weekend, September 12–14, all hopes were pinned on two potential buyers: Bank of America and Barclays of the United Kingdom. However, once Bank of America had taken a closer look at Lehman's business, it demanded $65 billion of guarantees from the Fed—more than twice as much as Bear Stearns had received. This shocked the administration. Having seen the huge hole in Lehman's balance sheet, it did not dare to put the taxpayers' money at risk. Indeed, Paulson has even claimed that he would not have been allowed to because the law required good collateral for any guarantees, which Bear Stearns (and the AIG insurance company) could produce but Lehman could not.

Bank of America withdrew from the deal on Saturday and instead made the first moves toward taking over Merrill Lynch, which was also in dire straits. Barclays, however, would be happy with a limited government guarantee. On Sunday morning, a group of banks agreed to support almost $60 billion of Lehman's bad loans while

Barclays would buy the rest. The Lehman negotiators cheered and exchanged high-fives: they had succeeded. But at 11:30 a.m., they received a message from the UK Financial Services Authority that killed off the good mood in one fell swoop. The deal was on only if Lehman's debts were guaranteed when the Asian markets opened on Monday morning. Barclays was happy to make such a guarantee, but the FSA now announced that the bank was not allowed to do that without first having obtained the approval of its shareholders, and that could take weeks. Nothing was finished until everything was finished.

Paulson called the chancellor of the exchequer (his opposite number in the United Kingdom) and other leading politicians, begging them to make an exception. But they all refused. U.S. officials believed this was because of a lack of confidence in the deal as such. In any case, they were losing the fight against the clock. On Sunday afternoon, it was too late to arrange a new deal—the markets were about to open. The directors of Lehman Brothers had no choice but to start preparing what would be the largest bankruptcy in U.S. history. At the last board meeting before the end, Richard Fuld said he felt sick. His beloved Lehman was no more.[32]

A few days later, Fuld had gone into the office to deal with unfinished business. He took a break and went down to the corporate gym, stepped on the treadmill, and started running as the machine monitored his cardiac rhythm. A former subject of his who was pumping iron noticed that "the Gorilla," who used to strike such terror into people, was in the room. He rose, walked up to Fuld, and hit him in the face.[33]

The titan lies knocked down on the gym floor. A few weeks later, he is dragged to congressional hearings, where members take turns humiliating him before the media of the whole world. A journalist tells her viewers that after listening to his answers, she too felt like hitting him in the face. It was like something out of a Tom Wolfe novel—a Master of the Universe, invincible. But then something goes wrong—an accident, a deal misfires, a phone call is made to the wrong person. Everything turns around, and a public that only yesterday was praising him to the skies is now mocking him and jeering at him. Suddenly, the giant is so incredibly small. And right there, on the gym floor or in front of the bullies of Congress and the media, it is impossible not to feel a hint of compassion for the family man who loved his company so much.

That is, until you think of the plastics manufacturer who is going to be told by his bank a few days later that it cannot roll over his loans because the credit market is frozen solid. Or of the young business assistant who will soon be going home to tell her husband and children that she has lost her job because the economy has stopped dead. Then the compassion goes away again.

The Scariest Week Ever

This was the scariest week he had ever experienced, one trader recounts. It was the week when the global economy almost had cardiac arrest. People at the offices of the other Wall Street firms drew up huge charts showing all Lehman Brothers' subsidiaries, with arrows and bars indicating their exposure to each of them. They finally concluded that it should work, there would be no systemic crisis, it was not the end of the world.

And there would have been no systemic crisis had it not been for that money-market fund announcing a loss while the family with children was being served their pigeon at the Stockholm restaurant. The money markets, which had seemed unsafe as far back as August 2007 because of mortgage-backed securities, now came across as downright lethal. By that Wednesday night, institutional investors had withdrawn almost $150 billion from them, more than one-twentieth of their total value. Panic-stricken money-market funds were selling commercial paper to be able to give investors their money back. On Thursday, Putnam Investments had to liquidate a $15 billion fund to cope with the pressure for repayments. The interest rate that issuers of commercial paper were forced to offer shot up from 2 to 8 percent as the market decided that safe Treasuries were the only things it wanted. One of the main financing mechanisms for ordinary businesses had jammed up.[34]

An investment bank the size of Lehman is involved in deals with other banks, funds, and companies to the tune of trillions of dollars. All the pledges and collateral that were part of these deals froze fast in the bankruptcy, meaning that those who had lent to Lehman could no longer get their money out. Several large hedge funds whose frightened investors wanted to withdraw their money had to watch as huge assets belonging to them were caught up in the bankruptcy estate. And if the 158-year-old Lehman could go down just like that, leaving only a crater behind, then anyone could. If you were to take a hit from such a collapse, there were now no longer any viable markets left where other liquidity could be obtained. Companies stopped trusting banks, banks stopped trusting each other, and few lent anything to anyone. And as the song from *Cabaret* teaches us, money is what makes the world go round. At that point, it felt as though the earth would stop turning.

The *Los Angeles Times* and *Newsweek* published a cartoon by Mike Smith where a customer comes into a big bank office and says, "I'm here to ask you for a loan." The clerk replies, "Funny, I was going to ask you the same thing." That was not far from the truth. Scared banks were cutting the amounts they lent, the maturities of their loans, and the number of borrowers. A few banks were standing on solid ground, such as HSBC of the United Kingdom whose stock was actually rising thanks to a more prudent corporate culture and early crisis management, but the general feeling was that almost all were vulnerable.

That was the week when the investment banks—the pride of Wall Street—were wiped out. Their existence harked back to President Roosevelt's New Deal, when banks were forbidden from being both commercial banks and investment banks. That is, banks were allowed either to accept deposits from ordinary savers or to issue and sell securities, but not both. This ban was abolished when President Clinton signed the Gramm-Leach-Bliley Act in 1999. Universal banks had existed in other countries for a long time and now began to develop in the United States as well, for example, J. P. Morgan, Chase, and Citigroup. But some stuck to the old division. And the foremost of the investment banks were Bear Stearns, Lehman Brothers, Merrill Lynch, Morgan Stanley, and Goldman Sachs.

They had all taken insane risks in the mortgage market, and without access to more stable financing in the form of ordinary savers' deposits, they had no prospect of riding out the financial crisis, which had grown increasingly acute. In March 2008, J. P. Morgan Chase bought Bear Stearns for less than one-fourth of what it had cost to build the Manhattan skyscraper where the investment bank had its headquarters. On Monday, September 15, after the attempted bailout had failed not because of diehard laissez-faire ideology but because of British bureaucracy, Lehman Brothers was declared bankrupt. On the same day, Merrill Lynch was bought by Bank of America, which actually paid 70 percent more than the price quoted on the stock market the previous Friday. At that point, Merrill had lost about $50 billion on mortgage-backed securities.

Now it dawned on Morgan Stanley and Goldman Sachs that they were the next dominoes to stand or fall. Everybody had their eyes on them, and their stocks plummeted. Investors withdrew their money and started looking for safer places for it, such as Treasuries. On Sunday, September 21, 2008, one week after the failed bailout of Lehman, the Fed announced that it had granted applications from Morgan Stanley and Goldman Sachs to convert into bank holding companies, meaning that they would be able to build up commercial-banking operations and accept deposits from the general public. This was in fact the solution that Timothy Geithner at the New York Fed had discouraged Richard Fuld from choosing for Lehman Brothers.

The Gramm-Leach-Bliley Act was often—particularly before the financial crisis had reached its full dimensions—cited as an example of the kind of deregulation that was supposedly at the root of the problems. That was because it gave commercial banks such as Citi-group a license to enter the fray and go in for financial instruments and mortgage-backed securities. This argument fell somewhat out of use, however, once it turned out that those hardest hit were the investment banks that went on as if deregulation had never happened. As Bill Clinton has pointed out, deregulation—if any-thing—helped stabilize the situation.[35] Without it, it would have been illegal for J. P. Morgan Chase to buy Bear Stearns and for Bank of America to acquire Merrill Lynch. Morgan Stanley and Goldman Sachs would not have been able to save themselves by turning into bank holding companies. Considering the scale of the earthquake that shook the world when *one* Wall Street giant went down, we can only speculate about what would have happened if Lehman Brothers had been joined by the other four on its way down.

But investment banks were not the only ones to collapse during this fateful week. A huge stash of new financial weapons of mass destruction had just been discovered, and something was now going very wrong with them, potentially causing a series of explosions throughout the financial system. They were "credit-default swaps" (CDSs), a kind of insurance policy that you can take out against the risk of a company or a security collapsing. The history of the CDS begins at the Boca Raton, a pink luxury hotel in Florida where about

80 people from J. P. Morgan & Co. took part in a conference in 1994. Legend has it that the young, successful bankers partied so wildly that they ended up throwing each other into the pool fully dressed. And yet the thoughts they thought were even wilder. The problem they had been given to solve was the following: J. P. Morgan was about to hit the ceiling set by banking regulations. How could it free up the huge amounts of capital it was forced to hold as insurance in the event that the corporations and governments it lent to should suspend payments?

J. P. Morgan was famous for its group culture. While other banks encouraged individualists who did their own thing, people there made a point of sticking together and developing new products as a team. Many of them later moved on to senior positions in other businesses after J. P. Morgan's merger with Chase Manhattan in 2000, but the "Morgan Mafia" is renowned for tight relationships among former colleagues, a bit like people who have been to the same boarding school.

The meeting at the Boca Raton was presided over by Peter Hancock, who had been appointed head of J. P. Morgan's derivatives division at the age of 29. He had gravitated toward the derivatives market because it gave him the same feeling of creative problem solving that he had experienced as a science student at Oxford University. Now he encouraged his colleagues to think freely and toss out any idea that occurred to them. The most exciting of the ideas they later worked on in the conference room, at the pool, and in the bar involved mixing derivatives and credit. The concept was for an outside party to take over the risk that a bank's counterparty might go bust. In exchange for regular payments, that outside party would step in and compensate the bank if something went wrong. This was similar to an insurance policy, with premiums and payments in the event of an accident, but the difference was that anyone could buy it—you could take out insurance against Sweden's or Lehman Brothers' suspending payments even if you yourself had no business with them.[36]

The new credit derivative became incredibly popular in the market, because now banks could buy default swaps on, say, the institutions they had lent money to and then tell their supervisory authorities they no longer ran any risk if their debtors were to go belly-up. Somebody else had taken over that risk, meaning that the banks were suddenly entitled to free up their capital and invest it. The problem, of course, was that they still ran one risk, namely, the party that had sold them the CDS would not be able to pay out the compensation—and if, as it were, everybody can take out insurance on my car, then there is an awful lot of money to be paid out if I drive carelessly. In the eye of the government regulations, however, the risk had gone away. And the banks could not care less, because even though the risk was not that much smaller, they were now able to free up capital. They no longer had to think about the risks represented by thousands of counterparties and could therefore act more aggressively. Bank regulation had spawned a new, exotic credit derivative, which itself was unregulated.

When Lehman Brothers fell, it was suddenly clear that future payments on CDSs could involve pretty large amounts. People looked around and realized for the first time that the value insured by credit derivatives had almost doubled every year. After the collapse of corporations like Enron, more and more people had felt a need to reduce their risk in this way. Now the market seemed to have reached about $55 trillion in notional value. The only question was who was sitting on all those risks right now. Could they really afford to pay? What if only a tiny proportion of default swaps were to default, and the related losses were to cause a bank to collapse, which would trigger more CDSs, creating new losses and triggering new CDSs, and so on in a long series of explosions that might end up knocking out the entire financial system?

That is why dark glances were now being cast at AIG, the American International Group. It was not only the world's largest insurer, with 116,000 employees and operations in 116 countries, but also a leading seller of credit-default swaps. On the same day that Lehman went down—Monday, September 15—the rating agencies downgraded AIG. Since it had been able to apply tiny margins to its insurance agreements only on the strength of its earlier grade, AIG was now forced to raise new collateral to the tune of many billions of dollars in short order, and its stock fell by 60 percent as soon as the stock market opened. One of those participating in talks with the administration and the Fed about AIG was Lloyd Blankfein, who was CEO of Goldman Sachs—the job Hank Paulson had had before he became Treasury secretary. Blankfein was particularly worried, because if AIG collapsed, his bank would lose around $20 billion worth of insurance policies, according to reports in the *New York Times*. But it never came to that. Instead, there was yet another large-scale government intervention. On that Tuesday, the Fed made $85 billion available to AIG in exchange for the departure of its CEO and an opportunity to buy a majority share of the company stock.[37]

Credit-default swaps have been characterized as engines of doom, but if you take a closer look at them, you find that, if correctly used, they may in fact be a good insurance solution. Blaming them for, say, the poor quality of the mortgages they insured is a bit like being against fire insurance because houses lack smoke detectors. The possibility of taking out insurance against the collapse of an investment or a counterparty is obviously very valuable to those who want to avoid being pulled along down. That such insurance can also be used by outsiders to bet on a certain event happening to somebody else means that more information and a multitude of perspectives help ensure that the price of the insurance comes closer to representing a reasonable assessment of probability. If it suddenly becomes more expensive to take out insurance against a certain institution, that amounts to an early warning of future problems that may give that institution time to address the cause of those problems.

However, the CDSs shared a defect with the securitized mortgages they often insured: There was no exchange allowing the market to determine their prices. Instead, CDSs were traded in more haphazard ways, sometimes through undocumented deals over the phone, and for a long time the seller of a CDS did not even have a way of knowing whether the other party had sold it to someone else. Since nobody knew who was sitting on what risks, the stage was set for tumult in times of crisis. The lack of transparency fueled excessive panic—many believed that Lehman swaps could have triggered payments of hundreds of billions of dollars, but the real figure was only $6 billion.[38] The absence of an open marketplace also prevented the emergence of armies of profit seekers who would have scrutinized every nook and cranny of the CDSs to find out what they were worth. And compared with the problem of mortgage-backed securities, things were twice as bad with CDSs: Here we were dealing with swaps without market valuation insuring mortgage-backed securities without market valuation. There was simply a gargantuan scope for arbitrariness and mistakes.

That scope was exploited in 2004 by AIG's financial division in London when it came up with the lucrative idea of insuring mortgage-backed securities. Since the rating agencies had approved its product, AIG concluded that it would be able to charge high fees without ever having to pay anything—it was "money for nothing." CDSs flowed out in all directions and money flowed into the tiny division, which accounted for 17.5 percent of AIG's total profit in 2005. Those who worked there were paid accordingly. Each member of the fairly small London team averaged more than $1 million per annum.[39]

By December 2007, AIG had sold default swaps on various securities worth about $440 billion. More than one-tenth were backed by subprime mortgages that were rapidly losing value. Its CEO assured investors at a meeting that the company's risk models, which analyzed the risk of the underlying mortgages, provided "a very high level of comfort." But no mathematical model, however complex, can be better than the data you put into it. When AIG made its deals, it did not reckon with the risk that the value of the securities would be written down or that policyholders would demand more collateral—which they were entitled to do if their securities lost value. The reason why AIG believed it was never going to lose anything was simply that it had skipped over the major risk factors when it had made its calculations.[40]

AIG's financial division was overseen by the Office of Thrift Supervision, an agency of the U.S. Treasury Department. However, the OTS, whose officials were constantly on the spot at AIG's Connecticut department, also did not think that demands for more collateral would cause any problems. It found the CDSs "fairly benign" since their credit ratings were high, and it also felt that the underlying assets were "low-risk," as they too had been given good grades by the rating agencies.[41]

There was just one hitch. To its seller, a CDS can never be equivalent to an ordinary insurance policy. If you are in a car crash or your house burns down, this typically does not entail that everybody else is now more likely to bump into things in traffic or to have their homes consumed by fire. It means that your insurer can compensate you out of the premiums paid by all other car owners or homeowners and still make a juicy profit on the difference. But in the financial markets, sorrows often come in battalions. If one bank falls or one security loses its value, it is a sign that others are in trouble, in some cases actually *because* of the first event. An insurer may therefore quickly be left with nothing but losses. The numerous banks and funds that had also sold CDSs were in a better position since they had bought CDSs at the same time to guarantee their business, so their losses and gains could cancel each other out if the market ran into major trouble. But AIG was different. It just sold.

As securities began to head south, Goldman Sachs and other buyers repeatedly demanded that AIG accumulate more collateral. Since the market value of CDSs was falling at the same time, the insurer was also forced to write down the value of its assets dramatically. AIG needed more and more capital from a market that was less and less keen to provide it. That set in motion a spiral of losses that, in the absence of a bailout, could have dealt a very heavy blow to the banks and financial companies that had built CDSs and secured all their deals with them. Instead, the spiral was stopped by the bailout on September 16, 2008.

The week after taxpayers had been forced to step in, senior executives of AIG's life insurance business took part in a long-planned retreat in California. Together with their agents, they amused themselves with spa treatments, rounds of golf, and banquets to the tune of almost half a million dollars. The next day, it was reported that the Fed would lend AIG almost $40 billion more. A week or so later, it emerged that AIG had gone through with an exclusive hunting trip to England in which several of its senior executives participated at the same time as the loan negotiations were being conducted. And all the while, the demands for AIG to raise collateral to guarantee its CDSs kept increasing. In the subsequent month, it was reported that AIG had spent a further $343,000 at an exclusive resort in Arizona— just before the announcement of a third bailout package that brought the total sum of loans and stock purchases to $152 billion. But on that occasion, AIG hid all corporate logos and told hotel staff not to mention the company's name under any circumstances. The idea, one must assume, was to ensure that no angry taxpayer would spot the executives and go punch them in the nose.

Mark-to-Nothing

One reason why mortgage-backed securities were written down so fast and by so much was that the accounting rules in force made the write-downs self-reinforcing. U.S. government agencies had long worried that the rules were too lax and facilitated creative accounting. During the dot-com bubble, many companies had used strange methods to calculate the value of their assets, and the energy-trading company Enron had managed to trick investors by entrusting that task to complex mathematical models. To address this situation, the U.S. financial authorities now required mark-to-market accounting. Under this model, which has been used by companies in the United States since 1993, an asset is not valued according to the price it was once bought for, the price it is expected to be sold for in the future, or the return it yields in the meantime. Instead, it has to be "marked to market," that is, valued at the price it would fetch on the market if it was sold right now. The accounting rules were made tighter and stricter in 2007: hard-to-value securitized assets, including mortgage-backed securities, now also had to be marked to market. "If you think banks are writing off large amounts of assets now, wait until new accounting rules take effect this month," prophesied the financial news website CFO.com in early November 2007.[42]

The new rules came into force at the same time as the market for mortgage-backed securities collapsed. Chastened by earlier scandals, the auditing firms wanted to avoid being taken to court over incorrect valuations and insisted that the new rules be applied. They immediately set about making huge write-downs of securities. Since nobody believed in the credit-rating agencies anymore, it was hard to find anyone anywhere in the world who wanted to buy securitized mortgages. There was no liquid market, and the few willing buyers offered peanuts. Some commentators thought that this was a temporary problem and that once the credit market had calmed down and transparency increased, people would eventually be willing to pay more for the assets. The regulatory provisions contained wording to the effect that mark-to-market could not be used if there was no active market, but the SEC did not allow that emergency exit to be used. In March 2008, it emphasized that assets had to be marked-to-market so long as there were any buyers left in the market. The write-downs accelerated.

There is something natural and self-evident about mark-to-market—about simply accepting today's market prices as the highest wisdom rather than performing strange calculations where there is always room to manipulate and to cover up losses. There are strong arguments that this should be the default option, but its weakness is that the exclusive focus on today's prices amplifies the business cycle. If the stock market goes up, all institutions seem to be worth much more than before, so they can reduce their equity capital and buy more on credit, which pushes up asset prices even more, which further increases the perceived value of the institutions, and so on. In bad times, the same institutions seem to be worth much less and they have to sell off more assets, which pushes prices down further, which makes their auditors write down the value of their remaining assets even more, and so on, this time in a downward spiral. The former head of the Federal Home Loan Bank in Chicago warned the SEC:

> In the midst of a severe bust, where we are now, this rein-
> forces the downward cycle of panic—falling prices–losses–il-
> liquidity–credit contraction–more panic–further falling pric-
> es–greater reported losses–no active markets.[43]

Moreover, in many contexts, write-downs also led to holders of mortgage-backed securities being forced to pay back money to those who had lent them the cash to buy the securities (with them as collateral). Under some contracts, lenders were entitled to get their money back if a security sank below a predetermined price. In other words, holders had to raise new capital even as the value of their securities was collapsing. Banks with huge holdings were thus in a situation resembling that of a family that is seeing house prices plummet and suddenly gets a call from the bank asking to have all the mortgage loan back.

One of the harshest critics of mark-to-market was William Isaac, who was head of the Federal Deposit Insurance Corporation between 1981 and 1985. He considered that the financial problems in the 1980s were worse than those now experienced by the United States. Then as now, there was a mortgage crisis, and the banks were up to their ears in bad loans to the developing countries of the world. If mark-to-market had been applied back then, Isaac said, every major U.S. bank would have collapsed, and the country would have entered a severe depression.[44] "Historians will look back some day and say that the government drove companies into bankruptcy by creating artificial losses," added former Speaker of the House Newt Gingrich.[45]

93

On September 30, 2008, the SEC finally accepted that there was no active market for mortgage-backed securities. The mark-to-market rules were suspended, and companies were allowed to value their assets based on the cash flow they generated. If the authorities wanted to save the investment banks of Wall Street, the world's biggest insurer, and two government-sponsored mortgage institutions, however, they acted one month too late. They were also too late to save a small, affluent country in the northern part of the Atlantic.

The Raven Goes Down

Iceland, a creation of the lava ejected where the Eurasian and American tectonic plates meet in the North Atlantic, has been for a thousand years the place with the best stories, or "sagas" as the locals call them. Barren landscapes, steep shores, and majestic mountain formations make it one of the most beautiful countries in the world. The heat in the earth's interior makes itself felt even today through geysers spraying boiling water from the rocky ground and through still-active volcanoes. In one of the world's most sparsely populated countries, with only 320,000 inhabitants, the elements feel more tangible than anywhere else. This small, northern Atlantic island nation has room for fantasies and dreams.

In the past two decades, Iceland has experienced a saga of such drama and tragedy that it could almost have been written by Snorri or Sturla. David Oddson, a prime minister with bushy, curly hair who penned short stories and poems in his spare time, liberalized the national economy in the 1990s. The government lowered taxes and privatized companies, and it pulled off the almost unparalleled feat of finding a way to manage fish stocks—based on ownership rights—which both avoids overfishing and generates income. The Icelandic economy grew fast, and the small island, where stories of poverty and famine are still told, became one of the richest countries in the world. Its highly educated citizens started successful companies in information technology, energy, and biotechnology, and Icelanders bought both West Ham United, a London soccer club, and House of Fraser, a large British department store chain. Whatever others may be saying today, don't you believe them—back then everybody envied the small band of modern-day Vikings who were all drive and no fear.

Today, Iceland is virtually bankrupt. Its stock exchange fell 90 percent in 2008, and its economy is expected to shrink by more than 10 percent in 2009. Unemployment and the rising cost of living have ruined thousands. In October, someone with a black sense of humor offered up the entire country for sale on eBay: "Unique opportunity to buy a Northern European country . . . admittedly a somewhat sketchy financial situation." Bidding started at $1.75. Those who laughed probably choked when they found out that the Icelandic government was trying at that time to obtain a large rescue loan from the increasingly authoritarian Russian Federation. "We have not received the kind of support that we were requesting from our friends," the prime minister explained, "so in a situation like that one has to look for new friends."[46] Soon after, the International Monetary Fund stepped in.

The reason for Iceland's deep fall should be sought in what was until not long ago its greatest source of pride: its banking industry. Even today, opinion is divided about what went wrong. Some claim that a banking system that has been poorly developed until recently is prone to making beginner's mistakes; others say that the ancient Viking spirit encouraged too aggressive expansion. A third explanation homes in on the fact that, as a manifestation of nationalism and to humor opponents, foreign buyers were not allowed when government assets were privatized. In such a small country, that meant that the banks were taken over by people without banking experience, sometimes by former politicians and their aides.[47] At any rate, it is completely beyond doubt that the country was too small to have such a large and internationally active banking sector under a system based on central banks as lenders of last resort.

Indeed, the country's small size was the reason the recently privatized banks soon expanded abroad. Their domestic market was not big enough. The daredevil growth they engaged in was based on borrowing to an extent, relative to the size of their country, which has few counterparts in history. In mid-2008, the three banks—Glitnir, Landsbanki, and Kaupthing—accounted for three-fourths of the Iceland Stock Exchange, and their assets including loans were more than 10 times their home country's GDP. Kaupthing increased its assets 30-fold between 2000 and 2008. Iceland was a high-risk fund dressed up as a sovereign state, according to a joke doing the rounds of the financial markets.

The Central Bank of Iceland kept interest rates much higher than elsewhere in response to the overheated economy and the high rate of inflation. This made it possible for the banks to attract foreign money by offering generous interest rates—up to 7 percent on one-year deposits. The high interest rates kept the exchange rate of the króna high, making it cheap for Icelanders to import exclusive goods from other countries. To buy such luxury items, and to buy their homes, they borrowed in other currencies, such as Swiss francs or Japanese yen, to avoid having to pay the high interest rates prevailing on their island. This was very risky. If the króna were to fall, they would be hard put to pay back in other currencies. But all they were doing was following the example set by banks and business—which bought foreign companies, raised loans on them, and bought more. On September 15, 2008, Glitnir's management realized that its dependence on credit could land it in disaster. The bank had financed its expansion with loans from European banks, and 600 million euros' worth ($850 million) of loans would fall due one month later. But Lehman Brothers had just collapsed, and the temperature of the global financial markets was way below zero. Where on earth would Glitnir get 600 million euros? Few had the courage to lend even to the largest and most creditworthy banks, and unlike its Icelandic peers, Glitnir had no foreign deposits to take from. Many other banks in many other countries had similar problems at about the same time. If Glitnir had been in Germany or the United States, the central bank would have lent the money, savers would have felt safe, and the whole story would have been long forgotten by now. What's more, the loans of the Icelandic banks were not exposed to U.S. mortgages—they were good-quality loans, and capital-adequacy ratios were pretty good compared with those of many other banks.

But Glitnir and the other two banks were not headquartered elsewhere. They were domiciled in a country with a population of just under 320,000, a tiny central bank, and even tinier foreign-exchange reserves. There was no way Iceland alone could keep Glitnir afloat for an extended period. But when it asked other countries for help, they refused because they felt Iceland did not give an open and honest account of its precarious situation. On September 28, the government instead announced an offer to take over 75 percent of Glitnir in exchange for 75 percent of its shares. This caused bank stocks to plummet and led to credit-rating cuts both for the banks and for Iceland as a country. It also made concerned British savers start to withdraw their money from Landsbanki, which had established itself successfully in the United Kingdom under the name of Icesave. Iceland's government and central bank did all they could to get hold of liquidity and even asked the central banks of other countries where the banks had operations for loans, but to no avail.

The Icelanders had nowhere left to go. On October 6, Prime Minister Geir Haarde asked for broad powers to handle the banking crisis, concluding his speech with the words *Guð blessi Ísland*—"God help Iceland." The next day, the government used its new powers to nationalize Landsbanki. It promised that it would guarantee the money of Icelandic savers while foreign savers would be given compensation, if possible, up to 20,000 euros ($27,000), in line with European guarantee agreements. But it also hinted that there probably was not enough money even for that, at least not right away.

Iceland's biggest bank, Kaupthing, looked in better shape. It had not been the subject of any bank runs and seemed able to obtain the credit it needed. Throughout that Tuesday, long into the night, its management worked on a proposal to save the Icelandic banking system by taking over Glitnir and selling foreign assets. On Wednesday morning, the bankers then got started on the main part of their task, when suddenly they were all transfixed by their TV monitors. What they saw and heard was shocking: The British government, whose willingness to compromise was the basis for any solution, had decided without previous warning to take over Kaupthing's UK subsidiary because it was concerned about its viability and doubted that Iceland would compensate British savers. Destroying any remaining confidence, this drastic action crushed Kaupthing and killed the rescue plan for the banking industry. The Icelandic government was forced to take over Kaupthing the next morning and eventually Glitnir as well.[48]

The British government also froze Landsbanki's assets in the United Kingdom. The method it chose probably set a world record for abuse of legislation. It applied an anti-terrorism law enacted in 2001 that was designed to freeze the assets of foreigners planning to damage the United Kingdom or its economy. Icelanders, whose country habitually tops international rankings of freedom, democracy, and noncorruption, could suddenly visit the website of Her Majesty's government and find themselves listed alongside terrorists and rogue states: al

Qaeda, the Taliban, North Korea, Iran. . . .[49] And as if this was not enough, Prime Minister Gordon Brown also mistakenly said that the British government would freeze any Icelandic assets it could lay its hands on and demanded that Iceland compensate British savers in a way that would slap a burden of debt per capita on it, not dissimilar to that imposed on Germany at Versailles.

Even if the British government had consciously tried to find the best way to shatter the global markets' confidence in Iceland, it is hard to believe that it could have come up with a more cunning plan. In a world shaken by crisis, a deeply indebted terrorist nation with a reduced credit rating inspires only so much confidence. The rest of the world immediately severed all economic ties with Iceland. Many banks refused even to transfer money there, and it became impossible to get hold of foreign currency.[50] "Kaupthing was the last, best hope of the Icelandic banking system, and it was killed there and then," explains Icelandic journalist Andres Magnusson. "This really was the last straw. A lot of Icelanders are asking, 'Excuse me: who's the terrorist here?'"[51]

In a single day, the Icelandic króna lost 27 percent of its value against the euro. The stock exchange was closed for three days. When it opened again, it fell 77 percent, reflecting the weight of the banks. Capital controls were introduced, meaning that nobody wanted to bring foreign currency into the country. Businesses could not renew their loans, and it became virtually impossible to import food, which is particularly devastating for a cold, barren country that does not really have an agricultural industry. At the end of the month, the central bank raised its benchmark rate from 12 to 18 percent to cushion the fall of the króna. Successful companies were smashed to pieces, and unemployment ballooned.

A young Icelandic couple had recently taken out a loan in foreign currency to buy a home. After the collapse, their interest payments— as expressed in a króna that just would not stop falling—almost doubled. The crumbling housing market meant that the value of the house they had bought plummeted. In the course of a few days, the prices they had to pay for fruit and vegetables increased by 50 percent. At that point, the man was laid off from his job.

Out there atop the Mid-Atlantic Ridge, for more than a thousand years, Icelanders have struggled back on their feet time and again after volcanic eruptions and earthquakes. But financial tectonic plates can collide, too.

5. Madly in All Directions

Crackbrained meddling by the authorities ... may aggravate an existing crisis.

—Karl Marx, in a letter to Friedrich Engels

"If we don't do this," said the balding and bearded Fed chairman Ben Bernanke as he riveted his usually kind eyes on the leaders of the Senate and the House of Representatives, "we may not have an economy on Monday." A dead silence fell on House Speaker Nancy Pelosi's conference room. Those who were there say you could have heard a pin drop.

Bernanke and Treasury Secretary Paulson had hastily convened this emergency meeting on the evening of Thursday, September 18, 2008, three days after the fall of Lehman Brothers. Panic reigned in the credit markets. Without the ability to borrow money, companies choke, which leaves people out of a job, which makes consumption go away, taking the whole economy with it. The economy was about to suffer cardiac arrest, as the most fashionable metaphor would have it. The administration and the Fed had recently given out improvised electric shocks to get the economy beating again, but to no avail. Bernanke and Paulson now felt an overall approach was necessary.

The program that they proposed to Congress—and that its leaders now quickly endorsed—was intended as a defibrillator working at maximum power. They wanted the government to guarantee the money-market funds and to ban the shorting (selling stocks you do not own) of shares in financial companies, and above all, they wanted $700 billion. The largest bailout package in history would enable the treasury secretary to buy bad mortgages from the banks, so that the markets would regain confidence in them and they would be able to start circulating again. The difficult question, of course, was how much the government should pay for the mortgages. If the banks had wanted to sell at the price the market was willing to pay, they could have done so at any time. In other words, the bailout would entail the banks' being paid more than the market wanted to give for the mortgages. Critics concluded that this was tantamount to giving taxpayers' money to banks that had screwed up, *because* they had screwed up: "cash for trash."

The Great Delusion

Paulson and Bernanke had secured support for their proposal earlier that day in the Roosevelt Room, a classic meeting room in the West Wing of the White House with no windows but fake daylight coming from a false skylight. This meeting, in the words of one of those present, "scared the hell out of everybody." The Treasury secretary and the Fed chairman had told President Bush about the panic in the credit markets, explaining that if he did not sign off on the biggest bailout in history, the United States would be hit by a crisis bigger than the Great Depression. The president had been speechless, almost stunned, for a moment. Then he had sprung into action.[1]

That is how mention of the Great Depression affects Americans, even those who are too young even to have parents who lived through it. It is a national trauma, and the photos and stories of people lining up for soup kitchens or the rare jobs that were available give regular reminders. They are testament to the fact that even a prosperous country can be thrown, for no apparent reason and in very short order, into destitution and hopelessness. The torment lasted for over a decade, unemployment peaked at almost 25 percent, and the stock market lost around 90 percent of its value. "Not on my watch," says each Fed chairman, prepared to pump endless sums into the economy at the very thought of the Great Depression; "Nor on mine," echoes each president, signing off on any spending package imaginable just to avoid going down in history with that blemish on his record.

The Great Depression would be mentioned repeatedly in the early stages of this crisis, by politicians, businesspeople, and journalists. After frightening the president, Paulson held a conference call with Republican members of Congress, telling them things would get "far worse than the Great Depression in the '30s" if they did not vote for his plan.[2] Media watchers have found that in just the first four months of 2008, the three major TV networks—ABC, CBS, and

NBC—drew comparisons with the Great Depression no fewer than 40 times.[3]

The Great Depression was cited to tickle viewers and readers, to give a historical parallel to what was happening, to scare people into action, and above all to explain why the government could not remain passive and let the market forces clean out the failed investments. This is because most people today believe that the Republican president Herbert Hoover was such a dogmatic advocate of laissez faire that he stayed passive after the 1929 stock market crash and let the economy collapse because he was waiting for the free market to solve the problems. Another widespread misconception is that salvation came because his Democratic successor Franklin D. Roosevelt pursued a policy involving more government intervention. These two misrepresentations of history together justify the conclusion that, in a time of crisis, it is always better for the government to do too much than too little. In other words, our approach to the present crisis has been based on a delusion about history. It builds on an incorrect idea of Hoover's policies and of the impact of Roosevelt's.

There was in fact an interwar depression in the United States that was met with minimal government intervention, but that was back in 1921. The newly elected Republican president, Warren Harding, had just taken over an economy where the GDP had fallen more than 3 percent and unemployment was shooting up. Harding was a protectionist but otherwise stuck to old American ideals of free markets and limited government. His response to the crisis was to lower taxes, to halve federal spending in two years, and to abstain from preventing wages from falling and companies from competing with one another. As a result, bad companies were wound up while more competitive ones were able to attract more capital and cheaper labor. This led to a fabulously fast recovery. Even in 1922, the economy grew by 6 percent and the number of unemployed fell from 4.9 million to 2.8 million. The little depression was over in a year, and few remember it today.[4]

Herbert Hoover was already around at that time—as a critic. He was an early adopter of the tenets of "social engineering," convinced that all human problems had political and technological solutions.[5] The statist faction of the Republican Party had managed to squeeze Hoover in as commerce secretary in the Harding administration, and in that capacity, he called in vain for more government coordination of the economy. He then stayed on in the same job under President Calvin Coolidge, who was less than appreciative: "That man has offered me unsolicited advice for six years, all of it bad."[6]

As president, however, Hoover would get a chance to try his interventionist ideas in practice. Very soon after the 1929 stock market crash, he launched the most ambitious political response to a recession in the history of the United States. He and the Republican-controlled Congress immediately pushed through the notorious Smoot-Hawley tariff, which erected the second-highest tariff barrier ever around the country. The rest of the world protested and quickly responded by raising its own tariffs, meaning that not only imports into the United States but also exports from the country were knocked out. International trade broke down, and the Depression spread across the world. As a matter of fact, the stock market crash at the end of October 1929, which is generally viewed as the starting point of the crisis, actually happened soon after it became widely known that the coalition in Congress that had been blocking the tariff increases had come unstuck.[7]

Hoover also increased government spending, launched federal public works programs on an unprecedented scale, and began to subsidize the agricultural sector he had smashed to pieces by starting a trade war. Since he believed that the most important thing was to prevent a fall in consumption, he was willing to do anything to keep wages from dropping—as until then they had always done in times of crisis. "Labor is jubilant," a contemporary witness says about how the American Federation of Labor reacted when hearing of Hoover's plans, which it saw as "a remedy for unemployment which, at least in its philosophy and its groundwork, is identical with that of labor."[8] What's more, Hoover drastically raised taxes right when the downturn was in the offing.

The reports dispatched in 1930 by a junior Swedish diplomat paint a picture of President Hoover that is not at all consistent with the belief commonly held today that he subscribed to some sort of extreme laissez-faire ideology. Rather, he emphasizes that "it must be recognized that [Hoover] has not stood idly by but has taken resolute action to tackle great problems" and that this means that "the foundation has probably been laid for important constructive work in the future." Sweden's best-known economist at the time,

Gustav Cassel, was not equally optimistic. In December 1929, he wrote that Hoover's public projects and attempts to keep wages up were based on an exaggerated faith in the government that could make the crisis worse:

> Under the energetic leadership of President Hoover, it appears that the government wishes to intervene quickly and powerfully to prevent an economic depression. . . . There are, for this reason, grounds for grave concern across the world about a government intervention the real purpose of which is to destroy American savings through uneconomical investments in America. The intervention made by the government is therefore obviously harmful in this case. It would be vastly better to leave business to its own devices.[9]

The only area where it may be justified to talk about passivity on the part of the government under President Hoover is its behavior when banks were collapsing left and right and the money supply contracted. Even there, however, it was more a question of policy failure than market failure, as shown by Milton Friedman and Anna Schwartz in their classic work, *A Monetary History of the United States.* The recently founded Federal Reserve had been entrusted with the task of adding liquidity, which entailed that businesses did not think it necessary to stay away from weak banks and that banks themselves no longer felt the need to resort to the methods they had previously used to end bank runs (such as restrictions on the right of withdrawal during the 1907 crisis). But when the New York Fed started to inject capital after the crash, it was blocked by the Federal Reserve Board in Washington, D.C.—not because the latter considered that the wrong thing to do but because it wanted to outmaneuver the New York office, which had effectively been running the entire Federal Reserve system under its appropriately surnamed chairman, Benjamin Strong. He had died in 1928, and the central board in Washington now saw a chance to grab power. The New York Fed repeatedly called for action, but the people in Washington refused. Instead, the Fed system accumulated reserves in the midst of the severe crisis, and in the fall of 1930, it actually increased interest rates. In this way, the Federal Reserve Board took control of U.S. monetary policy, but at the cost of a drop of around one-third in the money supply from 1929 to 1933—an unprecedented monetary collapse. The many negative effects of deflation included making people's debts even heavier and making tariffs (which were fixed nominal amounts per unit of weight) even higher.[10]

The reason that over 10,000 U.S. banks went under during the Great Depression was overconcentration. That, in turn, was a consequence of legislation banning them from running operations and branches outside their home states. This made them completely dependent on local businesses. If a small number of depositors withdrew their savings or a small group of borrowers ran into trouble, the entire bank became insolvent. North of the border, where the crisis may actually have hit even harder than in the United States, the system was different. Canadian banks were free to expand across province lines and could spread their risk and help branch offices that encountered difficulties. Not a single bank went bankrupt in Canada during the Great Depression. And the country did not even have a central bank until 1935.[11]

What determined the depth of the Great Depression more than anything else was that President Hoover kept wages up at the same time as the money supply and thus prices were falling. This combination led to a strong increase in real wages, which went up by 10 percent in manufacturing during the two years after the stock market crash instead of falling by as much, which had been the pattern of earlier crises. Consequently, companies now had to pay more for labor in a situation where they could not raise capital and had a hard time selling their goods either in the United States or abroad. Hoover boasted during the 1932 election campaign that in the midst of the deepest crisis ever, U.S. real wages were the highest in the world.[12] He just forgot to mention that the result of that policy was an unemployment rate of almost 25 percent.

Hoover was proud of his interventionist experiment. He declared: "No President before had ever believed there was a governmental responsibility in such cases. . . . Therefore, we had to pioneer a new field." Right from the start, the objective was that "the Federal government should use all of its powers," which Hoover saw as a "program unparalleled in the history of depressions in any country and any time."[13] Then again, no president before him had created such a long, deep, and global economic depression, either.

Those who believe that Hoover was an advocate of laissez faire often base that assumption on the fact that his Treasury secretary, Andrew Mellon, was against the government bailouts and recommended bitter medicine instead: "Liquidate labor, liquidate stocks, liquidate the farmers, liquidate real estate." What they ignore then is that Mellon opposed Hoover's policies and that Hoover himself declared, "We determined that we would not follow the advice of the bitter-end liquidationists."[14]

This picture of President Hoover has not been dug out by historians only recently. It is how his contemporaries perceived him. During the 1932 election campaign, his challenger Franklin D. Roosevelt accused him of being a spendthrift, tax-raising, protectionist centralist; Roosevelt promised instead to restore free trade, deregulate, achieve budget balance, and cut federal spending by one-fourth. His vice-presidential candidate went even further, raging about Hoover's "leading the country down the path of socialism."[15] Laissez-faire free-marketers such as Ayn Rand, H. L. Mencken, and Isabel Paterson voted for Roosevelt, not least because of their intense dislike for Hoover, who in 1932 campaigned for further constraints on trade and immigration.

At first Roosevelt's team included people like his budget director Lewis Douglas, who claimed that the Depression was not at all the result of the free market but rather a consequence of government actions in the 1920s undermining the free market: low interest rates, tariffs, and subsidies that had inflated prices.[16] But Douglas soon quit once Roosevelt had explained that there were two federal budgets: the ordinary one, which was the one he had promised to bring into balance, and the emergency one, which needed to be deep in deficit to finance all the support programs that had to be developed. In fact, Roosevelt did not have an explicit plan for what was going to happen after the election and he was prepared to listen to proposals and to experiment. Within the Democratic Party, suggestions for managing the crisis that verged on socialism had begun to emerge. And even though Roosevelt lowered tariffs and ended Prohibition (do not underestimate the extent to which that helped restore Americans' confidence in the future), he also started building on his predecessor's government controls and job programs. As time went by, Roosevelt stole Hoover's old clothes garment by garment, presenting them as part of his New Deal. One of the architects of Roosevelt's new policy program, Rexford Guy Tugwell, confessed years later, "We didn't admit it at the time, but practically the whole New Deal was extrapolated from programs that Hoover started."[17]

However, President Roosevelt went even further with regulations, subsidies, agricultural programs, and infrastructure projects at an unprecedented scale. The man who had complained in the 1932 election campaign that "government—Federal and State and local—costs too much"[18] tripled federal spending even before the war started. Instead of fostering competition, he tried to create monopolies and trusts, and business happily connived. Companies were to decide price and wage levels together; at times, there was a ban on selling goods below certain minimum prices. He also gave organized labor a stronger role and created the Social Security system.[19] Some of the things he did considerably reduced people's suffering during the crisis. Millions of unemployed were given jobs by the government, and federal pensions and unemployment insurance must have enormously increased the sense of security in a situation where there was nothing else to rely on, even though the associated costs made hiring even more expensive for companies. Other projects, by contrast, caused immediate harm. One example was the idea of increasing food prices to support farmers. To achieve that, the government destroyed huge amounts of agricultural land, crops, and meat; all it led to was more hunger and more unemployment among agricultural laborers.

Despite the strong enthusiasm aroused by President Roosevelt as a person and as a leader, the New Deal was a disappointment. In particular, the expansive monetary policy pursued—the only genuine difference compared with Hoover's policies—created very high rates of growth in 1934, 1935, and 1936, and yet when the unemployment rate was at its lowest, in 1937, it was still over 14 percent, more than four times the 1929 level. For an economy with so much unused capacity, this was an incomprehensibly slow recovery. Moreover, that was the year before tighter monetary policy and higher taxes led to "a depression in the Depression," bringing unemployment back up to 19 percent. The UCLA economists Harold Cole and Lee Ohanian have estimated that the New Deal caused both wages and prices to be about one-fourth higher than they would otherwise have been, meaning that companies could ill afford to hire. Cole and Ohanian think that this policy prolonged the Great Depression by seven years.[20]

The common denominator of the myriad different projects was that they all contributed to turning the United States into a giant experimental laboratory where all conceivable and inconceivable political projects were being launched, reinforced, canceled, and transformed into their direct opposite. One moment big corporations were to be given total power over the economy, the next they were to be persecuted. One day saving was the big thing, the next spending. Many intellectuals admired this feverish spirit of experiment and this willingness to test unconventional ideas at full scale without really knowing where they would take the country. For people in business, by contrast, all this made it difficult to find a sure footing and a clear horizon so that they could start planning, investing, and getting back to work in order to bring the country out of the Depression. Economic historian Robert Higgs calls the problem "regime uncertainty."[21] In the mid-1930s, private-sector investment was just one-third of what it had been a decade before. Net investment—total investment less consumption of assets—fell each year from 1930 to 1935 and took 12 years to return to its 1929 level.[22]

Against a backdrop of a constant flow of new regulations, increasingly fierce anti-capitalist rhetoric, and attacks on the independence of the judiciary, businesses did not know what the future would bring. Communications and infrastructure companies would be able to invest huge sums, said James Farley, who was both a member of the cabinet and chairman of the Democratic Party, "if they knew where they were heading." The big investor Lammot du Pont was of the opinion that under President Roosevelt, all that had been solid melted into air:

> Uncertainty rules the tax situation, the labor situation, the monetary situation, and practically every legal condition under which industry must operate. Are taxes to go higher, lower or stay where they are? We don't know. Is labor to be union or non-union? . . . Are we to have inflation or deflation, more government spending or less? . . . Are new restrictions to be placed on capital, new limits on profits? . . . It is impossible to even guess at the answers.[23]

Even British economist John Maynard Keynes, who was fond of the New Deal and partly inspired it, wrote a personal letter to President Roosevelt criticizing him for scaring off businessmen by his unpredictable regulatory enthusiasms and angry rhetoric: "You could do anything you liked with them, if you would treat them (even the big ones), not as wolves or tigers, but as domestic animals by nature, even though they have been badly brought up and not trained as you would wish."[24]

An opinion poll from March 1939 shows this to have been how Americans themselves felt, too: 54 percent said that Roosevelt's attitude to business was delaying the recovery while only 26 percent did not think so. A 1940 study showed that almost 60 percent of senior executives knew of others who hesitated to sign contracts with the armaments industry, and most of them thought this was because they did not believe that you could do business with an administration that was so hostile to companies. If Roosevelt had managed to make corporations shrink even from lucrative deals, you can only imagine what their thinking may have been about riskier, more long-term investments. Executives' worries about the future were even more apparent in a survey conducted in the subsequent year, when over 40 percent guessed that after the war, the United States would develop into a semisocialist economy or a full-fledged fascist or communist dictatorship.[25]

Henry Morgenthau, who was Roosevelt's Treasury secretary for over a decade, suspected all along that the huge government expansion they brought about was of very little use. In May 1939, he complained to his diary:

> We have tried spending money. We are spending more than we have ever spent before and it does not work. And I have just one interest, and now if I am wrong somebody else can have my job. I want to see this country prosper. I want to see people get a job. I want to see people get enough to eat. We have never made good on our promises. I say after eight years of this administration, we have just as much unemployment as when we started. And enormous debt to boot.[26]

A survey of economists in 1995 showed that almost half believed the New Deal had made the Great Depression longer and deeper.[27] What it took to get to the beginning of the end of the Depression was not a new deal, but a new world war. As European manufacturing became paralyzed by World War II, U.S. exports (not the least of which was military equipment) to friendly countries increased by ridiculous amounts. When the United States later joined the war, Americans lost some of their purchasing power but probably did not notice much since goods were rationed anyway. And if 9.5 million people are jobless and you draft 12 million young men into the armed forces, it is going to make a bit of a dent in your unemployment statistics.

The big economic boost for the United States came after the war. Keynesian economists had predicted that demobilization and the associated steep fall in government spending would lead to a depression. But business stepped in instead, and private production increased by almost 30 percent in one year. Under a different set of assumptions—that business works best when it is free and operates under clear rules—however, this development was entirely logical: Wartime economic controls were phased out, the New Deal was over, and the new president, Harry Truman, was felt to be more stable and more business-friendly than Roosevelt had been. Uncertainty about the future was a thing of the past, and now companies were again willing to bet on it.

Shorted Out

Many politicians blamed the 1929 stock market crash on shorting. Herbert Hoover accused investors of being unpatriotic for selling borrowed securities they believed were overvalued to pay back with ones bought more cheaply at a later time. He denounced their intent "to take a profit from the losses of other people." The New York Stock Exchange was regulated by New York State, so it would have been unconstitutional for Hoover to try to intervene in his capacity as president, but pressure was brought to bear, forcing the management of the exchange to reduce shorting opportunities. Federal restrictions were added later in the 1930s.[28]

It soon emerged that shorted stocks had accounted for a minuscule proportion of trade—only 0.0015 of shares were shorted on November 1, 1929. Those who owned stocks did not want to lend them; they wanted to sell them. If anything, shorting has a stabilizing effect on prices because it increases trading volume and brings more liquidity to the market, so that those who want to buy or sell can more easily find someone who is willing to do the opposite.[29] But this did not matter: "The average man does not apply severe logic in his reasoning on such matters," the *New York Times* wrote in October 1930. He is just looking for "something peculiar and abnormal" to pin the blame on.[30] Short selling thus often has to serve as a scapegoat when stock exchanges fall, simply because many people share President Hoover's dislike for people profiting from the failure of others. But their opportunity to sell short is exactly what gives investors a stake in exposing companies that are trying to manipulate the market or cook their books, or that have other skeletons in their closets. If shorting is unpatriotic, then it is also unpatriotic to be an investigative reporter.

The first of the proposals pushed through by Ben Bernanke and Hank Paulson after the fall of Lehman Brothers was a ban on shorting financial stocks. Just one day after the meeting with congressional leaders, on September 19, 2008, the Securities and Exchange Commission prohibited investors from shorting the stocks of 799 companies during a period of three weeks. The administration had found something peculiar and abnormal to blame. Immediately after this decision, the stock market rallied and financial stocks soared.

The United Kingdom had done the same thing the day before, and other countries followed suit with bans covering longer periods. Other government agencies also made assaults on speculators. The attorney general of New York State, Andrew Cuomo—whom we already met in his earlier guise as housing secretary in the 1990s, when he did all he could to ensure that noncreditworthy households would get mortgages—called for regulations and started investigations to find out whether shorters in the market had engaged in downward manipulation of prices: "I want the short sellers to know today that I am watching."[31]

The U.S. ban had been preceded by intense lobbying on the part of the major banks, which claimed that their shares were falling because speculators were selling them short. As other companies joined the chorus demanding protection, the list of untouchables expanded to over 900 corporations in only three days; all of a sudden, Ford, General Motors, and General Electric counted as financial companies. A few more days of lobbying added the computing giant IBM and the pharmacy chain CVS. But not all businesses were as keen on political protection for their stock price: When the Diamond Hill Investment Group found out that it was on the SEC's list of nonshortables, it immediately asked to be let off. Its CEO Rod Dillon explained that shorting is necessary for the market to work properly:

> What is so frequently misunderstood by so many, whether regular investors or C.E.O.'s, is that the goal of the marketplace is to have the stock price be an accurate reflection of fundamentals of your business. They think the goal is to have the stock price as high as it could be.[32]

Dillon was pointing out something important. Those who sell stocks short do so because they have, or think they have, obtained information that others lack, and information was exactly what investors would have needed during the days of confusion when suddenly it was virtually impossible to figure out where the risks were, causing everybody to sit on their money. The message sent by the Treasury Department, the Fed, and the SEC through the ban on shorting was that they believed there existed information that had better be kept away from markets. The Dow Jones index did rise just over 7 percent during the two days when the ban went from rumor to finalized decision, but that was in part because all those who had sold borrowed shares now had to buy them back at any price. And then the stock exchange lost 25 percent in two weeks. "Banning the short-selling of stocks," *The Economist* noted, "makes for a good headline; but it deprives markets of liquidity and information, the very things that they have lacked in this crisis."[33]

The mistakes of banks and others have often been exposed by short sellers. By prohibiting what they do, you remove a powerful incentive for market players to obtain more information. Swedish financier Mats Qviberg felt that the authorities were shooting the messenger: "The problem is not that people have shorted the banks. On the contrary, that has been the exact right thing to do; the banks have been badly run."[34] Hedge-fund manager James Chanos, whose work led to the exposure of Enron's bogus transactions, believes that in the hunt for cheaters, short sellers are the detectives of the market, whereas bureaucrats engage mainly in archaeology. As he saw it, the ban amounted to government protection for companies that had misbehaved: "We seem to have capitalism on the upside and socialism on the downside."[35] Paul Donovan at the Swiss bank UBS did not mince his words either:

> This can be characterized as a populist reaction of no positive value. Anyone who seriously thinks that the cause of this crisis arises from the actions of evil and manipulative speculators lacks the insight and knowledge to be allowed anywhere near the regulation of financial markets.[36]

The immediate consequence of the government action was to flatten out the category of financial-market institution that had thus far been the least damaged by the crisis: the unregulated hedge funds. These large mutual funds sell both short and "long" (i.e., stocks they actually own) to obtain a good return regardless of how

111

the stock exchange moves, meaning that they add a lot of liquidity to the market even in bad times. Now, however, half of their business model was banned, and the shares they had earlier borrowed to sell they now had to buy at prices that could be twice as high. This exacerbated the losses that the hedge funds had already started to make; investors began to withdraw increasing amounts from them, and plenty of funds closed up shop entirely. It was a massacre, as one person put it.

Three months later, studies of the shorting bans were carried out in the United States, the United Kingdom, Germany, France, and Italy. With the proviso that the period of the bans had been brief, they all concluded that the effect on stock behavior had been negligible and that the risk of large drops in prices had not decreased after the ban or compared with stocks that could still be sold short. The ban had had "minimal effect," as the headline in the *Financial Times* expressed it. That, however, does not mean that the ban had no impact. Volumes of trade had fallen and markets had become less liquid. Spreads between bid and offer prices had grown, and trade had became more fitful.[37] The SEC's own preliminary follow-up also pointed to unwanted consequences, such as reduced market liquidity. At the end of 2008, its chairman, Christopher Cox, was critical of the SEC's actions: "Knowing what we know now, I believe on balance the commission would not do it again. . . . The costs appear to outweigh the benefits."[38]

But it is not certain that the Treasury Department felt the ban to be a failure, because its main intention in introducing it had been to build crisis awareness and come across as strong and active. An official admitted to the *New York Times* that Treasury did not expect any practical results. It was a symbolic action "to scare the hell out of everybody," as that official put it.[39] As such, it was successful beyond expectations.

Socialism for the Rich

In her book *The Shock Doctrine*, Canadian writer Naomi Klein claimed that politicians and economists exploit crises to scare voters so that they can push through unpopular liberalizations, tax cuts, and privatizations. A look at the history of government in the Western world shows her to be right that politicians exploit crises, though seldom to liberalize and reduce the size of the state but rather to increase government control, public spending, and their own power.[40]

The Great Depression of the 1930s is one example of that; the week following the fall of Lehman Brothers in September 2008 is another. Treasury Secretary Paulson not only wanted to increase regulation of the financial sector and force taxpayers to finance the biggest bailout package in history.[41] He also wanted to exploit the crisis to amass as much power as possible in his own hands, in part at the expense of the directly elected representatives of the people of the United States whom he and Bernanke frightened in Nancy Pelosi's conference room. The draft of his $700 billion bailout plan, which ran to no more than three pages, included wording to the effect that, in practice, the Treasury Department would place itself above the ordinary rules and beyond democratic scrutiny. Most remarkable of all are the powers conferred on the U.S. secretary of the treasury by virtue of Section 8:

> Decisions by the Secretary pursuant to the authority of this Act are non-reviewable and committed to agency discretion, and may not be reviewed by any court of law or any administrative agency.[42]

This was nothing short of an attempt by Hank Paulson to turn himself into "economy czar." In practice, he was telling Congress, "You hand me $700 billion to do as I please with, and that's that!" The cover of the next issue of *Newsweek* featured Hank Paulson's somewhat angular head with its completely bald pate and the caption "King Henry." At the same time, *The Economist* penned a portrait of him under the heading "President Hank." Even without Section 8, he was now the leading powermonger in Washington, D.C.—the Treasury secretary who was telling the president what to do.

Paulson had come from the position as CEO of Goldman Sachs only two years previously, at which time *The Economist* had impishly inquired whether the reason why he accepted a lower salary and more bureaucracy might be that it gave him an opportunity to be "forced" into selling his $700 million worth of Goldman stock, which it would not look good for him to dispose of while he remained at the helm.[43] In early August 2007, after the housing bubble had burst and Bear Stearns's hedge funds had keeled over, and as Jim Cramer was hollering about Armageddon on CNBC, Paulson had told President Bush, "This is far and away the strongest global economy I've seen in my business lifetime." Now, one year later, he thought the opposite: "This is the most serious thing that we faced."[44] And it was his job to take care of it. His oft-mentioned optimism and confidence doubtless came in handy. As a football player in his youth, he had earned the nickname "the Hammer." But there was also an element of faith. Paulson, a teetotaler, is a Christian Scientist, thus convinced that illness, death, and the material world are not real. For someone who does not believe in the material world, he was now laying claim to discretionary powers over fairly large parts of it. Seven hundred billion dollars is almost 6 percent of the gross domestic product of the United States. Somebody calculated that if you took out that sum in $1 bills and lined them up lengthwise, you would get two-thirds of the way from the earth to the sun. Considering Paulson's background at Goldman Sachs and the large number of his aides who came from Wall Street, many wondered if there might not be conflicts of interest when he was to save his former employer and the rest of the financial sector—especially now that nobody was going to be allowed to scrutinize his actions. "After reading this proposal, I can only conclude that it is not only our economy that is at risk, Mr. Secretary, but our Constitution, as well," objected Sen. Christopher Dodd (D-CT), chairman of the Senate Banking Committee, when Paulson had presented his plan to the committee on September 23. The Republican and Democratic committee members alike declared the loosely drafted plan to be unacceptable.[45]

When the first shock had worn off, members of Congress started to pay more attention to the deluge of phone calls, e-mails, and letters raging against a plan that favored those who had thrown the country into the crisis in the first place. And 2008 was an election year. Anti-government Republicans and anti-business Democrats began to argue against the bailouts as a way of taking from ordinary people and giving to big finance. Why should taxpayers provide the money for the stratospheric salaries of the Wall Street executives? Several polls taken at this time indicated strong skepticism about government intervention. A Rasmussen poll showed that only 7 percent of voters wanted the government to rescue financial institutions in trouble, and a poll by Fox News/Opinion Dynamics indicated that most people, regardless of their political preferences, were against the bailout and that 76 percent of voters (including 66 percent of Democrats) felt that the financial crisis was a good opportunity to reduce the size of government and lower taxes.[46]

The economist Nouriel Roubini, who had predicted the problems several years earlier as he tried to identify the developing countries that were next in line for being struck by a financial crisis, was angrier than most. He characterized the bailout as "a disgrace" and "a total rip-off," as "socialism for the rich, the well-connected and Wall Street" that, at huge cost, would be of very little benefit to the financial system. Like many other economists, Roubini would have preferred a solution along the lines of that chosen by Sweden and Finland for their banking crises: having the government provide capital to the banks, but only in exchange for preferred stock that will earn all the dividends, so that the previous stockholders do not make any money from the bailout.[47] Direct injection of capital could be cheaper, given that $70 billion of capital enables a bank to lend over $700 billion.

In a letter to Congress, more than 100 U.S. economists of varying political complexions criticized the Paulson Plan on a range of counts. They considered it unfair given that, in practice, it was a way to favor certain financial institutions at the expense of taxpayers; and they believed it was possible to save the financial system without saving individual investors. Further, they felt that the description of the acquisition procedure was scandalously unclear and lacked monitoring and follow-up. Above all, though, they warned against implementing huge changes to the financial system based on short-term motives. This letter has been described as a sign of an "emerging consensus [of] academic economists."[48] At the same time, many other economists, along with certain heavyweight free-market commentators such as *The Economist* and Martin Wolf of the *Financial Times*, described Paulson's plan as bad, but better than nothing; one almost felt as though they had been inspired by the "politician's syllogism" from the British TV series *Yes, Prime Minister*: "Something must be done. This is something. Therefore it must be done."

The strong-willed Paulson did everything he could to get his $700 billion—at one meeting in the White House, he even half-jokingly went down on his knees, hands clasped, begging Nancy Pelosi, the Democratic Speaker of the House of Representatives, to continue supporting the package even if the Republicans started to hesitate.

On September 24, both presidential candidates—Barack Obama and John McCain—jointly expressed their support for a large bailout, and President Bush tried to wring a yes out of Congress in a televised speech that seemed designed to arouse concern. Instead of trying to calm his audience, the president spoke of imminent disaster: "The government's top economic experts warn that without immediate action by Congress, America could slip into a financial panic." He did not assure listeners that the situation was under control but instead declared that "our entire economy is in danger."[49] Investors could be forgiven for getting the impression that Bush had lost control and that it was time to pile up cash. "If markets are driven by animal spirits, then what they did that week was probably the most irresponsible scaremongering in the history of the United States," commented Matt Kibbe of the free-market organization Free-domWorks.[50] *The Economist* explained that this unusual rhetoric of panic could turn into a self-fulfilling concern: "So politicians ought to think twice about spreading despondency. That is the media's job."[51]

It is probable that key actors consciously exaggerated the threat of disaster to more easily push their policies through, which in turn helped fuel a panic in the markets. We are used to politicians behaving in a composed manner, saying that we really have nothing to fear but fear itself, so when one of them claims that panic is close at hand, he or she rarely inspires confidence. By contrast, Ben Bernanke, himself an expert on the Great Depression, calmed a Texas audience toward the end of the year by stressing that comparisons between then and now were "a lot of loose talk . . . there's no comparison."[52] And there was simply no risk that a country as rich and diversified as the United States, with such an extensive social safety net, could be affected by something similar: "Let's put that out of our minds; there's no comparison in terms of severity."

Fair enough, if it had not been for that meeting with ABC, in which President Bush explained why the administration had gone to Congress and asked for $700 billion:

> I can remember sitting in the Roosevelt Room with Hank Paulson and Ben Bernanke and others, and they said to me that if we don't act boldly, Mr. President, we could be in a depression greater than the Great Depression. . . . And my attitude is, is that if that's the case, this administration will do everything we can to safeguard the financial system. And that's what we've been doing.[53]

This, then, is the same Ben Bernanke who thinks that all comparisons are a lot of loose talk and that such a depression—let alone an even bigger one—could hardly happen in an economy as sophisticated as that of the United States. Unless we believe that Bernanke completely changed views over a period of a few months or that Bush has a bad memory, then there is very much to indicate that Bernanke tried to scare the president into action using arguments that he himself did not believe in, and that the president then used those arguments to scare the population and the market.

It worked, but not at first. On Monday, September 29, the House of Representatives voted down the Paulson Plan by a small margin, even though the czar clause had been removed and certain limits had been set for the remuneration of senior executives. Almost immediately, however, several members who had pushed the no button gave out the impression that they had only wanted to send a message to voters about their dissatisfaction and did not really want the package to fail, particularly not as the Dow Jones index reacted to their collective decision by falling almost 7 percent. The political, media, and business establishments raged at populist politicians who would risk a depression rather than disappoint their voters. This gave vent to a feeling that the Paulson Plan was the obviously right way to go and that anyone who failed to accept it right away was on the verge of imbecility. Dana Milbank of the *Washington Post* labeled its opponents "wing nuts," and conservative columnist David Brooks called them "nihilists." A science article in the *New York Times* tried to pin down the evolutionary bug that had caused the population to resist Paulson's bailout plan.[54]

But the "nihilists" were soon annihilated. Once the Senate had voted through a revised version of the Troubled Assets Relief Program on that Wednesday, the House got a second chance on Friday, October 3. Democrat Brad Sherman described a sense of panic among members, with increasingly absurd horror scenes being conjured up, for instance, that the stock exchange would collapse and a state of emergency would be proclaimed across the country if they voted no again.[55] However, they did not. The difference was that this time the package had been sweetened with an additional $110 billion of targeted tax breaks, including for alternative sources of energy and victims of natural disasters, as well as narrow business sectors that just happened to be important where skeptical members had their voters—Hollywood studios, owners of race courses, and producers of wooden arrows for children.

In the end, of course, it turned out that Congress was against the $700 billion only because it was too *little* money.

An Offer You Couldn't Refuse

However, the stock market continued to fall quickly. When the package had been voted down on September 29, 2008, the Dow Jones index lost 7 percent, which the advocates of the package saw as evidence that it was necessary. But during the five days after the package had been voted through, the stock market fell by more than 18 percent. More than anything else, the excited atmosphere and politicians' talk of panic had worried the markets. And the administration's handling of the TARP did not inspire confidence, either. "It's not based on any particular data point," a Treasury representative replied to a question from *Forbes.com* as to why the amount of $700 billion had been picked. "We just wanted to choose a really large number."[56]

A Wall Street executive who was involved in talks with Treasury after the package had been pushed through reveals that the government officials were asking him such basic questions about how to do things that he began to suspect that there was something fishy about the entire project: "It was clear they hadn't thought it through."[57] There was a simple explanation for why the people at Treasury had not devoted much thinking to the plan they had declared necessary to save the United States from a depression: They had already decided not to implement it. Hank Paulson admits today that he told his staff as far back as October 2, "We are going to put capital into banks first." Defining, pricing, and buying bad assets turned out to be an administrative nightmare—and it was not even certain that it was going to help. The nihilistic wing nuts had been right all along!

The day *before* the members of the House of Representatives voted on the TARP, which they were told had to be implemented in order for the United States to have an economy in the future, Treasury had thus already scrapped the proposed program. Instead, Treasury began work on the solution proposed by Nouriel Roubini and other economists, namely, to recapitalize banks in exchange for stock. Paulson had made sure that the legislation included wording that gave him the authority to buy almost any assets, including financial company stock. In retrospect, Paulson defends his explicit denials that that was the idea by saying that Congress would have been opposed to the federal government stepping in as part owner of a series of banks. "This is a very complicated and difficult sell," he later told the *New York Times*. "I don't know how to sell that." The Treasury secretary did not think he could persuade the elected representatives of the American people that a certain proposal was good, so instead he told them he was going to do something they were more willing to accept but slipped in powers to do what he really wanted to do. It was a $700 billion swindle.

Paulson's about-face came across as less dramatic than it really was because events in Europe were beginning to steal the limelight. On the evening of October 4, Italy's conservative prime minister, Silvio Berlusconi, said that the financial crisis had happened because the United States had developed a "capitalism of adventurers." Europeans, by contrast, were wiser and more prudent: "Europe is not facing and has never faced the risks in the American system."[58] But Europe soon would—the day after Berlusconi's statement, in fact. Then Italy's second-largest bank called an emergency meeting to raise more capital, and the German government was forced to bail out a mortgage institution and guarantee all bank accounts. It soon emerged that many European banks had had even less control of their business than their American peers. Iceland fell apart; countries such as Hungary and Latvia seemed to be heading the same way; and the International Monetary Fund began negotiating emergency loans.

The Belgo-Dutch banking and insurance group Fortis, one of the world's largest corporations, had been in trouble ever since it was involved in the acquisition of ABN AMRO in October 2007, in part because European Union rules to limit the concentration of ownership had forced it to sell large parts of the company at a loss. Raising new capital grew increasingly difficult for Fortis, and after Lehman's fall there began to circulate rumors of impending bankruptcy that caused customers to withdraw their money. On September 28, the governments of Belgium, the Netherlands, and Luxembourg divided the bank among themselves and sold off a large chunk to its French competitor BNP Paribas, which had already expressed an interest.

There was also concern in the world of finance that British banks such as HBOS and the Royal Bank of Scotland were only days away from collapse. To prevent a crisis, the British government announced an extensive bank package on October 8. It was going to inject up to £50 billion ($87 billion) into the country's major banks and other financial institutions, but it asked for something in return: either preferred stock on which all dividends would be paid or interest-bearing securities. Bank owners were the ones who should feel the pain, not taxpayers. At the same time, banks were to be offered easier access to credit. This resembled Sweden's and Finland's method of solving earlier banking crises, and it soon turned out to be the winning model. Four days later, leaders from European Union member states met in Paris, declaring that each of them would recapitalize its national banks. They also raised the level of deposit insurance—feeling they had no choice following Ireland's promise the previous week to guarantee all bank deposits, which had caused savings to flow into Ireland from other countries, forcing more and more other countries to extend their deposit guarantees.

These interventions calmed markets more than did those of the U.S. administration. When the grumpy but stable British prime minister, Gordon Brown, laid out the course, people at least knew where they were headed. The self-esteem this must have given Brown manifested itself in a fantastic Freudian slip. When the House of Commons was debating the financial crisis in early December, he mistakenly declared, "We not only saved the world . . . ."

There was the briefest of pauses, during which members looked at one another for some kind of confirmation that they really should believe their ears. Then an explosion of mirth drowned out Brown's correction, ". . . saved the *banks*." And it would not subside. While the opposition was naturally roaring with laughter, many members of the prime minister's own Labor Party were laughing openly while others, like the Roman guards hearing silly names in Monty Python's *Life of Brian*, had to contort their faces to refrain from bursting into guffaws. Members of Parliament were slapping their knees and waving pieces of paper in the air as they were choking with laughter. The Speaker had to call for order four times, and it was almost half a minute before Brown—the man who had created the British financial regulations that were now crumbling, who had refused to grant an administrative exemption to save Lehman Brothers, and who had branded Iceland a terrorist country to show British savers that he was a man of action—could resume his speech and tell the world what an immense debt of gratitude it owed him.

On Tuesday, October 14, Treasury Secretary Hank Paulson publicly announced that the first $250 billion of TARP money would be used to recapitalize banks while the government began to guarantee banks' loans, including to each other, for a modest fee. To begin with, new capital would be given to nine large banks and to smaller ones that requested it in exchange for preferred stock with a 5 percent dividend, rising to 9 percent after five years, and the opportunity to buy more stock. This was intended to ensure that the banks would have an incentive to raise other capital in due course and buy out the government. By not laying claim to voting rights, the government limited its sway over banks. All had to join, because if someone stayed outside, the others would look weak. This solution differed from what many economists had called for. In their book, recapitalization meant giving money to banks that would otherwise collapse. Paulson, by contrast, wanted to give money to all the banks, because then they would be able to start lending to business and get the economy going. The program was said to be voluntary, but very soon descriptions surfaced in the press indicating that the degree of voluntariness was the same as in the cartelization of business under the New Deal.[59] Back then, when General Hugh Johnson, whom President Roosevelt had placed in charge of the project, was asked what he was going to do about companies that did not voluntarily set the same prices, pay the same wages, and offer the same working conditions as their competitors, he replied, "They'll get a sock right on the nose."[60]

The press reports said that at 3:00 p.m. on the day before the announcement, Hank Paulson had lined up the top executives of the nine big banks along one side of a 20-foot mahogany table. They were seated in brown-leather chairs in alphabetical order—Bank of America at one end and Wells Fargo at the other. After describing the deal, Paulson declared that there was no scope for negotiation or compromise. All the bankers were given a one-page document that they were expected to sign, without grumbling, before they left the room—for their own good and that of their country. Some of them immediately showed interest, whereas others peppered the Treasury secretary with critical and anxious questions. At one point Ben Bernanke, who was also present, had to step in to emphasize that there was no need for such a confrontational atmosphere.

Most critical of all was Wells Fargo chairman Richard Kovacevich. He explained that his bank had stayed away from exotic mortgage deals and was in no need of a bailout. It was beyond his comprehension why he should transfer his stockholders' profits to the Treasury secretary in exchange for protection that his bank did not need. Then Paulson sharpened his tone. Sure, Kovacevich could take his chances and pass up the offer, but if Wells Fargo were to find it hard to raise private capital at a later stage and then asked for help, the administration would not be so generous.

It turned out to be an offer you couldn't refuse. "Nice little bank you've got there; wouldn't it be a pity if it had a little accident?"

At 6:30 p.m., all had signed the agreements.

Three days after Paulson's announcement, one of the strongest banks, J. P. Morgan Chase, held an internal conference call to decide what to do with the $25 billion it had just been given by taxpayers. What the participants did not know was that Joe Nocera of the *New York Times* had obtained a connection number so that he could hear them. He reported that not one word was said about the bank's lending more money—on the contrary, it was planning to lend less. Instead, one executive mentioned that the $25 billion could be used to buy other banks.[61]

When 21 banks that had received at least $1 billion each of taxpayers' money were asked by the Associated Press what they had done with that money that they otherwise would not have done, not a single bank gave a straight answer. Several said they did not know. The Morgan Stanley representative would reveal this only if she could remain anonymous, and the person from New York Mellon Corp. replied, "I just would prefer if you wouldn't say that we're not going to discuss those details." It is not a wild guess that the banks themselves would never grant a loan to someone who came strolling into one of their branches and gave that answer to the question of what he or she intended to do with the money.[62]

Still, despite all the shortcomings, the credit guarantees and the huge capital infusions into the big banks and then a few hundred other banks did ease worries about a wave of major bank collapses. The cost to banks of borrowing from one another started to fall, and the spread between that rate of interest and the one applying to safe, short-term loans to the Fed, which had just hit an all-time high, more than halved over the subsequent month. But even though the banks continued to amass capital and credit volumes continued to shrink, the general public now began to feel more confident that the financial infrastructure would remain operational. The ship was not moving forward, but at least it was not sinking any more. In that sense, Paulson's extortionary tactics at the long mahogany table can be seen as the end of the most acute phase of the financial crisis.

But some people felt this had come at a very high price. According to the economist Anna Schwartz, quoted in the *Wall Street Journal*, "They should not be recapitalizing firms that should be shut down." There was good reason for taking seriously her warning that the rewarding of failure will lead to more failure, because Schwartz, now 93 years old, is the coauthor, with Milton Friedman, of the most widely accepted explanation of how the Fed created the Great Depression. At a conference in honor of Friedman's 90th birthday in 2002, Ben Bernanke, himself an expert on the Great Depression and then one of the seven Fed governors, made a much-acclaimed speech: "I would like to say to Milton and Anna: Regarding the Great Depression. You're right, we did it. We're very sorry. But thanks to you, we won't do it again."

That was a witty speech, but Anna Schwartz herself feels that Bernanke's fixation on the Great Depression is a problem because what we are experiencing now is not a repeat of the problems of the 1930s. Back then, banks went under because they were illiquid. They actually owned enough capital; they just did not have time to get it back quickly enough when worries led to sudden runs on them. Then, the Fed ought to have stepped in, giving banks an opportunity to survive until they would once again have enough capital at hand. According to Schwartz, the Fed and the Treasury were doing in 2008 what they should have done in 1930. They were fighting the last war, oblivious to the fact that the battlefield had changed. In 2008, the problem was not just a shortage of liquidity but a lack of solvency—several banks really were unable to pay their debts because they had made bad business decisions, and it was imperative that they be made to take the consequences of their actions, Schwartz concluded: "Once that's established as a principle, I think the market recognizes that it makes sense. Everything works much better when wrong decisions are punished and good decisions make you rich."[63]

Schwartz was one of those who preferred the first Paulson Plan since the only way to get banks to function was to rid them of the bad loans so that they could start operating normally. Even as Paulson began using TARP money for other things, he still insisted that he was also going to buy bad loans. Only a month later, on November 12, however, he went back on that when he transformed his package once more. The remainder of the half of the $700 billion that Congress had already approved was now going to be used for more recapitalization and for entirely new forms of support, such as the financing of mortgages and guarantees in the market for student and credit card loans.

Only one thing was certain: The old plan was dead in the water. Paulson's "Troubled Assets Relief Program"—which it is still called—would never buy any troubled assets. Those who had sat on their bonds because they had been promised an opportunity to sell them to the government had their plans destroyed at the same time as their assets lost even more value. This decision triggered credit turmoil in the market for commercial real estate, and the cost to banks of borrowing from one another went up for the first time in a month as a result of new confusion about how the bailout package was going to be used. The Dow Jones index fell below 8,000 on November 19, its lowest level in over five years, with bank stocks sinking deeper than any other.

In times of crisis, the old dream of the strong man who knows what needs to be done and will brook no dissent tends to make a comeback. Evan Newmark of the *Wall Street Journal* noted that Hank Paulson had deceived Congress and forced banks to accept a package they did not want. On that basis, he concluded that the Treasury secretary was a "national hero."[64] However, Paulson somehow managed to combine tremendous will power with uncertainty about what to use it for. Again and again, he changed strategies, modifying the reasons he gave for making or not making certain decisions. Even two months after the TARP decision, the chair of the Congressional Oversight Panel thought that the administration seemed to lack a coherent strategy—it just kept staggering from one crisis to the next.[65] The administration's crisis management was oddly reminiscent of Lord Ronald in Stephen Leacock's story "Gertrude the Governess," who "flung himself upon his horse and rode madly off in all directions."

Hank Paulson has won plaudits for his pragmatism and his ability to change opinion as he goes along, but if it is true that investors need some sort of stable ground rules and a measure of predictability to make plans, then his method of first intimidating and then confusing was devastating for their chances of beginning to deal with the changed circumstances. The prices of the mortgage-backed securities that he was first going to buy up, then buy less of, and then not buy at all—and that the Fed soon thereafter announced its intention to start buying—were on a roller-coaster ride. The SEC kept changing its rules for asset valuation, and it first banned shorting, then extended the ban, then added more companies to the list, then even more, and then did away with the ban completely. On October 24, 2008, Joe Nocera of the *New York Times* guessed that one reason why financial markets remained volatile was that "investors no longer trust Treasury."[66] This resembles the combination of alarmist rhetoric and regulatory experiments that made Keynes ask Roosevelt to be more cautious if he wanted to bring back investment to the economy.

In mid-December, the Paulson Plan underwent its third change. This bailout threw all the floodgates wide open. Until then, all the bailouts had been linked in one way or another to the financial sector. The reason politicians always prioritize rescuing banks is that doing so is a way to save the economy rather than individual institutions. If an automobile manufacturer collapses, we buy cars made by someone else and if an airline goes bankrupt, we fly with another. But if central parts of the financial system are knocked out, it becomes impossible for both automakers and airlines to operate. This, however, did not prevent the senior executives of the Detroit Big Three automakers from taking their corporate jets to Washington, D.C., to ask Congress for taxpayers' money as they found themselves in acute insolvency. Paulson was urged to use money from his package, but even though he had managed to obtain huge powers for himself, Congress had after all restricted the package to financial institutions, so he refused emphatically at first. But when Congress had failed to agree before its Christmas recess, President Bush took action regardless. On December 19, he promised General Motors and Chrysler loans of $17.4 billion to keep them afloat until Congress returned. The money was taken from the TARP, that is, money that Congress had given to the administration on one explicit condition: that only financial institutions could share in it.

Robert Reich, Bill Clinton's first labor secretary, was one of those who wanted to give the money to the car industry, but he found that the way in which it was done showed that the administration felt able to do whatever it wanted in times of crisis:

> If TARP is a slush fund, everything's arbitrary. We're no longer a nation of laws; we're a nation of Treasury and White

House officials with hundreds of billions of dollars of taxpayer money to dispense as they see fit. Why rescue autos
and not, say, the newspaper industry, which is heading
for oblivion?"[67]

Why not indeed? Now it is no longer about saving the financial
system. It is about a large sum of money and a political battle to
decide who will get to favor their preferred groups at the expense
of others.

The CEO of Hudson City Bancorp in New Jersey, Ron Hermance,
wondered what Hank Paulson was doing to the economy. During
the mortgage bubble, Hermance's savings bank had stayed away
from the subprime market, and he demanded that clients pay 20
percent themselves if they wanted to borrow for a home. To the
extent that the Wall Street titans across the Hudson River spoke to
him, they probably sneered at him for clinging to quaint beliefs in
screening potential borrowers and showing restraint. But Hermance
had learned early in life that society needs its individualists, people
who think differently: "It's like my grandfather used to say. If everybody thought the same way, they would have married your
grandmother."[68]

That smidgen of worldly wisdom had slowly but surely built
Hudson City Bancorp into a major bank enjoying good health. As
the stock market crashed, its stock actually continued to rise. Hermance by no means opposed the administration's intervening to
ensure that the financial markets could function. But now he saw it
pumping billions of dollars into other banks, many of which had
been the worst sinners. In his opinion, there was a risk that the U.S.
government was now supporting banks that should fail because of
their mistakes.[69] Those who had earlier been able to compete more
aggressively with him because they took wild chances could now
socialize their losses and go on as if nothing had happened. Hudson
City Bancorp was up against a tough new competitor: the U.S. federal budget.

As more and more industries have been given government support, other people have come over to Hermance's views. It is under-
standable that politicians want to save companies—and the associated jobs—if they have run into trouble only because of the bad
economic times. But to do that, politicians have to take the money
from somewhere, either directly from taxes or by printing money

or borrowing more, which will eventually drive up interest rates. This means that others will have to pay for the government support while also facing tougher competition from businesses that are backed up by the government. All that will have been achieved is a redistribution of burdens, from those who were less competitive to those who were more so, and this will preserve old solutions and structures while making it more difficult for new businesses to expand and hire more people. What's more, centralization is a frequent outcome when politicians save the big fish—those that are too big to fail—at the expense of the little fish.

The sum of inventiveness is constant, so clever executives now adjusted their operations to make efficient use of the new support systems. In July 2008, the housing industry received a bailout as the Federal Housing Administration was told to guarantee a further $300 billion of subprime mortgages. This would stabilize home prices while taking the heat off Fannie Mae and Freddie Mac, which sit on many of those mortgages. In 2008, mortgages guaranteed by the government in this way accounted for as much as 26 percent of new home loans, compared with 4 percent the year before. This scheme enables Hank Paulson's old employer Goldman Sachs to buy bad mortgages for 63 cents on the dollar, convert them into taxpayer-guaranteed mortgages, and sell them as safe mortgages to someone else for 90 cents on the dollar. That is not a bad return on good relationships with the federal government.

Or you can do like Hector Hernandez in south Florida, whose mortgage company grants people FHA-insured loans to buy apartments in his own developments. Half of the FHA loans he has made since November 2006 have defaulted. Almost half of those borrowers paid interest for only three months or even less. More than 1 in 10 did not make a single payment. One of the borrowers revealed the business concept to *Business Week*: Hernandez had paid her $19,500 under the table to buy the apartment—a "cash-back opportunity," as he called it. He simply pays people to move in, enough by a wide margin to cover the tiny down payment that the FHA requires. The borrower then takes the money and moves out, Hernandez tells the FHA that yet another household has unfortunately failed to repay its mortgage, and the taxpayers have to step in to pay what Hernandez considers the borrower owes him. One study estimates that defaults on new FHA mortgages are going to cost taxpayers $100 billion over the next five years. But who is even going to notice another $100 billion in this humongous bankruptcy, anyway?[70]

Toward the end of his time in office, President Bush had drastically increased federal spending, introduced new controls and regulations, nationalized large swaths of the financial industry, and committed around $8 trillion to various types of bailouts and guarantees.[71] Now that the financial crisis was turning into a more traditional recession, he had also started intervening with taxpayers' money to support individual manufacturing companies. He defended himself in an interview: "I've abandoned free market principles to save the free market system."[72]

The question, of course, is how many free-market principles you can liquidate before you start liquidating the free-market system. At a certain point, as Karl Marx noted, quantitative change becomes qualitative change.

6. Tomorrow Capitalism?

Indeed, the world is ruled by little else [than ideas]. Practical men, who believe themselves to be quite exempt from any intellectual influence, are usually the slaves of some defunct economist.

—John Maynard Keynes, *The General Theory of Employment, Interest, and Money*

The container ships laden with goods that cross our oceans at all times of the day and night make up a large part of the everyday infrastructure of globalization. Now they were suddenly lying empty in the big Asian and American ports, waiting for cargo as containers were piling up on the docks. "The problem is not demand, and it's not supply because we have plenty of supply. It's finding anyone who can come up with the credit to buy," an analyst concluded.[1]

The banks were unwilling to issue letters of credit, which are necessary to guarantee that exporters will be paid on delivery, and some sellers stopped trusting the financial institutions that had issued guarantees. How could you know that they would still be able to pay next week? The financial storm had beached more ships than any natural storm ever did.

For an economy dependent on an international division of labor— on the work, components, and raw materials of other continents— this meant that breakdown loomed. If I cannot pay you until my customers have paid me, who is going to bear the risk in the meantime? As *The Economist* put it, the global business community moved in a single week from the just-in-time principle to the just-in-case principle—you had better amass as much cash as possible and do business with as few unknown counterparties as possible.[2]

No textbook or econometric study will ever be able to show the value of financial markets as clearly as the global economy did in the weeks after the fall of Lehman Brothers. How does a supplier dare to send goods across the globe to a buyer he or she does not know, and how does the buyer dare to pay before he or she has received the goods? How can we ever finance risky commitments, such as buying an apartment, making a credit card payment, expanding a company, or making a payment in another currency in one month's time, if there is no way to share exposure with others in a market willing to accept risk?

The transactions, credit agreements, and derivatives that may come across as so abstract and even as parasitic or unnecessary suddenly showed what they were worth in September and October 2008 by briefly ceasing to function. Like oxygen, we did not notice them until they were gone. Those were the scariest weeks in the lives of many leading business executives and policymakers.

The word "credit" comes from the Latin *credo*, which means "I believe." Credit is based on our belief or trust in the person we lend money to, on faith in another person's potential and willingness to make good use of the resources so that he or she will pay us back. But it is also based on our belief in ourselves and in our future. This confidence enables us to even out our income across our lifetimes by borrowing when we are financially weak and lending when we are doing well. The financial markets allow us to maintain a large-scale economy based on cooperation among individuals who have never met. Millions of people can combine their savings to build big corporations that will enjoy economies of scale. This is humanity's way of moving capital from where it is to where it can be more useful.

More than anything else, the financial market is a giant democratizing machine. Since there are millions of people who make individual decisions about their savings and investments, there is a chance that some of them will want to bet on newcomers and outsiders— on people who lack capital and contacts but have ideas and visions. Because such people can find others who are willing to take a chance on them, countries with sophisticated financial markets enjoy a much steadier stream of new, innovative companies that topple old giants. Being able to turn to open capital markets is the only way for the poor people of the world to escape their dependence on local loan sharks. As historian Niall Ferguson shows in his book on the history of money, the countries that have developed strong financial markets are the ones that have flourished in other respects as well. The application of Arabic mathematics to banking is what produced the Italian Renaissance. The tiny Netherlands defeated the Hapsburg

Empire, England defeated Napoleon, and the United States became history's strongest superpower in part because they all built superior financial institutions capable of financing government and developing their national economies. The powers of the Entente were victorious in World War I because they could finance their war effort by selling bonds in their global financial centers, such as Paris, London, and New York, while the Germans had to rely on their own resources.[3]

The liberalization of financial markets, for example, through competition among private banks and through open stock markets, seems to increase investment and raise productivity in an economy. The largest effect is due not to increased saving but to the fact that more capital ends up where it has the most impact. American studies show that the U.S. states that implemented the most financial deregulation in the 1970s are those that have since enjoyed the fastest growth. Research shows that the level of development that a country's financial markets had attained in 1960 was very important to its subsequent growth. A developing country that doubles the amount of private capital available to business and industry will increase its GDP by almost 2 percent per year. This means that, in 35 years' time, a country that does what it takes to make markets that liquid may be twice as rich as a country that is equally poor today but that does not take the action required.[4]

Because we have developed our financial markets, 43 percent of all wealth attained by the average human has been created in the past 30 years. Even a truly deep international recession will do no more than bring our global level of wealth back to where it was a couple of years ago. Because financial markets have made large-scale production and trade possible, extreme poverty has fallen by 74,000 people each day since the early 1980s. And even though the current crisis began in the United States, it remains a fact that countries with sophisticated financial markets have fewer financial crises than others.[5] One reason the peaks and troughs of the business cycle are evened out in developed countries is that people there can take out loans when times are bad.

Before They Knew the Answers

We cannot do without the confidence and cooperation that financial markets embody. But we have also seen how easy it is to develop confidence in the wrong people or business concepts. Toward the end of 2008, the worst financial storms had abated, at least for now, but this is also when the long and deep trough of the business cycle begins to make itself felt in earnest. As banks reduce their indebtedness and leverage, and as institutions that previously threw capital in all directions are wound down, companies, households, and in some cases even entire nations will be unable to borrow enough to cover their running expenses. This will lead to severe corporate collapses, high unemployment, and enormous budget deficits. In a single January day, 65,000 Americans lost their jobs. The global economy survived cardiac arrest; now the question is whether we will escape death by starvation.

What exactly happened? How could overenthusiastic homebuyers in the United States sink the global economy? Many politicians across the world quickly declared that the crisis must have come from inside the financial system, that the reason must have been that market players had been given too free a rein and made too big mistakes.

"Laissez-faire is finished," exclaimed President Nicolas Sarkozy of France. "The idea of the all-powerful market which wasn't to be impeded by any rules or political intervention was a mad one." According to the German finance minister Peer Steinbrück, the crisis revealed that the argument put forth by advocates of laissez faire "was as simple as it was dangerous," and Chancellor Angela Merkel drew the conclusion that more financial-market regulation was necessary. The finance minister of Silvio Berlusconi's Italy, Giulio Tremonti, raged that globalization had been invented "by a group of madmen, of mad illuminati. . . . Now all this has failed. Globalization has failed."[6]

Politicians who had never hesitated to claim credit for each one-tenth of one percentage point of growth or for each new job created now immediately went to great pains to pin the blame for the downturn on their lack of influence. But did they lack influence?

Critics say that the financial market was completely unregulated. But 12,190 people work full time on regulating the financial market in Washington, D.C., alone—five times as many as in 1960. The big wave of deregulation is said to have begun in 1980. Since then, the cost of the federal agencies in charge of regulating financial operators has increased from $725 million to $2.3 billion, adjusted for inflation.[7]

A "Hoover myth" is now developing about President George W. Bush to the effect that he was some kind of a deregulator. However, during his eight years in the White House, new federal regulations were added to the tune of 78,000 pages a year. That is the highest pace in the history of the United States. Bill Clinton reduced the number of federal bureaucrats by 969; Bush increased their number by 91,196. Clinton reduced the cost of financial regulation slightly; Bush increased it by 29 percent.[8]

A commonly heard argument is that we find ourselves in economic chaos because there are no international institutions entrusted with the task of coordinating and regulating globalization. But that is exactly the task of, inter alia, the International Monetary Fund, the World Bank, the multilateral (regional) development banks, the International Labor Organization, the United Nations Development Program, the United Nations Conference on Trade and Development, the United Nations Department of Economic and Social Affairs, the United Nations Industrial Development Organization, the Organization for Economic Cooperation and Development, the Bank for International Settlements, the Basel Committee on Banking Supervision, the Financial Stability Forum, the International Organization of Security Commissions, the International Association of Insurance Supervisors, and the International Accounting Standards Board.

Some of those who claim that the financial markets have been unregulated actually refer to the fact that private operators have been given regulatory responsibilities, for example, the credit-rating agencies. But if the government introduces new regulations and actually cedes control of them to private players who have a financial interest in turning them in a certain direction, it just makes for an even more toxic blurring of the line between government and business. This is the opposite of laissez faire, which is all about separating government from business.

Others who complain about a lack of regulation are thinking about the absence of supervision of the shadow banking sector and the lack of capital requirements for it. But that is just half the story; the other half describes how that sector suddenly became interesting only because regulations made normal—transparent—financial operations more expensive. Capital will go where it is wanted, and if the government closes some entrances, it will sneak in by the back door.

A third group talking about inadequate regulation simply means that the authorities did not understand the risks in the markets, paid attention to the wrong things, and made reasonable behavior harder and unreasonable behavior easier. Indeed. But that the government often acts incompetently is not news. And that is precisely why it is pointless to compare the real-life market economy, in all its imperfection, with an ideal image of how hypothetical, perfect authorities would govern the economy. It goes without saying that we must compare it with the real, imperfect authorities that we actually have.

The problem was not that we had too few regulations; on the contrary, we had too many, and above all faulty ones. Some readers may object that by pointing this out, I am mainly quibbling about the meaning of words and fighting an ideological battle. I grant you that you may have a point there. Please feel free to call the problem whatever you like if you have political reasons for doing so, just as long as you are aware of what it consists of. Because what would be fatal would be for slogans about "insufficient regulation" to give rise to the idea that the crisis happened because the government was absent, and that the government must therefore intervene and regulate more to avoid a repeat.

Before we give politicians, central bankers, and bureaucrats more power over the economy, shouldn't we first examine what they did with all the power and resources they already had when the biggest financial bubble in history was being inflated?

Let's look again at the historical background of the crisis. The housing bubble was pumped up and the hunt for ever-greater risk started when the Fed, not wanting the market to set exchange rates, cut interest rates to record-low levels as the emerging economies of the world began to send capital to the U.S. economy. U.S. politicians pumped up risk taking and house prices further through deductions, tax benefits for home savings accounts, and restrictions on new construction. By means of legislation, subsidies, and government-sponsored enterprises, they managed to generate mortgages even for people that the market deemed uncreditworthy.

The quasi-governmental institutions Fannie Mae and Freddie Mac developed the securitization of mortgages, which Wall Street fell madly in love with once the credit-rating agencies—which had been given a legally protected oligopoly by the government—declared them to be safe investments. Government-owned banks and municipalities across the world bought mortgage-backed securities like never before. International banking regulations agreed to in Basel, Switzerland, entailed that banks running classic banking operations had to pay extra, whereas those that moved such securities to special companies operating in a shadow sector got away cheap. The central position of Fannie Mae and Freddie Mac reinforced confidence that the government would intervene if the housing market ran into trouble. The Fed's safety net and the federal government's deposit insurance made banks dare to take big risks because they could privatize any gains but socialize any losses.

When home prices then began to fall and the market no longer wanted mortgage-backed securities, the financial authorities stepped in and decreed that banks had to write down the value of such securities radically, giving rise to several waves of panic selling. And when nobody wanted to finance the special companies anymore, the banks had to take them over, which put such a burden on their balance sheets that regulations forced them to pile up capital rather than make loans. President Bush and other leading policymakers whipped up a panic to push through the laws they wanted. And just as the financial markets were more worried than ever because they did not know where the big risks were, the authorities banned shorting, thus depriving the markets of liquidity and information when they needed it the most.

If this is laissez faire, then I would like to know what government intervention looks like. If politicians, central bankers, and bureaucrats had intentionally tried to create a crisis, they would have been hard put to find more effective actions. But I suppose they just got carried away, like the investment banks. At each stage, the government inflated the bubble at least as eagerly as the most enthusiastic of Wall Street traders. The only difference was that the government's pump was so much bigger.

The fundamental errors made by politicians and authorities do not mean that this crisis is entirely the fault of the government. Ordinary people, investors, and banks have made huge mistakes. Just because the central bank lowers interest rates drastically, households cannot make long-term home purchases on the assumption that the rates will remain at their new level forever. The government may wring out mortgages for households that cannot afford them, but nobody is forcing anyone to buy up those mortgages. If the credit-rating agencies exploit their statutory position to make systematic overvaluations, it does not relieve people of the responsibility to do some thinking for themselves about what various products may be worth and what risks they may be associated with.

Anyone who is not furious about the behavior of many senior executives and traders simply cannot be aware of what they have done.

Wall Street titans who had previously justified their stratospheric pay packages by referencing the huge responsibilities they had to shoulder have provided explanations after the fact along the lines that they were unlucky, that they did not understand, that it was not their fault. They fought until the bitter end to take their bonuses and dividends with them when they left. Many credit institutions engaged in completely irresponsible lending, and banks had remuneration systems that made their employees focus exclusively on maximizing sales and short-term profits without giving a thought to long-term risks. Investors failed to consider the absence of liquid exchanges capable of providing reasonable valuations of new types of securities and financial instruments, and they did not do enough to develop such exchanges. The insurer AIG relied completely on its imperfect computer models that did not take the unexpected into account, and its bosses allowed huge deals that they could probably not make heads or tails of.

They handled other people's money and they were given a free rein because the ownership structure of their institutions was weak: spread across a large number of funds that did not exercise adequate supervision over all the companies they had stakes in. As Adam Smith concluded long ago, this gives executives an opportunity to hijack companies and favor themselves rather than the owners: "The directors of such companies, however, being the managers rather of other people's money than of their own, it cannot well be expected, that they should watch over it with the same anxious vigilance with which the partners in a private copartnery frequently watch over their own."[9]

There are companies with strong owners and there are companies without them that have still succeeded in developing internal controls and systems of remuneration to ensure that the owners' long-term profit is what governs behavior. But when that is not the case, the problems will permeate the entire organization: from the CEO down to the lowliest employee, everybody will ignore the best interests of the company. Jérôme Kerviel, the young French trader at Société Générale who set his employer back almost 5 billion euros ($7.1 billion) (and thus undeniably has an axe to grind), has explained how things could go so far:

> The problem is that the bank never says, 'Attention guys! The money you're playing with is not virtual. At the other end of your computer, there are real people, with real lives, pay attention [to] what you do, you could do something very bad to them." Everything you do as a trader remains in the virtual world. It's a little like playing a computer game. Lose or win a few million: It only takes a few seconds.[10]

And almost without exception, senior executives and owners counted on the government and taxpayers to come to their rescue if something were to go wrong. Big corporations were the first to call for strong men who would put the free market and the rule of law to one side to save their operations. The head of the Securities and Exchange Commission has recounted how the CEO of one investment bank requested a freeze on normal trade in the entire U.S. market, comparing it to how Lincoln detained people without trial during the Civil War and how Roosevelt sent Japanese to internment camps during World War II: "That is how America made it through such crises, and we couldn't be too focused on maintaining the rule of law."[11]

This makes you want to exclaim in the words of one of Sweden's greatest 20th-century economists, the economic historian Eli Heckscher:

> There are few things more repugnant than the combination, in a large number of businessmen and corporations, of proud calls for freedom and independence in good times, and pathetic whimpers for assistance in the form of customs tariffs and government orders as soon as difficulty strikes and their ability to help themselves is truly put to the test.[12]

The principle ought to be straightforward, as Heckscher concluded: Either a company is viable, and then it needs no government support, or it is not viable, and then it deserves no government support. Those businesspeople and capitalists who choose to sign a pact with the devil anyway will soon realize who is the stronger party and who will constantly interpret the terms to his or her advantage. The government will support these businesspeople under their arms, but the price they will pay is having their hands and feet tied up. Abandon all hope indeed, ye who enter here.

The False Sense of Security

It is a fundamental misunderstanding that the market is rational and at some sort of equilibrium where all information and wisdom are incorporated in decisions. Neoclassical economic models filled with unrealistic assumptions about humans and the economy should always have warning stickers attached to them.

The market is nothing other than all the millions of decisions that we all take as we produce, act, and invest—and the tiniest bit of introspection is enough to realize that we do not behave like the textbook models. Since finding lots of information before acting takes time and costs money, we often go with our gut, following rules of thumb and copying what others have already done. That is why the market has a herd instinct. When others seem to be successful at something and get rich on it, you follow suit. After a while, the hollowness of the enthusiasm becomes apparent, and then it often changes into overblown fear that soon ushers in a recession.

A key lesson to be drawn from these events, however, is that borrowers, lenders, bankers, and brokers are not the only ones to be affected. Politicians, bureaucrats, and central bankers are at least as likely to succumb to the herd instinct—and they do not just have some sort of general power of influence; they have legal coercive powers. If you act in a different way from what they have approved, they may take your money or even send you off to jail. This gives them the ability to head up the march of the lemmings and force its pace.

Now the herd is saying that we need strict regulation to ensure that this will not happen again. Words are cheap. But if it is so easy to avoid crises, why did not the thousands of new pages of regulations written after the earlier crises steer us clear of this one? In fact, the story of this storm in the global markets is the story of how government intervention to solve previous crises laid the foundation for a new one. The Fed started making money cheap in 2001 to avoid deflation and a depression, and emerging economies exported capital because their fingers had gotten burned on capital imports during previous crises. Credit ratings became so exaggerated because financial authorities believed that government-sanctioned ratings would lead to more stable levels of risk. The capital requirements agreed to in Basel gave rise to increasingly exotic financial instruments and pushed assets off banks' balance sheets because those who had gone off to Switzerland had wanted to make banks safer—since previous government guarantees had made them less safe. The new requirements to mark assets to market were intended to prevent cheating, but in reality they served to amplify the downturn and knock out the investment banks. And so forth.

Nothing looks easier than retrospective regulation to ensure that we do not repeat the particular mistakes that messed things up so badly. But like generals, bureaucrats always fight the last war. The best outcome to be hoped for is that they will prevent market players from making exactly the same mistake they made last time—that is, the mistake everybody is focusing on avoiding anyway. And on top of that, you also get a whole new battery of regulations that may well make the next crisis considerably worse. We do not know where the next crisis will come from. From history we learn that we do not learn from history. Even Isaac Newton, one of the greatest geniuses of all time, lost a fortune in the South Sea Bubble. Not even those whose job it is to make forecasts know what will happen next. One of those who did that best, Economic Cycle Research Institute founder Geoffrey Moore, told his students that someone who can predict a recession at the exact time when it starts is a very successful forecaster.

Companies and investors hardly need more bureaucrats looking over their shoulders trying to guess what they are doing right or wrong. They need room to maneuver so that they can adjust or change their strategies as quickly as possible whenever there is new information about what is happening to demand, competition, and credit. Nothing is more dangerous than going too far in the search for safety, because that may lead to regulations that block the best paths of action in a crisis.

There is already a dangerous homogeneity in the market in that many rely on the same types of clever computer models that make them buy the same types of securities at the same time as everybody else. Piles of historical data are analyzed to identify a position in the market where the risk of losing money is less than 1 percent. However, even a 1 percent or 0.5 percent risk of being run over by a steamroller may be enough to make you abstain from jumping out before it to pick up small change. The writer Nassim Nicholas Taleb points out that it does not matter how sophisticated the models become, since the problem resides not in mathematics but in history, which does not always tell us what will happen next. Once in a while, we do get the 0.5 or 1 percent case, a Black Monday, a war, a Russian collapse, or a package that turns out to contain things that are not really AAA, and then there is a crash. We may increase the precision of our models, but the risk is that this will only cause us to rely ever more blindly on them. Spreading risk does not help all that much if, say, expansive monetary policy makes stocks, bonds, and real estate all move in the same direction. That is why nobody should be allowed to study these mathematical models without a pinch of salt close at hand. As Warren Buffett urges us all, we should "beware of geeks bearing formulas."[13]

For the exact same reasons, though, we should also beware of bureaucrats bearing plans. Strict regulations laying down what you may and may not do will add to this homogeneity. If the government prevents market players from holding securities below a certain credit rating, it means they will all sell at the same time when a security is downgraded past the limit. If the government's capital requirements favor certain ways of holding assets, all banks will hold their assets in those ways, and they will all be struck by the same type of problems at the same time.

After each crisis, the authorities investigate what worked better and then force market players to conform to this "best practice." All these attempts to make the system as safe as possible really make it extremely sensitive to small blows and changes. As Professor Lawrence Lessig of Stanford University concludes, a single virus gaining a foothold in the banking monoculture may knock out the market completely. All deviations, diversity, and mutations have been eradicated by precautionary principles and regulations, meaning that there is no resistance left anywhere.[14] At a conference in 2007, the risk-management officer of one company said that they were fortunate not to have much historical data on business risk, because if they did, the authorities would immediately force them to use those data to build risk models and act according to those models, rather than use common sense and develop various scenarios for future risks, as the company preferred to do.[15]

As business was becoming increasingly global, energetic work was undertaken to develop international rules on capital adequacy, accounting principles, and credit ratings. Politics had to catch up in order to increase stability and safety in the new Wild West. But the result was the same as that of national policies: a homogenization of the way banks and companies viewed risk, regardless of where they came from and where they operated. As long as things are going smoothly, this creates predictability and peace and quiet, making things very easy for us as customers. But it also gives everybody the same Achilles' heel. The likelihood of that particular part of the body being hit is small, but when it does happen, everybody will tumble to the ground in the same way in all countries.

All the salvage operations and bailouts that have been implemented this time will make the problem seven times worse next time, completely regardless of the effect that they may have had in the short term to prevent free fall. Banks and companies have learned that the more they do things just like everybody else—like the rest of the herd—the more likely they are to be saved by the government if things go wrong. Because then their operations or their market will be too big to be allowed to fail. Those who think differently and do things their own way pose no threat of a systemic crisis and cannot hope for any help. A prudent banker is one who is exactly as imprudent as the other bankers so that he goes bankrupt when the others do, as Keynes is claimed to have said. The European Commission is developing stricter supervision of the credit-rating agencies that made such complete fools of themselves during the present crisis. There will be more stringent regulations and national authorities will be able to review ratings that they dislike. Giving national governments power over the credit ratings awarded to companies in their countries is obviously the wrong way to tame grade inflation, but what is most dangerous is the aim as such, the belief that it is possible to obtain a correct grade for each institution and each security that everybody will then abide by. All this will do is accelerate the follow-the-leader culture, as *The Economist* predicts:

> Tying them even more tightly into the regulatory system is likely only to exacerbate these contradictions by raising barriers to new entrants and making the rating agencies

> appear even less fallible. Much better would have been less regulation, more competition and a requirement that bond issuers release any information they provide to the rating agencies to the public. Then everyone would have had a chance to get what they all say they want: investors who think for themselves.[16]

If we really want to make future financial storms less severe, we should be doing the opposite of what is happening now. We should remove the safeguards and untie the safety nets. We should abolish bailout plans and deposit insurance, so that banks would be forced to think about what risks they can really bear and how much capital they need to cover those risks. We should deprive the credit-rating agencies of their official role, so that investors would have to think for themselves about where they put their money. We should systematically put an end to the protections and guarantees that government authorities give to investors and savers, to leave room for their own common sense and their own responsibility. Those who do not trust themselves should not go anywhere near the riskiest markets.

No regulation has had greater effect on the risk taking of the banking sector than the lifeguard role of central banks (and now finance ministries as well). This has taught the major financial players to take hair-raising risks in the knowledge that they can privatize any gains and socialize any losses because they are far too big to fail. The dilemma, however, is that they would never have grown that big if they had not had that safety net. Present-day capitalism is sometimes attacked for being nothing but a "casino economy." But I know of no casino where the head of the central bank and the finance minister accompany customers to the roulette table, kindly offering to cover any losses. If there were such casinos, I am convinced that we would all be gambling much more, and much more wildly, than we do today. But that is how things are in our financial markets, especially now that government support and deposit insurance have become more extensive than ever before.

The problem is that we do *not* have a casino economy. To borrow a metaphor from child rearing, we have a *helicopter economy*. Helicopter parents constantly hover over their kids, preventing them from falling and hurting themselves. This means that their children never grow up and learn to see dangers for themselves. And for this very reason, such children will eventually fall in more serious and dangerous contexts instead, because risk is part of the human condition. The helicopter economy works in a similar way. The government hovers over banks and investors, making sure they do not get hurt too badly (and cleaning up any messes they leave behind). Whenever there is an accident, the benchmark rate is lowered, the central bank extends credit, and taxpayers' money is pumped in. The players never learn to look out for risks; they just continue their reckless behavior, and sooner or later they will fall off a ledge that they were not watching out for and pull us all down with them.

Capitalism without bankruptcy is like Christianity without hell—it loses its ability to motivate humans through their prudence and fears. If completely removing the safety net from under the financial market is not politically feasible, then it is necessary to make a division so that it protects only pared-down banks engaging in simple operations while all other financial institutions are told in no uncertain terms that the government's only responsibility if they fail is to wish them luck.

No matter how monetary policy is managed, there will always be a suspicion and a hope that it will be used to mitigate unpopular downturns irrespective of the long-term costs. Ever since President Richard Nixon abolished the remnants of the international gold standard in 1971, the door has been open for political manipulation of our money. I believe that it is crucial to rediscover the discussion about alternatives to a politicized monetary system. Perhaps we should reintroduce the gold standard or replace central banks with a computer that automatically adjusts the money supply upward in line with economic growth? Or perhaps we should even privatize currencies and ensure that competition keeps issuers in line, as Hayek proposed?[17] Such a discussion comes across as slightly bizarre to most people, but that is just because it has been absent while paper currencies controlled by independent central banks seemed to be a fairly good solution. Now we know better. It may be worth recollecting in this context that during the free-market period in the 19th century, Swedish banks were entitled to issue their own paper money. In his description of that "free-bank system," Per Hortlund points out that during the 70 years of its existence, not a single bill-issuing bank failed, no bill owner lost a krona, and no bank had to shut its windows even for a single day—a "world record for bank stability."[18] The Swiss economist Peter Bernholz tells us that "a study of about 30 currencies shows that there has not been a single case of a currency freely manipulated by its government or central bank since 1700 that enjoyed price stability for at least 30 years running."[19]

If we chop down the jungle of government support, protection, and requirements, investors and savers will be left to their own devices. That is tough. But thinking for yourself should be tough, because the intellectual exercise it provides will train skills that have lain dormant. And they are necessary. Just think about the hedge-fund fraudster Bernard Madoff, who may have cheated his established and well-heeled clients out of an unbelievable $50 billion. Despite the phenomenal returns reported by his fund, the big institutional investors stayed away. One of them explained that the fund made a nonserious impression "because when you get to page two of your 30-page due diligence questionnaire, you've already tripped eight alarms and said 'I'm out of here.'"[20] Madoff's fraud was hardly rocket science. It was a chain letter, the oldest con in the world: His returns were not spectacular at all; he just kept paying earlier investors with new investors' money until it ran out. But how come so many others entrusted Madoff with their fortunes? Like many other victims, the former textile businessman Allan Goldstein says that he trusted Madoff because he trusted the government: "Government has failed us. . . . We conducted our affairs in good faith in the belief that the SEC would never allow this sort of scheme to be conducted."[21]

Preventing fraud is one of the most fundamental duties of the government, and the law of the land very explicitly prohibits what Madoff did. The SEC did not manage to expose him despite a series of warnings and investigations, and even despite a 19-page report submitted in 2005 by an investor arguing that Madoff's hedge fund was a chain letter. Many people now call for even more rules, but the SEC apparently cannot even enforce the existing ones—and that is not because it has been lazy. In 2008, the SEC almost beat its record for the number of enforcement cases, and its budget has increased 110 percent in real terms between 2000 and 2009.[22]

As an investor, you may draw two opposite conclusions from this. Either you continue to give your life's savings to that nice man at the country club, hoping that the authorities will suddenly become competent, prioritize correctly, and see through any attempt on his part to do something fishy. Or you realize that bureaucracies will always have shortcomings, stop relying on them to solve all your problems, and acquire enough patience to get at least as far as page 2 of the due-diligence questionnaire before making your decision.[23]

Stockholm Syndrome

Some people believe that politicians and bureaucrats are somehow wiser and more enlightened, take a more long-term view, and are guided by more honorable motives than the millions of people who make decisions and set prices every day in the market economy. The Swedish left-wing oracle Göran Greider used the financial crisis as a pretext for claiming that the government must play a stronger part in the economy; this would lead to "long-termism" and "power to democracy."[24] He and others who think like him always compare the worst and most short-termist players in the market with their own ideals of how enlightened behavior the government could be capable of in the best of worlds. But as the Swedish writer and historian Vilhelm Moberg expressed it, "Their faith in the government as savior must have a purely metaphysical basis; it has no ground in reality as we have experienced it so far."[25]

Those who idealize government have failed to understand that politicians and bureaucrats have no fewer axes to grind than market players do. The former SEC commissioner Paul Atkins believes that the SEC failed to develop open marketplaces for mortgage-backed securities and credit-default swaps because it was "distracted"— devoting its time and resources instead to grabbing power from other government agencies by starting to regulate hedge funds and introducing new types of supervision of mutual funds.[26] One reason the regulation and supervision of the U.S. financial market are oddly divided among the Federal Reserve, the Securities and Exchange Commission, the Commodity Futures Trading Commission, the Treasury, and various government agencies is that these entities report to different congressional committees, and the politicians on those committees refuse to let go of areas of responsibility that guarantee them generous campaign contributions from financial companies and banks.

The countries negotiating in Basel, Switzerland, did not try to work out rational capital requirements; rather, they fought for rules that would favor their own banks at the expense of others. On first seeing the outcome of the many years of negotiations, an anonymous—but senior—person within one of the international regulatory agencies said, "It does read a bit as if it has been written without adult supervision." And considering all that this financial crisis has taught us about the shortcomings of risk models and credit-rating agencies, what else is there to say about the fact that the brightest international bureaucratic brains have arrived at a Basel II, which increases the regulatory importance of mathematical models and credit ratings?[27]

Those who believe in the government as savior should study not only how it laid the foundation for this crisis but also how it dealt with the subsequent financial tumult: how the U.S. administration tried to scare the nation out of its wits and constantly changed strategies, and how lobbyists and corporations control politics. They should have been there when the Treasury secretary tried to escape democratic scrutiny and tricked $700 billion out of Congress or when carmakers and pharmacy chains were redefined as financial companies so that they would enjoy a protection from investors that Treasury knew would be meaningless.

They could talk to Yves Leterme, who had to resign as prime minister of Belgium after the country's supreme court found that his government had tried to influence a judicial process concerning the nationalization of the Fortis bank group. They should ask a delighted President Bush how it feels not to end up in the history books on the same page as the closure of General Motors simply by dint of passing the problems and debts on to his successor. But the best would perhaps be for them to have a chat with those who have to deal with the inner contradictions of politics. The former European commissioner Mario Monti has described how finance ministers from European Union member states would often come to see him in Brussels. They would explain that they had made promises to their voters at home about giving subsidies to local companies, but as they were aware that doing so would be economically destructive, they now asked Monti to say that those subsidies were illegal under European antitrust law. This enabled the ministers to return home and blame the big bad European Union for not letting them keep their promises. "I am sure they do the same today," Monti says.[28]

Banks removed assets from their balance sheets and were forced to make huge financial commitments when they had to put them back. This strongly resembles what Congress did with Fannie Mae and Freddie Mac: The government-sponsored enterprises were put outside the federal budget to improve figures, but now they are back, costing the federal government hundreds of millions of dollars. Both politicians and market players have a tendency toward short-termism. The difference is that the latter can get out of it because decisionmakers in markets usually number in the millions and compete with one another, rather than being a small group as in politics. In the market, those who do something that will be profitable in the longer term are the ones who attract investment. If a company shows that its profits will be higher in 10 years, people already want to bet their money on it today, it will find it easier to raise capital, and its stock price will rise. A whole arsenal of market mechanisms is available for use if others are too short-termist in their thinking: if the stock market overvalues a stock, you can short that stock; if the market has become too fixated on quarterly reports to appreciate the business model of a company, that company can delist and focus on long-term growth.

Politics finds it harder to extract itself from short-termism because if an administration makes an investment today to obtain a result in 10 years, it has to explain the cost burden that is placed on people today while another administration in 10 years' time will be able to boast about the result. And conversely, if you shower voters with cheap money and build up a deficit today, you will win their love, while the next administration will have to explain why there has been a financial crisis and pay for the cleanup. As Austrian economist Ludwig von Mises concluded about the administrations of the world:

> They have all sold their souls to the devil of easy money. It's a great comfort to every administration to be able to make its citizens happy by spending. For public opinion will then attribute the resulting boom to its current rulers. The inevitable slump will occur later and burden their successors.[29]

This has nothing to do with what politicians are in power at the moment or in what country they are to be found. This book has dealt mainly with the United States because its economy is so big that mistakes made there were capable of tipping over the entire global economy. But similar stories could be written about many, many other countries.

For example, U.S. politicians are not alone in having created mortgage institutions to "push down mortgage rates so ordinary people can realize their housing dreams." In fact, that phrase is taken from a bill submitted to the Swedish parliament by the Social Democratic Party, which speaks proudly of SBAB, the Swedish government-owned mortgage corporation. With backing from the national government, SBAB has progressively loosened the requirements imposed on borrowers in the Swedish market. It was the first to offer a mortgage of up to 95 percent of the value of a home, and to lend money for the entire down payment. In all, SBAB has reduced mortgage rates by around 0.4 percentage points. It has attracted new borrowers to the market, which has reinforced the rising trend for prices. SBAB has made many households borrow 100 percent of home prices that they will be unable to recover for many, many years.[30]

As the crisis approached, the Swedish government *stepped up* its interventions. The right-wing government chose in March 2008 to set aside 5 billion kronor ($840 million) for government mortgage guarantees intended for those "who had been close to qualifying for a loan." That was more than six months after Jim Cramer of CNBC had professed that Armageddon had come to the markets and the CEO of Countrywide had talked about a housing collapse reminiscent of the Great Depression. For a fee, the Swedish government guaranteed that annual interest payments of up to 100,000 kronor ($16,900) would be made. The various agencies and organizations asked to comment on the government's proposal had warned that financially weak groups could be lured into taking out mortgages that they might be unable to afford in the longer term, but the minister for financial markets, Mats Odell, had brushed that criticism aside: "I'm responsible for the supply of homes in the Kingdom of Sweden, and that means my job is to make sure more people get a home."[31]

At the end of May 2008, when the U.S. mortgage market was in free fall and Bear Stearns had thrown in the towel, the opposition Social Democrats criticized the government's credit guarantee—*for not being extensive enough.* The Social Democrats' housing-policy group disliked that borrowers had to pay for their government insurance.[32]

Let there be absolutely no mistake: There are also cases of companies sacrificing long-term viability for short-term gain—but those companies have felt the need to cover that up and pretend to be long-term sustainable and productive, because that is what those who are going to entrust them with their capital are demanding. And there are also plenty of politicians who have sacrificed the short term to do what will make society better in the longer term—but then they have had to give the impression that people are in for immediate gain, because that is what those who are expected to entrust them with their votes are demanding.

One important difference, however, can be observed in how others react. When businesspeople and senior executives do a bad job, they are—eventually, at any rate—thrown out on their ear. When politicians and financial authorities do a bad job, however, they get *more* power. As chancellor of the exchequer (finance minister), Gordon Brown gave the United Kingdom a poorly functioning set of financial regulations; as Fed governor, Ben Bernanke convinced his colleagues to pump up an inflationary bubble to avoid a crisis; as U.S. housing secretary, Andrew Cuomo did all he could to foist mortgages on people who could not afford them. When the bubble burst, Brown, Bernanke, and Cuomo had all moved on to other positions and were given even more power so that they could save us from the chaos they themselves had helped bring about. After government authorities had helped create the worst financial crisis in generations, the climate of ideas has now shifted dramatically in the direction of *bigger* and *more active* government.

This situation is disturbingly reminiscent of Ludwig von Mises's 1949 conclusion that many will blame the recession on free markets and will respond by closing them down:

> Public opinion has become convinced that such happenings are inevitable in the unhampered market economy. People did not conceive that what they lamented was the necessary outcome of policies directed toward a lowering of the rate of interest by means of credit expansion. They stubbornly kept to these policies and tried in vain to fight their undesired consequences by more and more government interference.[33]

Create a crisis, and people will give you more power to fight it. This could be called the "Stockholm syndrome" of politics—our utter dependence on our hostage taker makes us develop a relationship with him and start taking his side against the rest of the world. That which does not work in the world of business loses out in competition and is closed down. It does not matter that an operation is very popular, that management believes it is going well, or that customers love it. It will still not survive unless it creates something that is valued more highly than the raw materials, components, ideas, capital, and labor from which it is made. And it will die even if nobody understands what happened. Politicians who distribute pork they cannot afford are reelected; butcher shops that sell pork they cannot afford go bankrupt.

That is why the Austrian economist Joseph Schumpeter identified *creative destruction* as the core of capitalism. Competition from other companies and free choice for customers entail that less good operations are constantly being eliminated so that resources go instead to more promising business concepts and operations. Many people today see the recession as a crisis for capitalism. It is not. It is just a crisis for certain capitalists—we have discovered that a number of business models do not work. That is an important insight. The market economy is sometimes described as a system to maximize profits, but profits are not all that matters. Losses are at least as important. We need to know what works and what does not. Any system is capable of launching projects and spending enormous resources on implementing them. The government sector is good at that, and so were centrally planned economies. One key to success, however, is to stop in time.

Strictly speaking, the problem is not the bust that we are now experiencing. The problem was the boom, because that was when bad investments were made based on hidden inflation and overly optimistic forecasts. The bust is the cure: It is when we wind up operations that do not work and let capital and labor move to the areas that work better, so that they can start lifting the economy. When the entire world is hit by a crisis at the same time and we cannot rely on the markets of other continents to pull us out of it, having that kind of flexibility in our domestic economies is more important than ever. Anything that prevents the prices of overvalued assets from falling will delay the recovery process. Bankruptcies of course entail problems for those involved, but for society they are the only way to separate the wheat from the chaff and ensure that the overall cake grows larger. This may sound unfeeling, but in fact moving on is the only way to minimize the human and financial cost of business models that have stopped working. A crisis is an opportunity to get rid of the junk that is standing in the way of new experiments and projects, not to pile up even more junk. It would of course have been better if many of the corporate closures and reorganizations could have been carried out earlier, during the boom, to avoid our societies' being hit by all restructuring problems at the same time. But then again, try saying that to all those who protested that it was unreasonable and unfair for companies to lay off staff and make their operations more efficient when times were good and corporate profits were high.

The problem with the present form of crisis management is that politicians, who have a short-term interest in maximizing votes, strive to make business as short-termist as they are. Country after country now chooses to cling to old solutions and to pump capital into companies that have their future behind them, such as certain carmakers. These companies are not to blame for all their problems. In a credit crunch, everybody finds it hard to borrow money and consumers stay home. But those problems affect everybody, and when the government singles out a few companies or industries for support, that is not free. The subsidies must be paid for by other companies through higher taxes or through government borrowing, which will lead to higher interest rates for everybody. These other companies are also suffering from problems that they cannot be blamed for. The only difference is that they are now also forced to take the hit for the problems of others.

Government support for companies is thus not a way to save jobs, as politicians try to make us believe. It is a way to move jobs from good companies to bad companies. It entails that the more competitive companies get access to less capital, that fewer can afford to buy from them, and that they have to pay higher taxes. It undermines the companies that could have started earlier to expand and recruit, and it reduces incentives for the credit stricken to deal with their problems themselves. This is just the way to prolong a recession and to be in a more fragile condition when finally coming out of it than you would otherwise have been.

As Treasury secretary, Hank Paulson was under the spell of short-termist political logic and threw taxpayers' money at anything that moved (or had stopped moving). But in the 1990s, he was in business and not restricted by political feasibility. Then he warned the Japanese that their policy of shelling out taxpayers' money and bailing

151

out a steady stream of companies risked causing a long recession with zombie corporations unable to get the credit market started, to expand their operations, or to recruit new employees. In the words he used back then, "It's a heavy tax on your markets and your society if you don't let institutions fail."[34]

The Second Time as Farce

There is a broad consensus that the way was paved for this financial crisis by record-low interest rates, huge deficits, and large-scale, credit-financed consumption. Today, governments across the world are trying to solve the crisis—by means of record-low interest rates, huge deficits, and large-scale, credit-financed consumption. Many people now agree that the Fed's record-low rates in 2001–2005 contributed to the crisis. Many observers now think it was utterly senseless of Alan Greenspan to cut rates drastically without worrying about the credit boom that might ensue. I would be more understanding of their moralizing if those same observers were not also demanding that central banks do exactly the same today. Greenspan simply wanted to avoid a depression and deflation in the only way he could. For the same purpose—avoiding depression and deflation—the central banks of the world are now cutting rates significantly faster and further than he did, without worrying about the inflationary boom that may ensue. The feeling, the intentions, and the arguments are the same: *Now* we have a crisis, tomorrow we will worry about when it comes, in the long run we will all be dead.

It was Karl Marx who said that history repeats itself, the first time as tragedy and the second time as farce. But he probably could not have guessed that the interval can be as short as eight years.

There is no saying where all this will end, but dark clouds are looming. Banks and financial institutions have been wholly or partially nationalized: Governments have intervened to save the financial systems and aim to wind down their commitments soon. But how do you do that when many governments wish to sell at the same time? We are going to see long-term government participation in the financial sector, and that risks leading to calls for loans to political favorites, local businesses, and national champions, which not only would distort competition but would also lead to further losses. History shows with disturbing clarity that the only thing worse than private ownership is public ownership. Politicians in many European countries have already started making more or less subtle demands that banks lend mainly to domestic businesses. Growing financial protectionism is throwing more and more sand into the gears of finance. There is a risk that capital will be locked in behind national borders so that it will be less able to come to the rescue when it is needed elsewhere.

As Western countries build ever-larger deficits, they scour markets for capital, meaning that businesses and developing countries will not be able to find any. The gigantic public works programs are being justified by reference to Keynes's teachings that the government can stimulate demand. In the absence of private demand, public spending is to fill the void and get the business cycle moving upward. But Keynes developed his ideas during the Great Depression and saw them as a way to get a completely stationary economy moving again. He was much more skeptical about whether public works could be used to control the business cycle. In 1942, he warned, "They are not capable of sufficiently rapid organisation (and above all cannot be reversed or undone at a later date)."[35] In fact, the delayed impact may reinforce the subsequent upturn, leading to overheating and a new crisis. Moreover, people may become worried if the government is overreacting, seeing it as a signal to stop consuming because they will have to pay for it in the future. Earlier action to stimulate demand seems to have had a limited effect. The Berkeley economist Alan Auerbach writes in a summary analysis that there is "little evidence that these effects have provided a significant contribution to economic stabilization, if in fact they have worked in the right direction at all."[36]

The U.S. Congressional Budget Office estimates that only 7 percent of the infrastructure spending in Barack Obama's stimulus package will benefit the economy during the current budget year. More than half of the road-building expenditures will materialize only after four years. Commentators believe that the economy will begin to change for the better at the end of 2009 or in 2010. The large government stimulus actions will have an impact only after that.[37] And then the projects will actually have been implemented unusually fast, because we are dealing with old plans that are to be reused. As one critical economist has noted, these projects have already been "drawn up, reviewed and rejected" by the authorities.[38] In other words, the coming boom will be reinforced by huge government borrowing to finance projects previously found unsuitable for funding—money that could instead have gone to competitive companies and enabled them to hire new workers.

The outcome is hardly going to be a quicker turnaround for the economy, only a new wave of misguided investment and deep indebtedness in many countries. And who is going to buy all the government bonds needed to finance debt as public finances come under increasing strain? There are already signs that investors are beginning to hesitate: Bond auctions have failed in several countries, and the yields demanded by buyers are rising fast in the United States. Big countries will face an overwhelming temptation to switch on their printing presses so that they can use inflation to pay back their debts. The last leading statesman who confessed to being a convert to Keynesianism was President Richard Nixon in 1971. The inflationary fire he lit caused a meltdown of the monetary system and the United States introduced price and wage freezes. The Western world's attempts to control the business cycle resulted in a witches' brew called stagflation—unemployment and inflation at the same time. A lost decade ensued.

There is also another risk, a smaller but more lethal one. The economists Fredrik Erixon and Razeen Sally at the free-trade institution ECIPE in Brussels warn that the extensive bailouts and government support actions now being carried out look like a repeat of the 1970s. When one country supports its steel industry or its carmakers, all others are worse off because of it and will want to stop imports from that country.[39] We have already seen the signs. The U.S. stimulus package contains a clause to the effect that key products used in the projects must be bought from U.S. manufacturers, and Prime Minister Gordon Brown talks about British jobs for British workers. President Nicolas Sarkozy has encouraged French carmakers to close down their plants in central and eastern Europe in exchange for government support, and the prime minister of Slovakia has responded by saying that the first thing his country will do if France starts acting in that way is to send the natural gas company Gaz de France home to Paris.[40]

The first shots have been fired in what could escalate into a full-scale trade war. And that would make the financial crisis we have experienced so far feel like a tea party. A global economy where the simplest of products may consist of components from 30-odd countries would collapse; hundreds of millions of people would be thrown into poverty. Then all the comparisons with the Great Depression would finally be relevant. The fact that all decisionmakers know this to be so means that we will probably not end up there, but even failures to undertake free-trade reforms and minor conflicts over tariffs may cause a great deal of suffering and delay the recovery.

The return of government, runaway public debt, support for old companies, and a risk of inflation and protectionism—there is a distinct whiff of the 1970s. But what if there is a possible happy ending after all? The 1970s did end with the 1980s. Governments had laid the foundation for an economic crisis with controls, public support, and taxes, and they were convinced that the only thing that could solve the crisis was even more controls, public support, and taxes. People may dream beautiful dreams about the enlightened and benevolent way in which the government could solve all our problems, so long as they have never seen it in full action. But as politicians accumulated power and began to act as owners, such dreams were no longer possible. Unemployment and inflation were pushed up to record highs as more and more resources were pumped into activities that had already failed. That was when alternatives became conceivable and when the insight that politics has its limitations returned. The outcome was liberalization and privatization. But as I have shown in this book, today's crisis is in many ways the result of our failure to break sufficiently free from the 1970s mentality and from the dream of the government as supervisor, monitor, helper, and supporter.

Each time people have seen the true consequences of large-scale government intervention, the spell has been broken. The longing for liberation has been reawakened. It remains to be seen how long it will take us this time to get back to the insight that the government has its limitations, and what torment our societies will have to endure in the meantime.

7. Oops, We Did It Again

"Insanity is repeating the same mistakes and expecting different results."

—*Narcotics Anonymous, 1981*[1]

Every politician, central bank, and regulator in the developed world spent 2008 and 2009 saying: "This must never happen again." *This* being the financial meltdown that almost took down the world economy. They differed in their proposed solutions but held one demand in common: Banks must never again take the kind of highly leveraged risks in exotic securities so widespread at the tail end of the housing bubble. Financial institutions should instead build a large buffer of risk-free investments that will always be liquid and never result in losses.

The crisis-resistant buffer to end all crisis-resistant buffers? Government bonds. The economic consensus after the financial collapse was that banks should lend more money to governments. Politicians and regulators demanded it, twisted arms, and wrote new rules to make that happen.

In the final chapter (chapter 6) of the first edition of this book, I wrote:

> If the government's capital requirements favor certain ways of holding assets, all banks will hold their assets in those ways, and they will all be struck by the same type of problems at the same time. . . . After each crisis, the authorities investigate what worked better and then force market players to conform to this "best practice." All these attempts to make the system as safe as possible really make it extremely sensitive to small blows and changes.

Since 2009, this warning has been tested on a continent-wide scale. European governments told banks that sovereign bonds were risk free, that they didn't need to be backed by additional capital, and that they were necessary. The new liquidity requirements in the

Basel III agreement on global regulatory standards, written as a response to the financial crisis, obligated banks to hold more government bonds on their balance sheets. The banks predictably loaded up. When the European Central Bank (ECB) lent financial institutions 442 billion euros in June 2009, they used half the amount to buy still more government bonds.

At the end of 2010, Europe's 90 biggest banks had lent more than 760 billion euros to the PIIGS countries–Portugal, Italy, Ireland, Greece, and Spain. As I write this, due to the losses from those bonds, the entire European banking system is on the verge of collapse.

The problem is not faulty valuations on particular securities; those have been wrong before, and they will be wrong again. The problem is the false conceit that regulators can protect financial markets from risk simply by deciding what is less risky, then getting everybody to march in that one direction. This just gives every bank the same weakness. If the defense is breached, everybody will tumble to the ground together.

A Greek tragedy

The euro crisis has followed the pattern of the 2007–08 financial crisis almost perfectly: Both were the result of cheap money, dangerous homogeneity, and the promise of bailouts. When problems appeared, the rule of law and bureaucratic predictability were replaced with erratic and contradictory behavior from policymakers, making it impossible for investors to plan long term.

European authorities did not begin regulating in favor of government bonds only in 2009. Their interpretation of previous Basel requirements assumed that a bank's exposure to risk through the holding of sovereign debt in its own currency was zero. Government bonds that were rated AAA- and AA- never required additional capital to cover them. American regulations were similar: Banks had to hold capital against all the other assets on their balance sheets, but not sovereign debt. Even low-rated foreign government bonds were subsidized in this way. Debt from, for instance, Brazil, Russia, and Turkey required no more than 2 to 4 percent of the bond's value in buffer capital, whereas a loan to a company holding the same investment rating required around 8 percent. "This is at the core of the crisis and it was I think the biggest accounting scam in history,"

Hans Hoogervorst, chairman of the International Accounting Standards Board, said at an industry conference in September 2011.

Markets also began to ignore important differences between euro governments when considering the risk of sovereign bonds. Why? Because there was the assumption that if weaker governments started wobbling on their bonds, the euro-zone's stronger governments would bail them out. So sovereign bonds were subsidized by regulation and capital requirements, then guaranteed as being essentially too big to fail.

There were no *formal* guarantees that a government in trouble would be bailed out. In fact, politicians insisted that no such thing would ever happen. But markets look at what you *do*, not what you say. The whole system was built on the promise of bailouts. European banks could buy the bonds of any euro-denominated country and hand them over to the central bank as collateral for new loans. The bank treated all these bonds the same. That sent a powerful message about what would happen when things went bad.

Before the euro system was created, investors usually kept one eye on the financial track record of European governments. If countries had a recent history of recklessness and default, markets demanded higher interest rates for lending to them. The euro system changed this. Now traditionally profligate countries like Greece and Spain were protected under tightwad Germany's credit umbrella, and all participating governments could borrow liberally at a low rate.

Interest rates started to converge in 1995, in anticipation of the new currency being formed four years later. At that time, the yield on a Greek 10-year bond was 18 percent. Italy's 10-year bonds were at 12 percent, and Spain and Portugal were at 11 percent, compared to just 7 percent for Germany. The interest-rate penalty for fiscally irresponsible borrowing was a powerful incentive to not borrow too much. But by 2005, the yields for all these countries were just below 4 percent. This was a triumph for the euro, boasted ECB president Jean Claude Trichet at the time. "Yields are driven by common news," he said at a conference in New York, "and only a very small fraction can still be explained by local risk factors."

But by trying to subsidize these local risk factors out of existence, European planners only encouraged deadbeats to be more reckless. Now governments could live with and even add to an already huge debt burden without swallowing the medicine of reform. Many of the countries in southern Europe lost ground on the exports market, especially to Asian countries, but they did not respond by liberalizing markets or increasing competition to stimulate productivity. Rather, they just imported more, increased the size of their governments, and increased wages.

From 1997 to 2007, government expenditure increased by around 6 percent annually in Spain, Portugal, and Greece (while population growth in each remained relatively stable). It increased by 4 percent a year in Italy, even while the economy shrank. Most importantly, Italy, Greece, Spain, and Portugal rapidly increased unit labor costs, an important measure of competitiveness. From 2000 to 2009, Greece's unit labor costs increased by 34 percent, adjusted for inflation, Italy's by 32 percent.

Such an economic approach hurts exports and growth, especially considering that the Eurozone's most important economy, Germany, was busy pushing ahead with labor market reforms while holding unit labor costs down. Portugal, Italy, and Greece bought more than they sold, and paid for it all with loans, private and public. Between 2000 and 2010, Portugal increased its public debt as a percentage of annual GDP from 49 to 93 percent, Italy from 109 to 118 percent, and Greece from 103 to 145 percent.

Some governments that are now experiencing crisis were not as reckless with public finances. Spain and Ireland actually reduced their public debt before 2008. But their private sectors made up for it by borrowing like mad. When the ECB created a single eurozone-wide short-term interest rate, the level was much too low for these two rapidly growing countries, thus inflating a large housing bubble. When that crashed, so did the countries' banks. Ireland then made the mistake of guaranteeing all its banks, which ruined public finances.

When financial markets ground to a halt in 2008, banks had to reduce their leverage. Debt was once again perceived as risky, causing a balance-of-payment crisis for several Eurozone nations. Greece, Portugal, and Ireland were bailed out by their European partners, but this only increased debt burdens and spread concerns about long-term unsustainability.

When fears about big economies like Italy and Spain began to surface, markets started worrying that even mighty Germany might not be able to bail everybody out. Germany's 10-year yield as of early 2012 was below 2 percent, but the convergence that Trichet once boasted of is history: Spain's 10-year yield was at 5.3 percent, Italy was at 5.6 percent, Ireland at 8 percent, Portugal at 12 percent, and Greece at a stunning 33 percent.

This balance-of-payments crisis could have been solved if prices and wages had been reduced to the levels of 10 years ago, before they were inflated. Such austerity would have increased exports, reduced imports, and attracted more capital from abroad. But regulated labor markets prevented costs from coming down rapidly in most crisis economies, except for Ireland and the Baltic countries. Meanwhile, bailouts and ECB purchases of Italian and Spanish government bonds reduced the pressure on those countries to reform. In Italy, unit labor costs actually increased during the first years of crisis.

Officially, Eurozone technocrats kept insisting they would never bail out a member nation in trouble. But as soon as Greece got into trouble, it got a bailout (on May 2, 2010). ECB president Trichet insisted at the time that fiscal discipline would be upheld because the central bank would never accept government bonds rated as "junk" as collateral for new loans. "Never" lasted until May 3, 2010.

Confidence was further undermined by the EU-wide "stress tests"—financial assessments conducted during the summers of 2010 and 2011 that were supposed to reveal the health of the continent's banks. Instead, however, they gave premature clean bills of health to at least two large banks that went on to fail: Allied Irish Banks (which went under in 2010) and Dexia (which folded the following year).

It wasn't that EU managers didn't move quickly enough in the crisis; it's that they seemed to move in all directions at once. The EU settled on a nominally voluntary write-down of Greek debt owed to private creditors, but this involved a lot of subsidies and arm-twisting. First the write-down amounted to a 21 percent haircut, then it became 50 percent, and now it looks like it might be even more, minus the "voluntary" aspect. When this spooked investors who feared that they would also have to accept losses on other countries' debt, the EU made another U-turn. At the end of 2011, leaders insisted that Greece was an exception, and that private bond-holders would not have to bear losses in future restructurings of sovereign debt.

Whatever the EU says today, we have no idea what kind of rules and interventions will be in place tomorrow. That is the worst climate for investment. "It's impossible to invest by looking at real data and the potential of different assets," one British banker tells me. "Instead we make money by trying to predict what politicians and central banks will be doing."

Future economic historians will puzzle over how European leaders turned a small liquidity problem in tiny Greece into a continent-wide risk of collapse in just two short years. The EU could have let Greece default. It would have been ugly for some banks, but such tough medicine would have created healthy incentives for the future, and predictability rather than uncertainty.

Instead, Greece was bailed out, and a climate of political uncertainty has prevailed ever since. Which banks are most exposed? Will there be another bailout for Greece, and then another, or will it finally default? Will there be a bailout for the next country in line, or not? Will private bondholders be forced to bear losses, or not? It's hardly surprising that in this atmosphere of utter uncertainty, the problems of Greece have began to be confused in investors' minds with countries that are not insolvent but merely illiquid, like Italy and Spain.

Instead of facing up to the problems and cutting its losses, Europe has continued to play a game of double or nothing. Just before Christmas 2011, the European Central Bank lent €489 billion for three years to European banks at a 1 percent interest rate, and the ECB handed over another €530 billion to them in February 2012. The ECB is now grossly leveraged. It wouldn't take big losses on loans to stressed banks and governments for the central bank's capital base to be wiped out, and in need of a bailout itself. That money might have saved Europe from a credit crunch in the short term, but it is also an attempt to get banks to start lending to governments again. As the optimistic French president Nicolas Sarkozy put it, "Italian banks will be able to borrow at 1 percent, while the Italian state is borrowing at 6–7 percent. It doesn't take a financial specialist to see that the Italian state will be able to ask Italian banks to finance part of the government debt at a much lower rate."

There you have the Eurozone solution to the problem of banks lending too much to governments: get the banks to lend even more. If the financial institutions prove too reluctant, the central bank will just lend them more money, guaranteed by taxpayers and printing presses, so that they loosen up the purse strings.

The only reasonable long-term solution to this mess is market discipline. If lenders know they have to bear their own losses should loans go bad, they will be more cautious with their money. The crisis economies of Southern Europe need to reduce expenses by increasing the retirement age, to liberalize product and labor markets to increase growth, and to reduce wages and prices to competitive levels. And they should change a worst-of-both-worlds system of very high taxes (Italy is the 170th worst out of 183 countries on total corporate tax rate, according to the World Bank) and lax collection.

But the EU is not ready to force governments to live within their means, and the guarantees are just getting larger. Since the Germans are no longer willing to fund reckless governments, they will have to impose discipline on Southern European spending policies from afar. The current idea seems to be getting unelected bureaucrats in Brussels to inspect the budget of democratic governments and levy economic punishments against the reckless.

What happens when leaders don't fall into line? Get rid of them, seems to be the drastic answer. The EU brain trust has already helped push out democratically elected leaders in Greece and Italy by delaying finance deals and temporarily suspending ECB purchases of sovereign bonds. Who has replaced them? Technocrats who promise to do what it takes. "What we need, in effect, is a suspension of democracy for 18 to 24 months so difficult decisions can be made," one Italian business leader told the *Financial Times*.

This whole process of handing weak economies money but taking control of their policies is the equivalent of giving your teenage son your credit card but then insisting on following him around everywhere to make sure that he doesn't use it in a reckless manner. He is almost guaranteed to wreak havoc and kick off a spiral of humiliation and recrimination.

Europe's dismantling of borders and trade barriers since the end of the Cold War has been an astounding success. After a 20th century of war and genocide, to come out on the other side in peace and unity was a cooperative triumph.

But not all forms of cooperation contribute to a spirit of community. If it entails a power struggle over who gets to take money out of the public coffers or who gets to decide things for others, then it can create tension and hostility. Right now, we are in a situation where Germany pays and decides, a set-up disliked by both contributor and receiver. Greeks and Italians now face harsh austerity measures, tax increases, and unemployment, and the decisions are being made in Brussels and Berlin. Protesters cry "EU out of Greece," the German embassy in Athens has been defaced with swastikas, and pictures of Angela Merkel often get touched up with a Hitler moustache. The Greek deputy prime minister pinned the crisis on Germany for stealing Greece's gold reserves during World War II.

On the other side of the conflict, it is now once again politically possible in Germany to talk about Southern Europeans as lazy, corrupt cheats. "Sell your islands, you bankrupt Greeks . . . and the Acropolis too," ran a headline in the popular German tabloid *Bild*, atop an article featuring interviews with MPs from Germany's governing coalition.

Some of the worst parts of modern European history are back again. Protesters, populists, and nationalists are gaining ground. And this is just at the beginning of the crisis. The years to come will bring more recession and austerity, if not an outright collapse. What happens if there are chaotic government bankruptcies, if banks fail, and people don't get their social security checks and salary payments? What happens in young democracies where there is no trust in the politicians?

The banking system in parts of Southern Europe survives only because of cheap loans from the European Central Bank. Insolvency, along with regulatory capital requirements, are forcing banks to shrink on a historic scale. Morgan Stanley is forecasting a €1.5–2.5 trillion near-term deleveraging for European banks as a whole. This would include a cut in lending of up to €1 trillion. Households will not be able to borrow, and small- and medium-sized enterprises will be denied the loans they need to stay in business.

European banks and governments are in a lethal embrace. Banks are in bad shape partly because they have lent so much money to desperate governments. Those governments become weaker every time they bail out the banks, making both parties look even riskier. "It seems we have created a machine from hell, that we cannot turn off," one senior official from Germany concluded at a dinner in Brussels in late 2011.

164

Enough problems with just one

In September 2011, at the annual International Monetary Fund (IMF)-World Bank meeting in Washington, D.C., French finance minister Francois Baroin had a hard time explaining the euro system. When talking to reporters, Baroin said that it was very difficult for Americans to understand how a currency could work with so many parliaments—but he added that the United States seemed to be having enough problems with just one.

The average eurozone country's public debt is around 85 percent of GDP, while America's public debt—federal, state, and local—has crossed the 100 percent threshold. The United States has a higher budget deficit than Spain, Portugal, Italy, and Greece, and the debt matures faster. If we look at both the deficit and the renewal of old loans, the U.S. government is borrowing 30 percent of its GDP in 2012. For comparative purposes, Italy needs to borrow 24 percent, Portugal 22, Spain 21, Greece 17, and Ireland 14 percent of its GDP.[2]

Baroin, it seems, had a point. Congress is too divided to agree on much, especially when it comes to reining in spending on pet programs. Democrats won't touch entitlement spending—Social Security in particular—which would save money without hurting growth. Republicans protect military spending and tax breaks, even though the latter are stealth subsidies that create an unpredictable tax system with countless loopholes. And President Barack Obama himself seems paralyzed when it comes to the long-term survival of the country.

Even under the best possible conditions, Republicans and Democrats seem incapable of agreeing, as demonstrated by the failure of the so-called supercommittee in November 2011. This bipartisan congressional group was supposed to agree on measures to reduce the deficit by no more than 0.6 percent of GDP over 10 years. That amounts to less than 3 percent of what the federal government would spend over the period. The committee members had exceptional powers: When Congress voted on their proposal it could not be burdened by amendments or blocked by filibusters. They also had ample incentives: If they failed, there would be painful cuts to defense and health care to compensate. Nevertheless, after three months, the supercommittee announced that it had fallen flat.

Yet, as I write this, markets are still quite sanguine about America's prospects—much more than I would have expected. The government can sell its bonds at close to record-low yields, and investors seem inclined to send even more money to the United States every time events make them fear for the world economy. After all, if America collapses, all other countries would have likely collapsed already. After all, in a situation where America's economy fails completely, most other economies would have likely failed already. The United States is still considered a safe haven, it remains the most liquid bond market in the world, and the dollar continues to be the world's reserve currency

But if this crisis has taught us anything, it is that perceptions can change rapidly. Since U.S. government loans must be renewed on average every five years, the United States is very exposed if markets begin to demand a higher interest rate. Even printing money would not help much: Creditors would immediately sense that the government was paying them back in dollars that weren't worth much anymore, and they would in turn demand a much higher yield on U.S. treasury bonds. Simply put, America is sitting on a fiscal time bomb.

Barry Eichengreen, one of the world's foremost experts on monetary systems and reserve currencies, warns that, in the absence of action, investors will one day start perceiving U.S. debt as a Ponzi scheme:

> If history is any guide, this scenario will develop not gradually but abruptly. Previously gullible investors will wake up one morning and conclude that the situation is beyond salvation. They will scramble to get out. Interest rates in the United States will shoot up. The dollar will fall.
>
> The United States will suffer the kind of crisis that Europe experienced in 2010, but magnified. These events will not happen tomorrow. But Europe's experience reminds us that we probably have less time than commonly supposed to take the steps needed to avert them.[3]

One traditional approach to reducing a mountain of debt is to grow your way out of it. But at today's levels, that would require much more growth than is conceivable. In order to merely maintain current ratios of debt to GDP a decade from now, for example, France would need a nominal growth rate (including inflation) of 4.6 percent a year, Italy 5.4 percent, the United States 5.9 percent, Britain 6.4 percent, and Portugal 13.2 percent. If we wanted debt levels to be reduced to a safer level of 60 percent of GDP, France would have to grow by 6.4 percent annually for a decade, Italy by 9.2 percent, the United States by 8.9 percent, Britain by 6.6 percent, and Portugal by 19.9 percent.[4]

Debt is a drag on growth, since the government's thirst for resources leaves less for households and private businesses. Higher taxes, inflation, and political uncertainty all follow logically in debt's wake. After having looked at 44 countries' experience over 200 years, economists Kenneth Rogoff of Harvard and Carmen Reinhart of the Peterson Institute for International Economics found in a February 2011 study for the National Bureau of Economic Research that when public debt is higher than 90 percent of GDP, median growth falls by 1 percent, and average growth falls even more. [5]

The timing couldn't be worse, given the even-bigger debts that changing demographics are inflicting on ill-prepared retirement and health care systems. In the United States, the number of workers per retiree is projected to decline from 4.5 workers today to 3 in 2035. In the EU, the number is slated to go from 3.5 today to 2 in 2035. We will have less work and less tax revenue to pay for more old-age pensions and health care.

As is now customary during a recession, the governments of the United States, Britain, Europe, and emerging markets flooded the system with cheap money, on a larger scale than ever, with record stimulus packages, zero interest rates, and massive quantitative easing. But the price of money has consequences. If it's too low, pension funds and insurance companies can't meet their return targets, and investors start hunting for yield in more exotic corners of the market. If there is a lot of liquidity but a lack of good business prospects, money moves to emerging markets and inflates bubbles there, and bubbles show up in assets and resources and increase the price of food and energy globally. This makes life even more difficult for populations who suffer from unemployment and wage restraint.

The International Monetary Fund thinks that easy money is necessary for recovery, but nonetheless acknowledges that it is leading to irresponsible credit decisions in the United States and other rich economies, which could "threaten financial stability." In a recent report, the IMF warns that "the sustained period of low yields has prompted some investors (especially those with return targets) to take on more credit, liquidity, structural, and duration risk or to increase leverage to enhance returns." If policymakers persist with this easy money policy, it could result in credit excesses while leaving balance sheets vulnerable to a new recession.[6]

Since banks are still mending and not eager to lend, low interest rates mean that more credit is being diverted to more opaque non-bank channels, that is, the shadow banking system, where big corporations can easily fund themselves. The *Financial Times* summed up the results this way in September 2011: "big companies get capital too easily, while bank-reliant smaller companies get none." [7]

Chinese bridges to nowhere

Between 2007 and 2012, the world's richest economies grew by 3 percent. Over the same five years, developing countries grew by 30 percent, India by 45 percent, and China by almost 60 percent. In other words, while Europe and America suffered, the emerging economies rebounded quickly, continued to grow strongly, and reduced poverty even further. It has been a very impressive feat, one that reinforces the conventional wisdom that a big economic shift from the West to the East is taking place.

Some of this strength is the result of how many low- and middle-income countries have liberalized their economies, which has allowed them to take advantage of international markets and new technologies. But some of it is also the short-term result of government stimulus programs and the subsequent asset bubbles. The last time around, easy money fuelled a gigantic housing bubble. It has happened this time as well—in emerging markets—but the housing bubble has not burst in that half of the world—at least, not yet.

Considered by many to be the current engine of the world economy, China is the most conspicuous example of this mounting fiscal catastrophe. Over the next six years, China will increase its number of skyscrapers by 87 percent. Since the crisis of 2008, property prices have increased by 60 percent. They have more than doubled in some of the wealthiest cities, and inflation is moving onto consumer goods, prompting the government to tighten its policies. "Money, money everywhere," Beijing economist Patrick Chovanec recently said of the situation. "Awash in luxury cars, condos and expensive jewelry, the Chinese are enjoying what looks to be an unstoppable boom."[8]

China, in other words, is drunk on easy money—a result of the country's aggressive response to the financial crisis. In addition to receiving inflows from the West, China has printed money and initiated its own stimulus package—one that was as aggressive as America's even though the economy is a third of the size. And yet the biggest stimulus has come from local governments. Estimates suggest that state-owned investment companies have run up $1.7 trillion in debt on assets and infrastructure, a sum that may double once future commitments are factored in.[9] This local spending binge is six times bigger than the stimulus package itself.

There are new bridges and roads to nowhere and empty housing complexes all over China. In August 2010, China's largest energy company reported that more than 65.4 million residences did not consume any electricity in the last six months. There are entire ghost towns, like the lavish new urban center of Ordos in northern China where thousands of new buildings stand empty. Real estate prices there doubled in three years before the bust. In cities like Shanghai and Beijing, apartments are sold for as much as 30 times the average annual income. Compare this to the United States, where before the crisis the worst subprime properties sold for six times the average annual income. Property prices have made it so expensive to bury corpses in Shanghai that the government is encouraging burials at sea.

Few Chinese borrow to buy a home, which makes many foreigners relaxed about the situation. Nevertheless, the developers borrow to build, and local governments and state-owned companies have gone deep into debt to support the stimulus. Since many of these projects lack long-term commercial prospects, this debt is unlikely to be repaid. And since local governments are now dependent on land sales for more than half of their finances, a slump would have political consequences as well.

China also has its own version of a shadow banking sector—made up of the opaque borrowing vehicles of these local governments—which have allowed them to borrow cheaply from banks in order to increase spending on everything. Estimates suggest that there are probably more than 10,000 of these shadowy government investment vehicles, but no one knows for certain. They rarely have any plans to repay their debts—only to borrow more—which is often needed to complete their many projects. "In the past, Chinese banks could carry borrowers like this indefinitely," Charlene Chu of Fitch Ratings in Beijing explains. "But today they don't have the large cash reserves they used to [in order] to do this. I don't see how all of this doesn't turn into a major problem at some point."[10]

One of the worst aspects of government-directed credit is that it bolsters the government and its favored companies at the expense of competitors. This super stimulus is also an important driver of what the Chinese call *guojin mintui*: "the state advances as the private sector retreats." The government has increased its tendency to twist rules and pick winners, while at the same time discriminating against both domestic and foreign businesses. This is particularly troubling in light of the fact that China's state-owned enterprises are in urgent need of reform. If you factor in their low cost of borrowing and access to cheap land, they are probably destroying capital when they produce.

Many are hoping that China will carry the world economy over the next several years. But when taken together, the construction boom, the lack of reform, and China's reliance on weak export markets in Europe and the United States are cause for serious concern. Economies that grow at rates of 10 percent a year can often afford to make a mess once in a while. But once that growth falters, the situation could soon become overwhelming. In 2011, the Chinese governments' attempts to dampen inflation and tighten credit began to slow down the economy. Property prices have begun to fall, and land sales in 2011 were sharply down. Fearing the consequences, the government is now trying to reinflate the bubble.

Yet China is not the only emerging economy that has relied on easy money in recent years. Many have experienced an inflow of short-term capital from abroad, as the West has reduced the price of money. Rapid growth in domestic credit—especially to the household sector—could threaten financial stability. A sudden disturbance or a political crisis, and that money could disappear overnight and trigger a currency crash and a balance of payment crisis in countries like India, Brazil, and Turkey.

The bottom line

This increasingly global debt crisis is not really a *new* crisis but a continuation, because we never solved our old financial problems. Debts that were unsustainable in 2008 did not become any less unsustainable just because they were loaded onto governments; the difference just meant that what was once a private-sector crisis has now become public. Instead of winding down failed banks and letting bankrupt companies go out of their misery, governments

170

propped them up and bailed them out. Instead of letting asset prices return to levels where markets were interested in buying, central banks inflated prices with zero interest rates and quantitative easing. The result is that markets can't function properly. Investors are terrified by every new development, especially the risk that governments themselves are running out of money.

The German economist Hans-Werner Sinn has compared this alarming state of affairs to past failures at managing politically popular exchange rates: "This aspect, too, calls to mind the times when governments tried to maintain inappropriate exchange rates, or used up their reserves to temporarily stabilize them, causing even larger disruptions when they had to give up," Sinn wrote in October 2011 in an article on the Centre for Economic Policy Research website *Vox*. "A frightening scenario is, therefore, that each new flaring of the crisis will drain more money from the creditors' purses, until they run empty."

Investors no longer make money by allocating money to the best ideas and businesses anymore; they make money by trying to predict what the Eurozone's leaders are going to do next, or what the Federal Reserve might do. In just a few years, "We have gone from economic policy to a political economy," says Kent Janér at the Swedish hedge fund Brummers. It's not a market in which supply and demand set the prices any more, it's a political process in which governments are calling the shots. Will they support this or that? For how long? For how much?

In a climate of uncertainty, often the best option is to observe from the sidelines before making a move. Banks have deposited more than $600 billion at the European Central Bank at awful interest rates, because they don't dare do anything else with the money. Another $1.6 trillion dollars is now sitting at the Federal Reserve.

I ended the first edition of this book hopeful that the consequences of large-scale government intervention would inspire a reassessment of our current path. In the United States, this happened much sooner than even I imagined. The bailouts provoked a groundswell of resentment. The debt explosion created a widespread awareness of the unsustainability of the present solutions. But so far, these important trends have not been translated into political action. Our governments continue to fight fire with fire, debt with debt, and the consequences of easy money and government guarantees with even easier money and bigger guarantees.

Banks and their creditors came away from the 2008 crisis with the impression that they will always be guaranteed by the government. If no serious changes are made, this understanding will stick. And since banks know that they will be saved if they do make mistakes, governments are attempting to regulate them in order to preclude those mistakes. Rather than giving banks the freedom to act and the responsibility to sink or swim on their own, governments are doing the opposite: giving banks a helping hand, while simultaneously tying their hands and feet.

The financial industry is drowning in regulation. In 2011, financial services companies worldwide were hit with an average of 60 regulatory charges every working day. That burden has increased by 16–20 percent annually since 2008—and it reflects the triumph of hope over experience.[11] As we have seen, new crises are often the result of attempts to regulate after previous crises—a cycle that only reinforces the herd behavior in financial markets. Because the financial stakes are so high, there is a high degree of regulatory capture, whereby the big banks lobby for rules that benefit them at the expense of their competitors. And when transparent risk is restricted, the risks taken will be more opaque.

This is no longer a financial crisis, or even a debt crisis. This is now a *political* crisis, a crisis of governments. This is not just because loose monetary policies, guarantees, and regulation contributed strongly to the current fiscal situation, or that runaway spending and lack of reform deepened it in Europe. It is a crisis of governments. Investors don't trust politicians to get their financial houses in order or to produce economic growth, and voters are growing ever more cynical as politicians who promised them everything are starting to admit that they just can't deliver.

At the same time, politicians and government authorities are in many ways assuming even more power to deal with the problems that they themselves created. It brings to mind Milton Friedman's natural history of government intervention:

> In the end the effects are precisely the opposite of the objectives of the reformers and generally do not even achieve the objectives of the special interests. Yet the activity is so firmly established and so many vested interests are connected with it that repeal of the initial legislation is nearly inconceivable. Instead, new government legislation is called for to cope with the problems produced by the earlier legislation and a new cycle begins.[12]

My Debts

The word *credit* has to do with believing in somebody, and first of all I owe a warm thank-you to Sven Hagströmer's and Mats Qviberg's foundation for believing in this book and for providing financial support that made writing it possible. While financial markets were frozen, moreover. That's what I call confidence.

I would also like to send big thank-yous to Mattias Bengtsson, Sofia Nerbrand, and Thomas Gür, who all in different ways gave me the idea of writing this book, even though only one of them knows that that is what happened as we were talking about it. And a small bonus thank-you to Nicolas Sarkozy, who made me realize it had to be written by making some unusually unexcogitated statements.

Anders Hjemdahl and Camilla Andersson helped me bring that idea down to the material world, and Eva Helmenius pointed me in the right direction at the exact time when my energy needed to find its outlet. My new friends at my Swedish publisher, Hydra—Björn Elzén and Barbra Bohannan—turned the entire project into what life on the trading floor is sometimes described as: an adventure at a fast pace, with great enthusiasm, and a happy ending.

Many people were kind enough to listen to my stories, read different parts of the manuscript, and to come back to me with wise comments, constructive criticism, and spontaneous ideas. Thank-you, Mattias Bengtsson, Håkan Borg, Mats Ekelund, Fredrik Erixon, Marius Gustavson, Teodor Koistinen, Peter Norberg, Cecilia Skingsley, and Mattias Svensson. Your kindness and helpfulness deserve an AAA.

All my blog readers and pen pals have contributed—as usual—ideas, tips, and criticism in a generous manner that I can only hope to be able to repay in some measure by my writings. Thanks are also due to a number of anonymous sources. I hope I have anonymized you enough to ensure that this book will not cost you your severance pay.

My greatest gratitude goes to my beloved Sofia, who is almost superhumanly patient about the espresso machine wheezing to life at odd hours of the night and about my devoting more time to global finance than to household finances—and to all four of Alexander's grandparents. Not least because their help when chickenpox raged meant that this book could be finished on time.

Notes

Preface

1. Ferguson, *Ascent of Money*, chap. 2.
2. Gainor, Seymour, and Ebel, "The Great Media Depression."
3. Santana, "Taiwanese Dogs Become the Latest Victims."
4. Jonung, "Ekonomer i krismöte."

Chapter 1

1. Doherty, "Can We Bank on the Federal Reserve?"
2. Nash, "A Laissez-Faire Pragmatist."
3. Lilleston and McCaleb, "Bush Endures Slaps from GOP Rivals."
4. Greenspan, *Age of Turbulence*, p. 228.
5. *Washington Post*, "The Chairman Speaks."
6. White, "How Did We Get into This Financial Mess?" p. 3.
7. Temkin, Johnson, and Levy, *Subprime Markets*.
8. Gross, "Location, Location—Deduction."
9. Bajaj and Leonhardt, "Tax Break May Have Helped Cause Housing Bubble."
10. Grant, *Mr. Market Miscalculates*, p. 129.
11. Samuelson, "The Boom in My Backyard."
12. Greenspan, "Understanding Household Debt Obligations."
13. Grant, *Mr. Market Miscalculates*, pp. 137–38.
14. Greenspan, *Age of Turbulence*, p. 231.
15. Grant, *Mr. Market Miscalculates*, p. 135.
16. Krugman, "That Hissing Sound."
17. O'Toole, "The Planning Tax."
18. Flandez, "With Market Hot, More People Now Have Third Homes."
19. Grant, *Mr. Market Miscalculates*, pp. 140–43.
20. *The Economist*, "Monetary Myopia."
21. Grant, *Mr. Market Miscalculates*, p. 122ff; O'Driscoll, "Asset Bubbles and Their Consequences."
22. Foust, "Alan Greenspan's Brave New World."
23. Doherty, "Can We Bank on the Federal Reserve."
24. Greenspan, remarks at the Economic Club of New York.
25. Bernanke, "Asset 'Bubbles' and Monetary Policy."
26. Despeignes, "'Greenspan Put' May Be Encouraging Complacency."
27. Grant, *Mr. Market Miscalculates*, pp. 110–11.
28. Cooper, *The Origin of Financial Crises.*
29. *The Economist*, "Paint It Black."
30. Wolf, *Fixing Global Finance*, p. 95.

31. A summary of the literature can be found in Berument and Froyen, "Monetary Policy and U.S. Long-Term Interest Rates."

32. U.S. Department of the Treasury, "Approaches to Improve the Competitiveness," p. 81.

33. Morgenson, "How the Thundering Herd Faltered and Fell."

34. Stelzer, "Do Deficits Matter?"

35. U.S. House of Representatives, Office of the Clerk.

36. Bartlett, *Impostor*, p. 18.

37. Mihm, "Dr. Doom."

38. Mises, *Omnipotent Government*, p. 262.

Chapter 2

1. U.S. Census Bureau, "Housing Vacancies and Homeownership."

2. Galbraith, *The Predator State*, p. 110.

3. Greenspan, *Age of Turbulence*, p. 233.

4. RealtyTrac, "Foreclosure Activity Increases 5 Percent."

5. Streitfeld and Morgenson, "Building Flawed American Dreams."

6. Gustavson, *Sosialisme på sparebluss*.

7. Stevenson, "The Velvet Fist of Fannie Mae."

8. White, "How Did We Get into This Financial Mess?"

9. First Union, press release.

10. Muolo and Padilla, *Chain of Blame*, p. 116.

11. Kurtz, "O's Dangerous Pals."

12. Minton, "The Community Reinvestment Act's Harmful Legacy."

13. Kurtz, "O's Dangerous Pals."

14. Liebowitz, "The Real Scandal."

15. Ibid.

16. Muolo and Padilla, *Chain of Blame*, p. 112ff.

17. Fannie Mae Foundation, *Case Study*, p. 121.

18. Simpson and Hagerty, "Countrywide Friends Got Good Loans"; Golden, "Countrywide's Many 'Friends'"; Mayer, "Fannie Mae and Freddie Mac Invest in Democrats."

19. Federal Reserve Bank of Boston, "Closing the Gap."

20. Ibid.

21. Day and Liebowitz, "Mortgage Lending to Minorities."

22. Day, "HUD Says Mortgage Policies Hurt Blacks."

23. *National Mortgage News*, "Fannie to Boost Subprime Activities."

24. Holmes, "Fannie Mae Eases Credit."

25. Barrett, "Andrew Cuomo and Fannie and Freddie."

26. Stiglitz, Orszag, and Orszag, "Implications of Risk-Based Capital Standard."

27. Duhigg, "Pressured to Take More Risk."

28. Barrett, "Andrew Cuomo and Fannie and Freddie."

29. Leonnig, "How HUD Mortgage Policy Fed the Crisis."

30. Becker, Stolberg, and Labaton, "White House Philosophy Stoked Mortgage Bonfire."

31. Bush, "President Calls for Expanding Opportunities to Home Ownership."

32. Becker, Stolberg, and Labaton, "White House Philosophy Stoked Mortgage Bonfire."

33. Office of Federal Housing Enterprise Oversight, "Report to Congress," p. 38. The OFHEO used similar language about Fannie Mae on p. 36.

34. Appelbaum, Leonnig, and Hilzenrath, "How Washington Failed to Rein in Fannie, Freddie."

35. Wallison and Calomiris, "The Last Trillion-Dollar Commitment."

36. Lerer, "Fannie, Freddie Spent $200M to Buy Influence."

37. Duhigg, "Pressured to Take More Risk."

38. Appelbaum, Leonnig, and Hilzenrath, "How Washington Failed to Rein in Fannie, Freddie."

39. Ibid.

40. Duhigg, "Pressured to Take More Risk."

41. Duhigg, "At Freddie Mac."

42. Appelbaum, Leonnig, and Hilzenrath, "How Washington Failed to Rein in Fannie, Freddie."

43. Krugman, "Fannie, Freddie and You."

44. Seeking Alpha, "Countrywide Financial Q2 2007."

45. Leonnig, "How HUD Mortgage Policy Fed the Crisis."

46. Wallison and Calomiris, "The Last Trillion-Dollar Commitment."

47. Shenn, "Fannie, Freddie Subprime Spree."

48. Lockhart, "Reforming the Regulation of the Government Sponsored Enterprises."

49. Wallison and Calomiris, "The Last Trillion-Dollar Commitment."

50. Taleb, *The Black Swan*, pp. 225–26.

51. Duhigg, "Pressured to Take More Risk."

Chapter 3

1. Dougherty, "German Bank Becomes First EU Victim"; *The Economist*, "Sold Down the River Rhine."

2. Muolo and Padilla, *Chain of Blame*, pp. 209–10.

3. Grant, *Mr. Market Miscalculates*, pp. 181–82.

4. Pollock, "The Human Foundations of Financial Risk."

5. Kindleberger and Aliber, *Manias, Panics and Crashes*, p. 13.

6. Greenspan, "Banks Need More Capital."

7. Nocera and Andrews, "Struggling to Keep Up."

8. Wolf, *Fixing Global Finance*, pp. 19–22.

9. *The Economist*, "Capital Ideas."

10. Rausa, "Basel I and the Law of Unintended Consequences."

11. *The Economist*, "On Credit Watch."

12. *The Economist*, "Spanish Steps."

13. Calomiris, "The Subprime Turmoil," p. 33.

14. Satow, "Ex-SEC Official Blames Agency for Blow-Up."

15. Labaton, "Agency's '04 Rule Let Banks Pile Up New Debt."

16. Satow, "Ex-SEC Official Blames Agency for Blow-Up." See also Calomiris, "Another 'Deregulation' Myth."

17. Muolo and Padilla give the background to this in *Chain of Blame*.

18. Morgenson, "How the Thundering Herd Faltered and Fell."

19. Henry and Goldstein, "The Bear Flu."

20. Dash, "Citigroup Saw No Red Flags."

21. Nakamoto and Wighton, "Citigroup Chief Stays Bullish on Buy-Outs."

22. *Charlie Rose Show*, WNET, October 1, 2008.

23. Jones, Tett, and Davies, "CPDOs Expose Ratings Flaw at Moody's"; Jones, "When Junk Was Gold."

24. Eisinger, "Overrated."

25. Morgenson, "Debt Watchdogs."

26. Committee on Oversight and Government Reform, *Credit Rating Agencies and the Financial Crisis*, p. 6.

27. Ibid., p. 5.

28. Morgenson, "Debt Watchdogs."

29. Lowenstein, "Triple-A Failure."

30. Morgenson, "Debt Watchdogs."

31. Committee on Oversight and Government Reform, *Credit Rating Agencies and the Financial Crisis*, p. 33.

32. Calomiris, "The Subprime Turmoil," pp. 32–33.

33. Lowenstein, "Triple-A Failure."

34. Keys, and others, "Did Securitization Lead to Lax Screening?"

35. Grant, *Mr. Market Miscalculates*, pp. 180–81.

36. Gorton, "The Panic of 2007," p. 57.

Chapter 4

1. *The Economist*, "Homing in on the Risks."

2. Reserve Primary Fund, press release.

3. Lowenstein, "Triple-A Failure."

4. Muolo and Padilla, *Chain of Blame*, pp. 9–10.

5. Ibid.

6. Ibid., p. 254.

7. Kelly, "Bear CEO's Handling of Crisis Raises Issues."

8. Search online for "we have Armageddon" and "Jim Cramer." The clip is a must-see.

9. Barr, "Moody's Downgrades 691 Mortgage-Backed Securities."

10. Birger, "The Woman Who Called Wall Street's Meltdown."

11. Morgenson, "Debt Watchdogs."

12. Tett and Davies, "Out of the Shadows."

13. Berkshire Hathaway Inc., *2002 Annual Report*, p. 13ff.

14. Krugman, "After the Money's Gone."

15. *Fortune*, "101 Dumbest Moments in Business."

16. *The Economist*, "On Credit Watch."

17. Stafford, "Traders Blind to Mounting Worries."

18. Dowd, "Moral Hazard and the Financial Crisis."

19. Reuters, "'US Homes Market Will Shed Investor Glut.'"

20. Hilzenrath, "Fannie's Perilous Pursuit of Subprime Loans."

21. *The Economist*, "Fannie and Freddie Ride Again"; Duhigg, "Doubts Raised on Big Backers of Mortgages."

22. Duhigg, "At Freddie Mac, Chief Discarded Warning Signs."

23. Paulson, oral statement on regulatory reform; Kopecki, "Fannie, Freddie 'Insolvent' after Losses"; CNBC, "Fannie & Freddie Takeover."

24. Duhigg, "At Freddie Mac, Chief Discarded Warning Signs."

25. Stiglitz, "Fannie's and Freddie's Free Lunch."

26. Bartiromo, "Bill Clinton on the Banking Crisis."
27. Gillespie and Welch, "'I Think the SEC Was Distracted.'"
28. Kelly, "Where in the World Is Bear's Jimmy Cayne?"
29. CNBC's Jim Cramer, who had warned of "Armageddon" as far back as August 2007, gave less impressive advice this time. On the March 11, 2008, edition of *Mad Money* he shouted, "No! No! No! Bear Stearns is fine! . . . Don't move your money from Bear! That's just being silly! Don't be silly!"
30. Davis, "Lehman Sought Millions for Execs."
31. Onaran and Helyar, "Fuld Sought Buffett Offer."
32. Dan Duyn, Brewster, and Tett, "The Lehman Legacy"; Onaran Helyar; Ohlsson, "Bushs nej blev starten på den globala finanskrisen."
33. Poor, "Knock Out."
34. Gullapalli and Anand, "Bailout of Money Funds."
35. Bartiromo, "Bill Clinton on the Banking Crisis."
36. Tett, "The Dream Machine."
37. Morgenson, "Behind Insurer's Crisis."
38. *The Economist*, "The Great Untangling."
39. Morgenson, "Behind Insurer's Crisis."
40. Mollenkamp and others, "Behind AIG's Fall."
41. Gerth, "Was AIG Watchdog Not Up to the Job?"
42. Taub, "FAS 157 Could Cause Huge Write-Offs."
43. Pollock, "Conceptual Problems."
44. Isaac, "How to Save the Financial System."
45. Katz, "Behind Schwarzman Spat."
46. BBC News Online, "Icesave Savers Warned on Accounts."
47. Lucas, "Konkurshotade Island kämpar för överlevnad."
48. Forelle, "The Isle That Rattled the World."
49. HM Treasury, "Financial Sanctions."
50. Someone I know remarks bitingly that Russia, by contrast, began to take an interest in Iceland only when it had just been branded terrorist (even though the Russian loan never actually came to anything).
51. Lyall, "Iceland, Mired in Debt."

Chapter 5

1. Becker, Stolberg, and Labaton, "White House Philosophy Stoked Mortgage Bonfire"; ABC News, "Charlie Gibson Interviews President Bush."
2. Poor, "Inhofe: 'Paulson Used Scare Tactics.'"
3. Gainor, Seymour, and Ebel, "The Great Media Depression."
4. Powell, "Not-So-Great Depression." GDP figures are from Maddison, *World Economy: Historical Statistics.*
5. Carlson, *Den sociala ingenjörskonstens rörelser.*
6. Johnson, *History of the American People*, p. 734.
7. Wanniski, "The Crash of '29."
8. Rothbard, *America's Great Depression*, p. 178.
9. Carlson, *Den sociala ingenjörskonstens rörelser*, pp. 73, 80–81 (quotation translated).
10. Friedman and Schwartz, *Monetary History of the United States*, chap. 10.
11. Hortlund, *Fribankskolan*, chap. 3.
12. Rothbard, *America's Great Depression*, pp. 283, 291.

13. Ibid., p. 186; Kennedy, *Freedom from Fear*, p. 52.

14. Johnson, *History of the American People*, p. 756ff.

15. Friedrich, "F.D.R.'s Disputed Legacy."

16. Ekirch, *Decline of American Liberalism*, p. 283.

17. Johnson, *History of the American People*, p. 757.

18. Roosevelt, address accepting the presidential nomination in 1932.

19. As the New Deal grew more radical, ex-president Hoover began to criticize it using traditional free-market arguments. This has contributed to the myth that Hoover was an advocate of laissez faire.

20. Cole and Ohanian, "New Deal Policies and the Persistence of the Great Depression."

21. Higgs, "Regime Uncertainty."

22. Ibid., pp. 566–67.

23. Kennedy, *Freedom from Fear*, pp. 351–52. Roosevelt characteristically chose to interpret this criticism to mean that business had gone on a "capital strike" to depose him; he even ordered the Federal Bureau of Investigation to find a conspiracy. See also Shlaes, *The Forgotten Man*.

24. Keynes, "The Maintenance of Prosperity Is Extremely Difficult."

25. Higgs, "Regime Uncertainty," p. 576ff.

26. Blum, *From the Morgenthau Diaries*, pp. 24–25.

27. Whaples, "Where Is There Consensus?"

28. Rothbard, *America's Great Depression*, pp. 219, 241.

29. Staley, *Art of Short Selling*, p. 247.

30. *New York Times*, "Shortselling."

31. Tsang, "Short Sellers under Fire."

32. Sorkin, "As No-Short-Selling List Grows." JMP Securities also asked to be struck from the list.

33. *The Economist*, "Shifting the Balance."

34. Lejland, "Finansrävarna" (quotation translated).

35. Chanos, "Short Sellers Keep the Markets Honest"; Tsang, "Short Sellers under Fire."

36. Donovan, "Investment Bankers of the World, Unite!"

37. Oakley, "Short-Selling Ban Has Minimal Effect."

38. Younglai, "SEC's Cox Regrets Short-Selling Ban."

39. Nocera, "Alarm Led to Action."

40. For critical scrutiny of her book, see Norberg, "The Klein Doctrine" (and for more exhaustive treatment of the issue in Swedish, Benulic and Norberg, *Allt om Naomi Kleins nakenchock*).

41. The next administration thinks along similar lines. On November 19, 2008, Barack Obama's chief of staff, Rahm Emanuel, treated the *Wall Street Journal* CEO Council to a description of the opportunity to create new political projects and regulate financial markets: "You never want a serious crisis to go to waste. . . . This crisis provides the opportunity for us to do things that you could not do before." Comically enough, Klein saw the bailout as confirmation of her thesis. Apparently, even the opposite of free-market economic liberalism can be characterized as free-market economic liberalism provided that the objective is to help banks. A *New Yorker* interview with her puts it this way: "Another difference, of course, was that the government wanted to enact not Friedman-style reforms but the opposite: enormous interference in the market. Still, since the point of this interference was to bail out

banks, this difference did not strike Klein as of much importance" (MacFarquhar, "Outside Agitator").

42. It is available online at http://www.nytimes.com/2008/09/21/business/21draftcnd.html?_r = 1&ref = business. Congress balked at that provision.

43. *The Economist*, "Riddle Solved."

44. CNNMoney.com, "Bush: US Economy Is Thriving"; Poor, "Inhofe: 'Paulson Used Scare Tactics.'"

45. Landler and Myers, "Buyout Plan for Wall Street."

46. Rasmussen Reports, "Just 7% Favor Fed Bailout"; Fox News Poll/Opinion Dynamics.

47. Roubini, "Not So Much Bail-Out as Rip-Off."

48. Acemoglu and others, letter to Congress; Wolfers, "Economists on the Bailout."

49. Bush, "President's Address to the Nation."

50. Cavanaugh, "Houses of Pain."

51. *The Economist*, "Weaken the Sinews."

52. Breitbart.com, "Bernanke Says Crisis 'No Comparison.'"

53. ABC News, "Charlie Gibson Interviews President Bush."

54. Cavanaugh, "Houses of Pain."

55. Sherman, press release.

56. Wingfield and Zumbrun, "Bad News for the Bailout."

57. Nocera and Andrews, "Struggling to Keep Up."

58. Schwartz, "European Banks Share Blame."

59. *Wall Street Journal*, "At Moment of Truth"; Landler and Dash, "Drama Behind a $250 Billion Banking Deal."

60. *Time*, "Sock on the Nose."

61. Nocera, "So When Will Banks Give Loans?"

62. Apuzzo, "Where'd the Bailout Money Go?"

63. Carney, "Bernanke Is Fighting the Last War."

64. Newmark, "Hank Paulson, National Hero."

65. Henriques, "Bailout Monitor Sees Lack of a Coherent Plan."

66. Nocera, "So When Will Banks Give Loans?"

67. Reich, "The Big Three and TARP."

68. Gross, "America's Smartest Banker."

69. Solomon and Enrich, "Devil Is in Bailout's Details."

70. Terhune and Berner, "FHA-Backed Loans."

71. Pender, "Government Bailout Hits $8.5 Trillion"; Goldman, "The $8 Trillion Bailout." The website of the *New York Times* includes a running update of the uses to which the Paulson Plan is put: http://projects.nytimes.com/creditcrisis/recipients/table.

72. CNN, *Lou Dobbs Tonight*, transcript.

Chapter 6

1. Greenwood, "Grain Piles Up in Ports."

2. *The Economist*, "All You Need Is Cash."

3. Ferguson, *Ascent of Money.*

4. Caprio, Honohan, and Feige, *Finance for Growth.*

5. Norberg, "Världens välfärd," p. 12; Chen and Ravallion, "Developing World Is Poorer than We Thought." This is based on the World Bank's old poverty measure

of $1 a day (adjusted for purchasing power and inflation), which it used from 1981 to 2005; according to the new measure of $1.25 a day, "only" 57,600 people per day have been lifted out of poverty (Calvo, Izquierdo, and Mejía, "Systemic Sudden Stops").

6. Sarkozy, "International Financial Crisis"; *International Herald Tribune*, "Germany: US Slipping as Financial Superpower"; Prashad, "Wealth's Apostles."

7. de Rugy and Warren, "Regulatory Agency Spending Reaches New Height," pp. 5–6.

8. de Rugy, "Bush's Regulatory Kiss-Off."

9. Smith, *Wealth of Nations*, V.i.e.18.

10. Jolly, "Ex-Trader Tells How He Lost So Much for One Bank."

11. Younglai, "SEC's Cox Regrets Short-Selling Ban."

12. Heckscher, *Gammal och ny ekonomisk liberalism*, pp. 96–97 (quotation translated).

13. Taleb, *The Black Swan*; Buffett on the *Charlie Rose Show*, WNET, October 1, 2008.

14. Lessig, "Why the Banks All Fell Down."

15. Dowd, "Moral Hazard and the Financial Crisis."

16. *The Economist*, "Negative Outlook."

17. Hayek, *Denationalisation of Money*. See also Rothbard, *What Has Government Done to Our Money?*

18. Hortlund, *Fribankskolan*, p. 77 (quotation translated).

19. Bernholz, "The Importance of Reorganizing Money, Credit, and Banking," p. 104, citing Parkin and Bade, "Central Bank Laws and Monetary Policy," pp. 24–39. Quoted in White, "Is the Gold Standard Still the Gold Standard?"

20. Varchaver, "Who Isn't a Madoff Victim?"

21. Goldstein, Financial Services Hearing.

22. de Rugy and Warren, "Regulatory Agency Spending Reaches New Height," p. 25.

23. Chapman, "The Empty Case for More Regulation."

24. Greider, "Vakna, vänstern" (quotations translated).

25. Moberg, "Staten—författarnas skyddspatron?" (quotation translated).

26. Gillespie and Welch, "'I Think the SEC Was Distracted.'"

27. Dowd, "Moral Hazard and the Financial Crisis."

28. *The Economist*, "Europe's Baleful Bail-Outs."

29. Mises, *Omnipotent Government*, p. 263.

30. Nilsson, "SBAB, ett svenskt Freddie Mac?" (quotation translated).

31. Lindqvist, "Kreditgaranti för första bostadsköpet" (quotation translated); Ingerö, "När sossarna gör så här så kallar vi det för fondsocialism" (quotation translated).

32. Backman, "Ägt boende och lånelättnad nytt i s-politik."

33. Mises, *Human Action*, p. 444.

34. Gunther, "Paulson to the Rescue."

35. Rizzo, "Keynes as Public Works Skeptic."

36. Auerbach, "Is There a Role for Discretionary Fiscal Policy?"

37. Taylor, "Much in Obama Stimulus Bill Won't Hit Economy Soon."

38. *The Economist*, "Days of Open Wallet."

39. Erixon and Sally, "1970s Déjà Vu."

40. Hall and Cienski, "Czechs Act over 'Protectionist' Paris."

Chapter 7

1. Narcotics Anonymous: *Basic Text*, *Approval Form*, November 1981. This quote has wrongly been attributed to Einstein and many others.

2. Pedro Amaral and Margaret Jacobson, "Why Some European Countries and Not the US?" *Economic Trends Articles*, December 2, 2011, Federal Reserve Bank of Cleveland.

3. Barry Eichengreen, "US Futures and Out-of-Control Deficits," *The Globalist*, December 5, 2011.

4. Fredrik Nerbrand, "The Allocator. Inflation of Default: Take Your Pick," July 29, 2011, HSBC Global Research.

5. Kenneth Rogoff and Carmen Reinhart, "Growth in a Time of Debt," prepared for the *American Economic Review Papers and Proceedings*, January 7, 2011.

6. International Monetary Fund, "Global Financial Stability Report," September 2011.

7. Lex: "IMF: Monetary Policy Is Part of the Problem," *Financial Times*, September 21, 2011.

8. Patrick Chovanec, "China Hides Rampant Inflation in Money Binge," Bloomberg News, October 19, 2010.

9. "Shell Game," *The Economist*, March 11, 2010.

10. Michael Forsythe and Henry Sanderson, "China Debts Dwarf Official Data With Too-Big-to-Finish Alarm," Bloomberg News, 18 December 2011.

11. Brooke Masters, "Financial Sector 'Drowning' in Regulation Flood," *Financial Times*, December 9, 2011.

12. Milton and Rose Friedman, *Free to Choose : A Personal Statement* (New York: Harcourt Brace Jovanovich, 1980).

References

ABC News. "Charlie Gibson Interviews President Bush." Transcript, December 1, 2008. http://abcnews.go.com/WN/Politics/Story?id=6356046.

Acemoglu, Daron, and others. "To the Speaker of the House of Representatives and the President Pro Tempore of the Senate." Letter to Congress, September 24, 2008. http://faculty.chicagogsb.edu/john.cochrane/research/Papers/mortgage_protest.htm.

Amaral, Pedro, and Margaret Jacobson. "Why Some European Countries and Not the US?" *Economic Trends Articles*. Federal Reserve Bank of Cleveland. December 2, 2011.

Appelbaum, Binyamin, Carol D. Leonnig, and David S. Hilzenrath. "How Washington Failed to Rein in Fannie, Freddie." *Washington Post*, September 14, 2008.

Apuzzo, Matt. "Where'd the Bailout Money Go? Shhhh, It's a Secret." Associated Press, December 22, 2008.

Auerbach, Alan. "Is There a Role for Discretionary Fiscal Policy?" National Bureau of Economic Research Working Paper no. W9306, November 2002.

Backman, Lars-Erik. "Ägt boende och lånelättnad nytt i s-politik." *Ekot*, May 27, 2008. http://www.sr.se/ekot/artikel.asp?artikel=2095283.

Bagehot, Walter. *Lombard Street: A Description of the Money Market.* Teddington, UK: Echo Library, 2005. First published 1873.

Bajaj, Vikas, and David Leonhardt. "Tax Break May Have Helped Cause Housing Bubble." *New York Times*, December 19, 2008.

Barr, Alistair. "Moody's Downgrades 691 Mortgage-Backed Securities." *MarketWatch.com*, August 16, 2007.

Barrett, Wayne. "Andrew Cuomo and Fannie and Freddie: How the Youngest Housing and Development Secretary in History Gave Birth to the Mortgage Crisis." *Village Voice*, August 5, 2008.

Bartiromo, Maria. "Bill Clinton on the Banking Crisis, McCain, and Hillary." *Business Week*, September 24, 2008.

Bartlett, Bruce. *Impostor: How George W. Bush Bankrupted America and Betrayed the Reagan Legacy.* New York: Doubleday, 2006.

BBC News online. "Icesave Savers Warned on Accounts," October 7, 2008.

Becker, Jo, Sheryl Gay Stolberg, and Stephen Labaton. "White House Philosophy Stoked Mortgage Bonfire." *New York Times*, December 21, 2008.

Benulic, Boris, and Johan Norberg. *Allt om Naomi Kleins nakenchock.* Stockholm: Voltaire Publishing, 2008.

Berkshire Hathaway Inc. *2002 Annual Report.* Omaha: Berkshire Hathaway Inc., 2003.

Bernanke, Ben S. "Asset 'Bubbles' and Monetary Policy." Remarks at the New York Chapter of the National Association for Business Economics, New York, October 15, 2002. http://www.federalreserve.gov/BoardDocs/Speeches/2002/20021015/default.htm.

Bernholz, Peter. "The Importance of Reorganizing Money, Credit, and Banking When Decentralizing Economic Decisionmaking," in *Economic Reform in China*, edited by James A. Dorn and Wang Xi, pp. 93–123. Chicago: University of Chicago Press, 1990.

Berument, Hakan, and Richard Froyen. "Monetary Policy and U.S. Long-Term Interest Rates: How Close Are the Linkages?" *Journal of Economics and Business* 61, no. 1 (2009): 34–50.

Birger, Jon. "The Woman Who Called Wall Street's Meltdown." *Fortune*, August 6, 2008.

Blum, John Morton. *From the Morgenthau Diaries: Years of Crisis, 1928–1938.* Boston: Houghton Mifflin, 1959.

Breitbart.com. "Bernanke Says Crisis 'No Comparison' to Great Depression." December 1, 2008. http://www.breitbart.com/article.php?id=081201213246 v50zx9ik& show_article=1.

Bush, George W. "President Calls for Expanding Opportunities to Home Ownership." Remarks by the president on homeownership, June 17, 2002. http://georgewbush-whitehouse.archives.gov/news/releases/2002/06/20020617-2.html

————. "President's Address to the Nation." White House Office of the Press Secretary, September 24, 2008. http://georgewbush-whitehouse.archives.gov/news/releases/2008/09/20080924-10.html.

Calomiris, Charles. "Another 'Deregulation' Myth." *On the Issues*, American Enterprise Institute, October 2008.

————. "The Subprime Turmoil: What's Old, What's New and What's Next." Paper prepared for the Federal Reserve Bank of Kansas City's Symposium, "Maintaining Stability in a Changing Financial System," Jackson Hole, WY, August 21–22, 2008. http://www.kc.frb.org/publicat/sympos/2008/Calomiris.10.02.08.pdf.

Calvo, Guillermo, Alejandro Izquierdo, and Luis-Fernando Mejía. "Systemic Sudden Stops: The Relevance of Balance-Sheet Effects and Financial Integration." Inter-American Development Bank Working Paper no. 637, July 2008.

Caprio, Gerard, Patrick Honohan, and Mark Feige. *Finance for Growth: Policy Choices in a Volatile World*. Washington: World Bank, 2001.

Carlson, Benny. *Den sociala ingenjörskonstens rörelser: Om Hoover, Hesselgren och hundra års händelser.* Lund, Sweden: Sekel Bokförlag, 2007.

Carney, Brian. "Bernanke Is Fighting the Last War." *Wall Street Journal*, October 18, 2008.

Cavanaugh, Tim. "Houses of Pain." *Reason*, January 2009.

CBS. *60 Minutes.* "McCain Blames Recession on Wall St." Transcript, September 21, 2008. http://www.cbsnews.com/stories/2008/09/21/60minutes/main4463340.shtml.

Chanos, James. "Short Sellers Keep the Markets Honest." *Wall Street Journal*, September 22, 2008.

Chapman, Steve. "The Empty Case for More Regulation." *Reason*, January 2009.

Chen, Shaohua, and Martin Ravallion. "The Developing World Is Poorer than We Thought, but No Less Successful in the Fight against Poverty." World Bank Policy Research Working Paper no. 4703, August 2008.

Cho, David. "Geithner Preparing Overhaul of Bailout." *Washington Post*, January 9, 2009.

Chovanec, Patrick. "China Hides Rampant Inflation in Money Binge." Bloomberg News. October 19, 2010.

CNBC. "Fannie & Freddie Takeover." Transcript, September 8, 2008. http://www.cnbc.com/id/26606180.

CNN. *Lou Dobbs Tonight.* Transcript, December 16, 2008. http://transcripts.cnn.com/TRANSCRIPTS/0812/16/ldt.01.html.

CNNMoney.com. "Bush: US Economy Is Thriving." August 8, 2007. http://money.cnn.com/2007/08/08/news/economy/bush/index.htm.

Cole, Harold, and Lee Ohanian. "New Deal Policies and the Persistence of the Great Depression: A General Equilibrium Analysis." *Journal of Political Economy* 112, no. 4 (2004): 779–816.

Committee on Oversight and Government Reform. *Credit Rating Agencies and the Financial Crisis.* Preliminary transcript, U.S. House of Representatives, October 22, 2008.

Cooper, George. *The Origin of Financial Crises: Central Banks, Credit Bubbles and the Efficient Market Fallacy.* New York: Vintage Books, 2008.

Dan Duyn, Aline, Deborah Brewster, and Gillian Tett. "The Lehman Legacy: Catalyst of the Crisis." *Financial Times*, October 12, 2008.

Dash, Eric. "Citigroup Saw No Red Flags Even as It Made Bolder Bets." *New York Times*, November 23, 2008.

Davis, Julie Hirschfeld. "Lehman Sought Millions for Execs while Seeking Aid." Associated Press, October 6, 2008.

Day, Kathleen. "HUD Says Mortgage Policies Hurt Blacks." *Washington Post*, March 2, 2000.

Day, Theodore, and Stan Liebowitz. "Mortgage Lending to Minorities: Where's the Bias?" *Economic Inquiry* 38 (1998): 3–28.

de Rugy, Veronique. "Bush's Regulatory Kiss-Off." *Reason*, January 2009.

de Rugy, Veronique, and Melinda Warren. "Regulatory Agency Spending Reaches New Height." In *2009 Annual Report*, pp. 5–6. Arlington, VA: Mercatus Center and Washington University in St. Louis, August 2008.

Despeignes, Peronet. "'Greenspan Put' May Be Encouraging Complacency." *Financial Times*, December 8, 2000.

Doherty, Brian. "Can We Bank on the Federal Reserve?" *Reason*, November 2006.

Donovan, Paul. "Investment Bankers of the World, Unite!" *UBS Daily Roundup*, September 19, 2008. http://uk.youtube.com/watch?v=36ZWywSq2V0.

Dougherty, Carter. "German Bank Becomes First EU Victim of U.S. Subprime Mortgage Woes." *International Herald Tribune*, July 30, 2007.

Dowd, Kevin. "Moral Hazard and the Financial Crisis." *Cato Journal* 29, no. 1 (2009): 141–66.

Duhigg, Charles. "At Freddie Mac, Chief Discarded Warning Signs." *New York Times*, August 5, 2008.

———. "Doubts Raised on Big Backers of Mortgages." *New York Times*, May 6, 2008.

———. "Pressured to Take More Risk, Fannie Reached a Tipping Point." *New York Times*, October 5, 2008.

The Economist. "All You Need Is Cash." November 22, 2008.

———. "Capital Ideas." August 28, 2008.

———. "Days of Open Wallet." December 11, 2008.

———. "Europe's Baleful Bail-Outs." November 1, 2008.

———. "Fannie and Freddie Ride Again." July 9, 2007.

———. "The Great Untangling." November 8, 2008.

———. "Homing in on the Risks." June 3, 2004.

_____. "Monetary Myopia." January 12, 2006.

_____. "Negative Outlook." November 15, 2008.

_____. "On Credit Watch." October 18, 2007.

_____. "Paint It Black." October 18, 2007.

_____. "Riddle Solved." June 15, 2008.

_____. "Shell Game." March 11, 2010.

_____. "Shifting the Balance." October 11, 2008.

_____. "Sold Down the River Rhine." August 9, 2007.

_____. "Spanish Steps." May 15, 2008.

_____. "Weaken the Sinews." October 4, 2008.

Eichengreen, Barry. "US Futures and Out-of-Control Deficits." *The Globalist*. December 5, 2011.

Eisinger, Jesse. "Overrated." *Portfolio.com*, September 2007.

Ekirch, Arthur A., Jr. *The Decline of American Liberalism*. New York: Atheneum, 1973.

Erixon, Fredrik, and Razeen Sally. "1970s Déjà Vu." *Wall Street Journal*, November 27, 2008.

Fannie Mae Foundation. *Case Study: Countrywide Home Loans, Inc.*, 2000. http://www.fanniemaefoundation.org/programs/pdf/rep_newmortmkts_countrywide.pdf (accessed December 27, 2008).

Federal Reserve Bank of Boston. "Closing the Gap: A Guide to Equal Opportunity Lending." April 1993.

Ferguson, Niall. *The Ascent of Money: A Financial History of the World*. London: Allen Lane, 2008.

Financial Times. "IMF: Monetary Policy Is Part of the Problem." September 21, 2011.

First Union. "First Union Capital Markets Corp., Bear, Stearns & Co. Price Securities Offering Backed by Affordable Mortgages." Press release, October 20, 1997. http://www.prnewswire.com/cgi-gin/stories.pl?ACCT=104&STORY=/www/story/10-20-97/340247&EDATE.

Flandez, Raymund. "With Market Hot, More People Now Have Third Homes." *Wall Street Journal*, January 5, 2005.

Forelle, Charles. "The Isle That Rattled the World." *Wall Street Journal*, December 27, 2008.

Forsythe, Michael, and Henry Sanderson. "China Debts Dwarf Official Data With Too-Big-to-Finish Alarm." Bloomberg News. December 18, 2011.

Fortune. "101 Dumbest Moments in Business." January 16, 2008.

Foust, Dean. "Alan Greenspan's Brave New World." *Business Week*, July 14, 1997.

Fox News Poll/Opinion Dynamics. October 10, 2008. http://www.foxnews.com/projects/pdf/101008_foxpoll.pdf.

Friedman, Milton, and Anna Schwartz. *A Monetary History of the United States 1867–1960*. Princeton, NJ: Princeton University Press, 1963.

Friedman, Milton, and Rose Friedman. *Free to Choose: A Personal Statement*. New York: Harcourt Brace Jovanovich, 1980.

Friedrich, Otto. "F.D.R.'s Disputed Legacy." *Time*, February 1, 1982.

Gainor, Dan, Julia A. Seymour, and Genevieve Ebel. "The Great Media Depression." Business & Media Institute, 2008. http://www.businessandmedia.org/special reports/2008/GreatDepression/GreatDepression_execsum.asp.

Galbraith, James. *The Predator State*. New York: Free Press, 2008.

Gerth, Jeff. "Was AIG Watchdog Not Up to the Job?" MSN Money, November 10, 2008. http://articles.moneycentral.msn.com/Investing/Extra/was-AIG-watchdog-not-up-to-the-job.aspx?page=all.

Gillespie, Nick, and Matt Welch. "'I Think the SEC Was Distracted.'" *Reason*, March 2009.

Golden, Daniel. "Countrywide's Many 'Friends.'" *Portfolio.com*, June 12, 2008.

Goldman, David. "The $8 Trillion Bailout." CNNMoney.com, January 6, 2009. http://money.cnn.com/2009/01/06/news/economy/where_stimulus_fits_in/index.htm?eref=rss_topstories.

Goldstein, Allan. Financial Services Hearing, U.S. House of Representatives, January 5, 2009. http://www.youtube.com/watch?v=uN-PieCA-4A.

Gorton, Gary. "The Panic of 2007." Paper prepared for the Federal Reserve Bank of Kansas City, Jackson Hole Conference, Jackson Hole, WY, August 25, 2008.

Grant, James. *Mr. Market Miscalculates: The Bubble Years and Beyond.* Mount Jackson, VA: Axios Press, 2008.

———. *The Trouble with Prosperity: The Loss of Fear, the Rise of Speculation, and the Risk to American Savings.* New York: Crown, 1996.

Greenspan, Alan. *The Age of Turbulence: Adventures in a New World.* New York: Penguin Books, 2008.

———. "Banks Need More Capital." *The Economist*, December 18, 2008.

———. "Gold and Economic Freedom." *The Objectivist*, July 1966. Reprinted in Ayn Rand. *Capitalism: The Unknown Ideal.* New York: New American Library, 1967.

———. Remarks at the Economic Club of New York, New York City, December 19, 2002. http://www.federalreserve.gov/BOARDDOCS/SPEECHES/2002/20021219/default.htm.

———. "Understanding Household Debt Obligations." Remarks at the Credit Union National Association's 2004 Governmental Affairs Conference, Washington, February 23, 2004. http://www.federalreserve.gov/boarddocs/speeches/2004/20040223.

Greenwood, John. "Grain Piles Up in Ports." *Financial Post*, October 8, 2008.

Greider, Göran. "Vakna, vänstern." *Aftonbladet*, November 18, 2008.

Gross, Daniel. "America's Smartest Banker." *Slate*, August 2, 2008.

———. "Location, Location—Deduction." *Slate*, April 14, 2005.

Gullapalli, Diya, and Shefali Anand. "Bailout of Money Funds Seems to Stanch Outflow." *Wall Street Journal*, September 20, 2008.

Gunther, Marc. "Paulson to the Rescue." *Fortune*, September 29, 2008.

Gustavson, Marius. *Sosialisme på sparebluss: USAs feilslåtte boligpolitikk.* Oslo: Civitanotat No. 13, 2008.

Hall, Ben, and Jan Cienski. "Czechs Act over 'Protectionist' Paris." *Financial Times*, February 10, 2009.

Hayek, Friedrich A. *Denationalisation of Money.* London: Institute of Economic Affairs, 1976.

Heckscher, Eli F. *Gammal och ny ekonomisk liberalism.* Stockholm: P. A. Norstedt & Söner, 1921.

Henriques, Diana. "Bailout Monitor Sees Lack of a Coherent Plan." *New York Times*, December 1, 2008.

Henry, David, and Matthew Goldstein. "The Bear Flu: How It Spread." *BusinessWeek*, December 31, 2007.

Higgs, Robert. "Regime Uncertainty: Why the Great Depression Lasted So Long and Why Prosperity Resumed after the War." *Independent Review* 1, no. 4 (1997): 561–90.

Hilzenrath, David. "Fannie's Perilous Pursuit of Subprime Loans." *Washington Post*, August 19, 2008.

HM Treasury. "Financial Sanctions: Current Regimes." 2008. http://www.hm-treasury.gov.uk/fin_sanctions_currentindex.htm.

Holmes, Steven. "Fannie Mae Eases Credit to Aid Mortgage Lending." *New York Times*, September 30, 1999.

Hortlund, Per. *Fribankskolan: Monetär laissez-faire i teori och praktik*. Stockholm: Timbro, 2002.

Ingerö, Johan. "När sossarna gör så här så kallar vi det för fondsocialism . . . ." Johan Ingerö's blog, October 16, 2008. http://ingero.blogspot.com/2008/10/nr-sossarna-gr-s-hr-s-kallar-vi-det-fr.html.

International Herald Tribune. "Germany: US Slipping as Financial Superpower." September 25, 2008.

International Monetary Fund. "Global Financial Stability Report." September 2011.

Isaac, William. "How to Save the Financial System." *Wall Street Journal*, September 19, 2008.

Johnson, Paul. *A History of the American People*. London: Phoenix, 1998.

Jolly, David. "Ex-Trader Tells How He Lost So Much for One Bank." *International Herald Tribune*, January 22, 2009.

Jones, Sam. "When Junk Was Gold." *Financial Times*, October 17, 2008.

Jones, Sam, Gillian Tett, and Paul Davies. "CPDOs Expose Ratings Flaw at Moody's." *Financial Times*, May 20, 2008.

Jonung, Lars. "Ekonomer i krismöte." *Dagens Nyheter*, January 29, 2009.

Katz, Ian. "Behind Schwarzman Spat with Wasserstein Lies Rule 115." Bloomberg.com, December 8, 2008.

Kelly, Kate. "Bear CEO's Handling of Crisis Raises Issues." *Wall Street Journal*, November 1, 2007.

———. "Where in the World Is Bear's Jimmy Cayne? Playing Bridge." Deal Journal blog/*Wall Street Journal*, March 14, 2008. http://blogs.wsj.com/deals/2008/03/14/where-in-the-world-is-bears-jimmy-cayne-playing-bridge.

Kennedy, David. *Freedom from Fear: The American People in Depression and War, 1929–1945*. New York: Oxford University Press, 1999.

Keynes, John Maynard. *The General Theory of Employment, Interest, and Money*. 1935. http://www.scribd.com/doc/11392072/The-General-Theory-of-Employment-Interest-and-Money.

———. "The Maintenance of Prosperity Is Extremely Difficult." In *New Deal Thought*, edited by Howard Zinn, pp. 403–9. Indianapolis: Bobbs-Merrill, 1966.

Keys, Benjamin, Tanmoy Mukherjee, Amit Seru, and Vikrant Vig. "Did Securitization Lead to Lax Screening? Evidence from Subprime Loans." European Finance Association 2008 Athens meetings paper, April 2008.

Kindleberger, Charles, and Robert Z. Aliber. *Manias, Panics and Crashes: A History of Financial Crises*. New York: Palgrave Macmillan, 2005.

Klein, Naomi. *The Shock Doctrine: The Rise of Disaster Capitalism*. London: Allen Lane, 2007.

Kopecki, Dawn. "Fannie, Freddie 'Insolvent' after Losses, Poole Says." Bloomberg.com, July 10, 2008. http://www.bloomberg.com/apps/news?pid=20601087&sid=a7NPAG.LEjHQ&refer=home.

Krugman, Paul. "After the Money's Gone." *New York Times*, December 14, 2007.

———. "Fannie, Freddie and You." *New York Times*, July 14, 2008.

———. "That Hissing Sound." *New York Times*, August 8, 2005.

Kurtz, Stanley. "O's Dangerous Pals." *New York Post*, September 29, 2008.

Labaton, Stephen. "Agency's '04 Rule Let Banks Pile Up New Debt." *New York Times*, October 2, 2008.

Landler, Mark, and Eric Dash. "Drama Behind a $250 Billion Banking Deal." *New York Times*, October 14, 2008.

Landler, Mark, and Steven Lee Myers. "Buyout Plan for Wall Street Is a Hard Sell on Capitol Hill." *New York Times*, September 23, 2008.

Lejland, Carl-Johan. "Finansrävarna: 'Blankning stabiliserar marknaden.'" *Dagens Industri*, September 23, 2008.

Leonnig, Carol. "How HUD Mortgage Policy Fed the Crisis." *Washington Post*, June 10, 2008.

Lerer, Lisa. "Fannie, Freddie Spent $200M to Buy Influence." Politico.com, July 16, 2008.

Lessig, Lawrence. "Why the Banks All Fell Down." *Newsweek*, October 27, 2008.

Lewis, Michael, ed. *Panic: The Story of Modern Financial Insanity.* London: Penguin Books, 2008.

Liebowitz, Stan. "The Real Scandal—How Feds Invited the Mortgage Mess." *New York Post*, February 5, 2008.

Lilleston, Randy, and Ian Christopher McCaleb. "Bush Endures Slaps from GOP Rivals in Fully Attended Candidate Forum." CNN.com, December 3, 1999.

Lindqvist, Roger. "Kreditgaranti för första bostadsköpet." *Dagens Nyheter*, September 13, 2007.

Lockhart, James. "Reforming the Regulation of the Government Sponsored Enterprises." Statement before the U.S. Senate Banking, Housing, and Urban Affairs Committee, February 7, 2008.

Lowenstein, Roger. "Triple-A Failure." *New York Times Magazine*, April 27, 2008.

Lucas, Dan. "Konkurshotade Island kämpar för överlevnad." *Dagens Nyheter*, October 10, 2008.

Lyall, Sarah. "Iceland, Mired in Debt, Blames Britain for Woes." *New York Times*, November 1, 2008.

MacFarquhar, Larissa. "Outside Agitator." *New Yorker*, December 8, 2008.

Maddison, Angus. *The World Economy: Historical Statistics.* Paris: Organization for Economic Cooperation and Development, 2003.

Masters, Brooke. "Financial Sector 'Drowning' in Regulation Flood." *Financial Times*. December 9, 2011.

Marx, Karl. Letter to Friedrich Engels, February 3, 1851. In *Marx/Engels Collected Works.* Vol. 38, p. 273. Moscow: Progress Publishers of the Soviet Union, 1975–2005. http://www.marxists.org/archive/marx/works/cw/index.htm.

Mayer, Lindsay Renick. "Fannie Mae and Freddie Mac Invest in Democrats." Capital Eye.org, July 16, 2008. http://www.opensecrets.org/news/2008/07/top-senate-recipients-of-fanni.html.

Mihm, Stephen. "Dr. Doom." *New York Times Magazine*, August 15, 2008.

Minton, Michelle. "The Community Reinvestment Act's Harmful Legacy," Competitive Enterprise Institute, OnPoint, No. 132, March 20, 2008.

Mises, Ludwig von. *Human Action: A Treatise on Economics.* Chicago: Contemporary Books, 1966. First published 1949.

———. *Omnipotent Government: The Rise of the Total State and Total War.* Spring Mills, PA: Libertarian Press, 1985. First published 1944.

———. *The Theory of Money and Credit.* Indianapolis: Liberty Fund, 1981. First published 1912.

Moberg, Vilhelm. "Staten—författarnas skyddspatron?" *Dagens Nyheter*, May 24, 1948.

Mollenkamp, Carrick, Serena Ng, Liam Pleven, and Randall Smith. "Behind AIG's Fall, Risk Models Failed to Pass Real-World Test." *Wall Street Journal*, October 31, 2008.

Morgenson, Gretchen. "Behind Insurer's Crisis, Blind Eye to a Web of Risk." *New York Times*, September 28, 2008.

_____. "Debt Watchdogs: Tamed or Caught Napping?" *New York Times*, December 7, 2008.

_____. "How the Thundering Herd Faltered and Fell." *New York Times*, November 8, 2008.

Munkhammar, Johnny, and Nima Sanandaji. *Finanskrisen—ett gigantiskt politikmisslyckande*. Munkhammar Advisory, Stockholm, October 16, 2008.

Muolo, Paul, and Mathew Padilla. *Chain of Blame: How Wall Street Caused the Mortgage and Credit Crisis*. Hoboken, NJ: John Wiley & Sons, 2008.

Nakamoto, Michiyo, and David Wighton. "Citigroup Chief Stays Bullish on Buy-Outs." *Financial Times*, July 9, 2007.

Narcotics Anonymous. *Basic Text, Approval Form*. November 1981.

Nash, Nathaniel. "A Laissez-Faire Pragmatist: Alan Greenspan." *New York Times*, June 3, 1987.

National Mortgage News. "Fannie to Boost Subprime Activities." March 3, 2000. http:// www.nationalmortgagenews.com/premium/archive/?ts=952102802.

Nerbrand, Fredrik. "The Allocator. Inflation of Default: Take Your Pick." HSBC Global Research. July 29, 2011.

Newmark, Evan. "Hank Paulson, National Hero." Deal Journal Blog/*Wall Street Journal*, October 15, 2008. http://blogs.wsj.com/deals/2008/10/15/mean-street-hank-paulson-national-hero.

New York Times. "Shortselling." October 18, 1930.

Nilsson, Per. "SBAB, ett svenskt Freddie Mac?" Report, Timbro, October 27, 2008.

Nocera, Joe. "As Credit Crisis Spiraled, Alarm Led to Action." *New York Times*, October 1, 2008.

_____. "So When Will Banks Give Loans?" *New York Times*, October 24, 2008.

Nocera, Joe, and Edmund Andrews. "Struggling to Keep Up as the Crisis Raced On." *New York Times*, October 23, 2008.

Norberg, Johan. "The Klein Doctrine: The Rise of Disaster Polemics." Cato Institute Briefing Paper no. 102, May 14, 2008. http://www.cato.org/pub_display. php?pub_id=9384.

_____. "Världens välfärd: Fyra decennier som förändrade planeten." Background Report no. 1 for the Swedish Globalization Council, Stockholm, Utbildningsdepartementet, 2007.

Oakley, David. "Short-Selling Ban Has Minimal Effect." *Financial Times*, December 18, 2008.

O'Driscoll, Gerald P. "Asset Bubbles and Their Consequences." Cato Institute Briefing Paper no. 103, May 20, 2008.

Office of Federal Housing Enterprise Oversight. "Report to Congress." Washington, June 2003.

Ohlsson, Erik. "Bushs nej blev starten på den globala finanskrisen." *Dagens Nyheter*, December 30, 2008.

Onaran, Yalman, and John Helyar. "Fuld Sought Buffett Offer He Refused as Lehman Sank." Bloomberg.com, November 10, 2008. http://www.bloomberg.com/apps/ news?pid=20601109&sid=aZ1syPZH.RzY&refer=home.

O'Toole, Randal. "The Planning Tax: The Case against Regional Growth-Management Planning." Cato Institute Policy Analysis no. 606, December 6, 2007.

Parkin, Michael, and Robin Bade. "Central Bank Laws and Monetary Policy: A Preliminary Investigation." In *The Australian Monetary System in the 1970s*, edited by M. A. Porter, pp. 24–39. Melbourne: Monash University, 1978.

Paulson, Henry. Oral statement on regulatory reform before House Committee on Financial Services. U.S. Department of the Treasury, July 10, 2008. http://www.ustreas.gov/press/releases/hp1074.htm.

Pender, Kathleen. "Government Bailout Hits $8.5 Trillion." *San Francisco Chronicle*, November 26, 2008.

Pollock, Alex. "Conceptual Problems with 'Fair Value' Accounting Theory." Testimony before the Securities and Exchange Commission, July 22, 2008. http://www.aei.org/speech/28370.

———. "The Human Foundations of Financial Risk." *Financial Services Outlook*, American Enterprise Institute, May 2008.

Poor, Jeff. "Inhofe: 'Paulson Used Scare Tactics to Force Bailout Legislation.'" Business & Media Institute, November 19, 2008. http://businessandmedia.org/articles/2008/20081119073313.aspx.

———. "Knock Out: CNBC Confirms Lehman CEO Punched at Gym." Business & Media Institute, October 6, 2008. http://www.businessandmedia.org/articles/2008/20081006150152.aspx.

Powell, Jim. "Not-So-Great Depression." *National Review*, January 7, 2009.

Prashad, Vijay. "Wealth's Apostles." *CounterPunch*, October 21, 2008. http://www.counterpunch.org/prashad10212008.html.

Presidential Vetoes (1789 to Present)." http://clerk.house.gov/art_history/house_-history/vetoes.html.

Rasmussen Reports. "Just 7% Favor Fed Bailout for Financial Firms." September 17, 2008. http://www.rasmussenreports.com/public_content/business/federal_bailout/just_7_favor_fed_bailout_for_financial_firms.

Rausa, Maurice D. "Basel I and the Law of Unintended Consequences." *Bank Accounting & Finance*, April 1, 2004.

RealtyTrac. "Foreclosure Activity Increases 5 Percent in October." November 13, 2008. http://www.realtytrac.com/ContentManagement/pressrelease.aspx?ChannelID=9&ItemID=5420&accnt=64847.

Reed, Christopher. "The Damned South Sea." *Harvard Magazine*, May–June 1999.

Reich, Robert. "The Big Three and TARP: What Happened to Democracy?" Robert Reich's blog, December 17, 2008. http://robertreich.blogspot.com/2008/12/big-three-and-tarp-what-happened-to.html.

Reserve Primary Fund. "A Statement regarding the Primary Fund." Press release, September 16, 2008. http://ww.ther.com/pdfs/Press%20Release%202008_0916.pdf.

Reuters. "'US Homes Market Will Shed Investor Glut'—Economist." January 17, 2007. http://www.reuters.com/article/companyNewsAndPR/idUSN1723482320070117.

Rizzo, Mario. "Keynes as Public Works Skeptic." ThinkMarkets blog, January 25, 2009. http://thinkmarkets.wordpress.com/2009/01/25/keynes-as-public-works-skeptic/#more-746.

Rogoff, Kenneth, and Carmen Reinhardt. "Growth in a Time of Debt." *American Economic Review Papers and Proceedings*. January 7, 2011.

Roosevelt, Franklin Delano. Address accepting the presidential nomination at the Democratic National Convention in Chicago, July 2, 1932. http://www.presidency. ucsb.edu/ws/index.php?pid=75174.

Rothbard, Murray. *America's Great Depression.* New York: Richardson & Snyder, 1983.

_____. *What Has Government Done to Our Money?* Auburn, AL: Ludwig von Mises Institute, 1990.

Roubini, Nouriel. "Not So Much Bail-Out as Rip-Off." *Guardian* (UK), September 20, 2008. http://www.guardian.co.uk/commentisfree/2008/sep/29/wallstreet. useconomy.

Samuelson, Robert J. "The Boom in My Backyard." *Newsweek,* December 30, 2002.

Santana, Wally. "Taiwanese Dogs Become the Latest Victims in Global Financial Meltdown." *Star Tribune,* November 6, 2008.

Sarkozy, Nicolas. "International Financial Crisis." Speech given in Paris on September 25, 2008, published by the French Embassy in London. http://www.ambafrance-uk.org/President-Sarkozy-speaks-to-French.html.

Satow, Julie. "Ex-SEC Official Blames Agency for Blow-Up of Broker-Dealers." *New York Sun,* September 18, 2008.

Schwartz, Nelson. "European Banks Share Blame." *International Herald Tribune,* October 13, 2008.

Seeking Alpha. "Countrywide Financial Q2 2007 Earnings Call Transcript." July 24, 2007. http://seekingalpha.com/article/42171-countrywide-financial-q2-2007-earnings-call-transcript.

Shenn, Jody. "Fannie, Freddie Subprime Spree May Add to Bailout." Bloomberg.com, September 22, 2008. http://www.bloomberg.com/apps/news?pid=20601109& sid=a.6kKtOoO72k&refer=home.

Sherman, Brad. "Statement of Brad Sherman regarding Financial Bailout Comment." Press release, October 10, 2008. http://www.house.gov/sherman/press_ room_2007_2008/morenews/BailoutComment.html.

Shlaes, Amity. *The Forgotten Man: A New History of the Great Depression.* New York: HarperCollins Publishers, 2007.

Simpson, Glenn, and James Hagerty. "Countrywide Friends Got Good Loans." *Wall Street Journal,* June 7, 2008.

Smith, Adam. *An Inquiry into the Nature and Causes of the Wealth of Nations.* Indianapolis: Liberty Fund, 1981. First published 1776.

Solomon, Deborah, and David Enrich. "Devil Is in Bailout's Details." *Wall Street Journal,* October 15, 2008.

Sorkin, Andrew Ross, ed. "As No-Short-Selling List Grows, Another Firm Chooses to Leave." Dealbook blog/*New York Times,* September 23, 2008. http://deal book.blogs.nytimes.com/2008/09/23/as-no-short-selling-list-grows-another-firm-chooses-to-leave/?pagemode=print.

Stafford, Philip. "Traders Blind to Mounting Worries." *Financial Times,* September 19, 2007.

Staley, Kathryn. *The Art of Short Selling.* New York: John Wiley & Sons, 1997

Stelzer, Irwin M. "Do Deficits Matter?" *Weekly Standard,* February 15, 2005.

Stevenson, Richard. "The Velvet Fist of Fannie Mae." *New York Times,* April 20, 1997.

Stiglitz, Joseph. "Fannie's and Freddie's Free Lunch." *Financial Times,* July 24, 2008.

Stiglitz, Joseph, Jonathan Orszag, and Peter Orszag. "Implications of the New Fannie Mae and Freddie Mac Risk-Based Capital Standard." *Fannie Mae Papers,* vol. 1, no. 2, March 2002.

Story, Louise. "On Wall Street, Bonuses, Not Profits, Were Real." *New York Times*, December 18, 2008.

Streifield, David, and Gretchen Morgenson. "Building Flawed American Dreams." *New York Times*, October 19, 2008.

Taleb, Nassim Nicholas. *The Black Swan: The Impact of the Highly Improbable.* London: Penguin Books, 2008.

Taub, Stephen. "FAS 157 Could Cause Huge Write-Offs." *CFO*, November 7, 2007. http://www.cfo.com/article.cfm/10097878/c_10098290.

Taylor, Andrew. "Much in Obama Stimulus Bill Won't Hit Economy Soon." *International Herald Tribune*, January 20, 2009.

Temkin, Kenneth, Jennifer Johnson, and Diane Levy. *Subprime Markets, the Role of GSEs, and Risk-Based Pricing.* Washington: U.S. Department of Housing and Urban Development, March 2002.

Terhune, Chad, and Robert Berner. "FHA-Backed Loans: The New Subprime." *Business Week*, November 19, 2008.

Tett, Gillian. "The Dream Machine: Invention of Credit Derivatives." *Financial Times*, March 24, 2006.

Tett, Gillian, and Paul J. Davies. "Out of the Shadows: How Banking's Secret System Broke Down." *Financial Times*, December 16, 2007.

Time. "Sock on the Nose." August 7, 1933.

Tsang, Michael. "Short Sellers under Fire in U.S., U.K. after AIG Fall." Bloomberg.com, September 19, 2008. http://www.bloomberg.com/apps/news?pid=20601087&sid=aTHLqfgpnFYw&refer=home.

Tvede, Lars. *Business Cycles: From John Law to the Internet Crash.* London: Routledge, 2001.

U.S. Census Bureau. "Housing Vacancies and Homeownership." http://www.census.gov/hhes/www/housing/hvs/historic/histt14.html (accessed January 12, 2009).

U.S. Department of the Treasury. "Approaches to Improve the Competitiveness of the U.S. Business Tax System for the 21st Century." Office of Tax Policy, December 20, 2007.

U.S. House of Representatives, Office of the Clerk, "Presidential Vetoes (1789) to Present." http://clerk.house.gov/art_history/house_history/vetoes.html.

Varchaver, Nicholas. "Who Isn't a Madoff Victim? The List Is Telling." *Fortune*, December 19, 2008.

Velleius Paterculus, Marcus. *Compendium of Roman History.* Translated by Frederick W. Shipley. Loeb Classical Library. Cambridge, MA: Harvard University Press, 1967. London: W. Heinemann, 1924.

Wallison, Peter J., and Charles Calomiris. "The Last Trillion-Dollar Commitment: The Destruction of Fannie Mae and Freddie Mac." American Enterprise Institute Financial Services Outlook, September 2008.

Wall Street Journal. "At Moment of Truth, U.S. Forced Big Bankers to Blink." October 15, 2008.

Wanniski, Jude. "The Crash of '29—A New View." *Wall Street Journal*, October 28, 1977.

Washington Post. "The Chairman Speaks." 2005. http://www.washingtonpost.com/wp-srv/business/articles/greenspan_comments.html.

Whaples, Robert. "Where Is There Consensus among American Economic Historians? The Results of a Survey on Forty Propositions." *Journal of Economic History* 55, no. 1 (1995): 139–54.

White, Lawrence H. "How Did We Get into This Financial Mess?" Cato Institute Briefing Paper no. 110, November 18, 2008.

———. "Is the Gold Standard Still the Gold Standard among Monetary Systems?" Cato Institute Briefing Paper no. 100, February 8, 2008.

Wingfield, Brian, and Josh Zumbrun. "Bad News for the Bailout." *Forbes.com*, September 23, 2008. http://www.forbes.com/home/2008/09/23/bailout-paulson-con gress-biz-beltway-cx_jz_bw_0923bailout.html.

WNET. *Charlie Rose Show.* October 1, 2008.

Wolf, Martin. *Fixing Global Finance.* Baltimore: Johns Hopkins University Press, 2008.

Wolfers, Justin. "Economists on the Bailout." Freakonomics blog/*New York Times*, September 23, 2008. http://freakonomics.blogs.nytimes.com/2008/09/23/econo mists-on-the-bailout.

Younglai, Rachelle. "SEC's Cox Regrets Short-Selling Ban." *Financial Post*, December 31, 2008.

Index

About the Author

Johan Norberg is a senior fellow at the Cato Institute and a writer who focuses on globalization, entrepreneurship, and individual liberty. Norberg is the author and editor of several books exploring liberal themes, including a history of liberal pioneers in Swedish history. His book *In Defense of Global Capitalism*, originally published in Swedish in 2001, has since been published in over 20 different countries. He is also the author of *När människan skapade världen*, 2006 (*When Mankind Created the World*), the coauthor of *Ett annat Sverige är möjligt*, 2006 (*Another Sweden Is Possible*), and *Global rättvisa är möjlig*, 2001 (*Global Justice Is Possible*), the coauthor of *Allt om Naomi Kleins nakenchock*, 2008 (*Naomi Klein's Baseless Shock*) and the coeditor of *Frihetens klassiker*, 2003 (*The Classics of Freedom*), all of which are available only in Swedish at this time. His personal website is http://www.johannorberg.net/. He wrote and hosted *Globalisation Is Good*, a documentary for Channel Four in Britain.

Norberg's articles and opinion pieces appear regularly in both Swedish and international newspapers, and he is a regular commentator and contributor on television and radio around the world discussing globalization and free trade. Before joining Cato, Norberg was head of political ideas at Timbro, a Swedish free-market think tank, from 2003 to 2005. He then served as a senior fellow for the Brussels-based Centre for a New Europe during 2006. Norberg received his master's degree from Stockholm University in the history of ideas.

Cato Institute

Founded in 1977, the Cato Institute is a public policy research foundation dedicated to broadening the parameters of policy debate to allow consideration of more options that are consistent with the traditional American principles of limited government, individual liberty, and peace. To that end, the Institute strives to achieve greater involvement of the intelligent, concerned lay public in questions of policy and the proper role of government.

The Institute is named for *Cato's Letters*, libertarian pamphlets that were widely read in the American Colonies in the early 18th century and played a major role in laying the philosophical foundation for the American Revolution.

Despite the achievement of the nation's Founders, today virtually no aspect of life is free from government encroachment. A pervasive intolerance for individual rights is shown by government's arbitrary intrusions into private economic transactions and its disregard for civil liberties.

To counter that trend, the Cato Institute undertakes an extensive publications program that addresses the complete spectrum of policy issues. Books, monographs, and shorter studies are commissioned to examine the federal budget, Social Security, regulation, military spending, international trade, and myriad other issues. Major policy conferences are held throughout the year, from which papers are published thrice yearly in the *Cato Journal*. The Institute also publishes the quarterly magazine *Regulation*.

In order to maintain its independence, the Cato Institute accepts no government funding. Contributions are received from foundations, corporations, and individuals, and other revenue is generated from the sale of publications. The Institute is a nonprofit, tax-exempt, educational foundation under Section 501(c)3 of the Internal Revenue Code.

CATO INSTITUTE
1000 Massachusetts Ave., N.W.
Washington, D.C. 20001
www.cato.org